SPRINGINTHEWORLDANDALLTH YOUNG

I

Birds called. Breezes played among branches just bursting into green. Daffodils, proud and erect, stood in clumps about the dazzling lawn. Young, pulsing, eager things elbowed their way through last year's leaves to taste the morning sun; the wide-eyed celandine, yellower than butter; the little violet, hugging the earth for fear of being seen; the sturdy bourgeois daisy; the pale-faced anemone, earliest to wake and earliest to sleep; the blue bird's-eye in small family groups; the blatant dandelion already a head and shoulders taller than any neighbor. Every twig in the old garden bore its new load of buds that were soft as kittens' paws; and up the wrinkled trunks of ancient trees young ivy leaves chased each other like school-boys.

Spring had come again, and its eternal spirit spread the message of new-born hope, stirred the sap of awakening life, warmed the bosom of a wintry earth and put into the hearts of birds the old desire to mate. But the lonely girl turned a deaf ear to the call, and rounded her shoulders over the elderly desk with tears blistering her letter.

"I'm miserable, miserable," she wrote. "There doesn't seem to be anything to live for. I suppose it's selfish and horrid to grumble because Mother has married again, but why did she choose the very moment when she was to take me into life? Oh, Alice, what am I to do? I feel like a rabbit with its foot in a trap, listening to the traffic on the main road—like a newly fledged bird brought down with a broken wing among the dead leaves of Rip Van Winkle's sleeping-place. You'll laugh when you read this, and say that I'm dramatizing my feelings and writing for effect; but if you've got any heart at all, you'd cry if you saw me (me of all girls!) buried alive out here without a single soul to speak to who's as young as I am—hushed if I laugh by mistake, scowled at if I let myself move quickly, catching old age every hour I stay here."

"Why, Alice, just think of it! There's not a person or a thing in and out of this house that's not old. I don't mean old as we thought of it at school, thirty and thirty-five, but really and awfully old. The house is the oldest for miles round. My grandfather is seventy-two, and my grandmother's seventy. The servants are old, the trees are old, the horses are old; and even the dogs lie about with dim eyes waiting for death."

"When Mother was here, it was bearable. We escaped as often as we could, and rode and drove and made secret visits to the city and saw the plays at matinees. There's nothing old about Mother. I suppose that's why she married again. But now that I'm left alone in this house of decay, where everybody and everything belongs to the past, I'm frightened of being so young, and catch looks that make me feel that I ought to be ashamed of myself. It's so long since I quarreled with a girl or flirted with a boy that I can't remember it. I'm forgetting how to laugh. I'm beginning not to care about clothes or whether I look nice."

"One day is exactly like another. I wander about aimlessly with nothing to do, nowhere to go, no one to speak to. I've even begun to give up reading novels, because they make me so jealous. It's all wrong, Alice. It's bad and unhealthy. It puts mutinous thoughts into my head. Honestly, the only way in which I can get the sort of thrill that I ought to have now, if ever I am to thrill at all, is in making wild plans of escape, so wild and so naughty that I don't think I'd better write about them, even to you, dear."

"Mother's on her honeymoon. She went away a week ago in a state of self-conscious happiness that left Grandfather and Grandmother snappy and disagreeable. She will be away four months, and every weekly letter that comes from her will make this place more and more unbearable and me more restless and dangerous. I could get myself invited away. Enid would have me and give me a wonderful time. She has four brothers. Fanny has begged me to stay with her in Boston for the whole of the spring and see and do everything, which would be absolutely heaven. And you know everybody in New York and could make life worth living."

"But Grandfather won't let me go. He likes to see me about the house, he says, and I read the papers to him morning and evening. It does me good, he considers, to 'make a sacrifice and pay deference to those whose time is almost up.' So here I am, tied to the shadows, a prisoner till Mother comes back—a woman of eighteen forced to behave like a good little girl treated as if I were still content to amuse myself with dolls and picture books! But the fire is smolderin Alice, and one fine day it will burst into flame."

A shaft of sunlight found its way through the branches of a chestnut tree and danced suddenly upon the envelope into which Joan had sealed up this little portion of her overcharged vitality. Through the open windows of her more than ample room with its Colonial four-post bed, dignified tallboys, stiff chairs and anemic engravings of early-Victorianism, all the stir and murmur of the year's youth came to Joan.

If her eyes had not been turned inward and her ears had not been tuned only to catch her own natural complaints, this chatter of young things would have called her out to laugh and tingle and dance in the haunted wood and cry out little incoherent welcomes to the children of the earth. Something of the joy and emotion of that mother-month must have stirred her imagination and set her blood racing through her young body. She felt the call of youth and the urge to play. She sensed the magnetic pull of the voice of spring, but when, with her long brown lashes wet with impatient tears, she went to the window and looked out at the green spread of lawn and the yellow-headed daffodils, it seemed more than ever to her that she was peering through iron bars into the playground of a school to which she didn't belong. She was Joan-all-alone, she told herself, and added, with that touch of picturesque phrasing inherited from her well-read mother, that she was more like a racing motorboat tied to a crumbling wharf in a deserted harbor than anything else in the world.

There was a knock on her door and the sound of a bronchial cough. "Come in," she said and darted an anxious look at the blond fat face of the clock on the mantelshelf. She had forgotten all about the time.

It was Gleave who opened the door, Gleave the bald-headed manservant who had grown old along with his master with the same resentfulness—the ex-prizefighter, sailor, lumberman and adventurer who had thrown in his lot with Cumberland Ludlow, the sportsman, when both were in the full flush of middle age. His limp, the result of an epoch-making fight in an Australian mining camp, was emphasized by severe rheumatism, and the fretfulness of old age was heightened by his shortness of breath.

He got no further than: "Your grandfather—"

"I know," said Joan. "I'm late again. And there'll be a row, I suppose. Well, that will break the monotony, at any rate." Seizing the moment when Gleave was wrestling with his cough, she slipped her letter into her desk, rubbed her face vigorously with her handkerchief and made a dart at the door. Grandfather Ludlow demanded strict punctuality and made the house shake if it failed him. What he would have said if he could have seen this eager, brown-haired, vivid girl, built on the slim lines of a wood nymph, swing herself on to the banisters and slide the whole way down the wide stairway would have been fit only for the appreciative ears of his faithful man. As it was, Mrs. Nye, the housekeeper, was passing through the hall, and her gasp at this exhibition of unbecoming athletics was the least that could be expected from one who still thought in the terms of the crinoline and had never recovered from the habit of regarding life through the early-Victorian end of the telescope.

Joan slipped into Mr. Cumberland Ludlow's own room, shut the door quickly and picked her way over the great skins that were scattered about the polished floor.

"Good morning, Grandfather," she said, and stood waiting for the storm to break. She knew by heart the indignant remarks about the sloppiness of the younger generation, the dire results of modern anarchy and the universal disrespect that stamped the twentieth century, and set her quick mind to work to frame his opening sentence.

But the old man, whose sense of humor was as keen as ever, saw in the girl's half-rebellious, half-deferential attitude an impatient expectation of his usual irritation, and so he merely pointed a shaking finger at the clock. His silence was far more eloquent and effective than his old-fashioned platitudes. He smiled as he saw her surprise, indicated a chair and gave her the morning paper. "Go ahead, my dear," he said.

Sitting bolt upright, with her back to the shaded light, her charming profile with its little blunt nose and rounded chin thrown up against the dark glistening oak of an old armoire, Joan began to read. Her clear, high voice seemed to startle the dead beasts whose heads hung thickly around the room and bring into their wide, fixed eyes a look of uneasiness.

Several logs were burning sulkily in the great open fireplace, throwing out a pungent, juicy smell. The aggressive tick of an old and pompous clock endeavored to talk down the gay chatter of the birds beyond the closed windows. The wheeze of a veteran Airedale with its chin on the head of a lion came intermittently.

They made a picture, these two, that fitted with peculiar rightness into the mood of Nature at that moment. Youth was king, and with all his followers had clambered over winter and seized the earth. The red remainders of autumn were almost over-powered. Standing with his hands behind him and his back to the fire, the old sportsman listened, with a queer, distrait expression, to the girl's reading. That he was still putting up a hard fight against relentless Time was proved by his clothes, which were those of a country-lover who dressed the part with care. A tweed shooting-coat hung from his broad, gaunt shoulders. Well-cut riding breeches, skin tight below his knees, ran into a pair of brown top-boots that shone like glass. A head and shoulders taller than the average tall man, his back was bent and his chest hollow. His thin hair, white as cotton wool, was touched with brilliantine, and his handsome face, deeply lined and wrinkled, was as closely shaved as an actor's after three o'clock. His sunken eyes, overshadowed by bushy brows, had lost their fire. He could no longer see to read. He too heard the call without, and when he looked at the young, sweet thing upon whom he was dependent for the news, and glanced about the room so full of memories of his own departed youth, he said to himself with more bitterness than usual: "I'm old; I'm very old, and helpless; life has no use for me, and it's an infernal shame."

Joan read on patiently, glancing from time to time at the man who seemed to her to be older than the hills, startlingly, terribly old, and stopped only when, having lowered himself into his arm-chair, he seemed to have fallen asleep. Then, as usual, she laid the paper aside, eager to be up and doing, but sat on, fearful of moving. Her grandfather had a way of looking as though he would never wake up again, and of being as ready as a tiger to pounce upon her if she tried to slip away. She would never forget some of the sarcastic things he had said at these times, never! He seemed to take an unexplainable delight in making her feel that she had no right to be so young. He had never confided to her the tragedy of having a young mind and an old body, young desires and winter in his blood. He had never opened the door in his fourth wall and let her see how bitterly he resented having been forced out of life and the great chase, to creep like an old hound the ancient dogs among. He had never let her suspect that the tragedy of old age had hit him hard, filling his long hours with regret for what he might have done or done better. Perhaps he was ashamed to confess these things that were so futile and so foolish. Perhaps he was afraid to earn a young incredulous laugh at the pathetic picture of himself playing Canute with the on-coming tide of years. He was not understood by this girl, because he had never allowed her to get a glimpse into his heart; and so she failed to know that he insisted upon keeping her in his house, even to the point of extreme selfishness, because he lived his youth over again in the constant sight of her. What a long and exquisite string of pearls there could be made of our unspoken words!

The logs glowed red; the hard tick of the pompous clock marked off the precious moments; and outside, spring had come. But Joan sat on with mutinous thoughts, and the man who not so long ago had stalked the beasts whose heads and skins were silent reminders of his strength, lay back in his chair with nodding head.

"He's old," she said to herself, "dreadfully, awfully old, and he's punishing me for being young. Oh! It's wicked, it's wicked. If only I had a father to spoil me and let me live! If only Mother hadn't forgotten all about me in her own happiness! If only I had money of my own and could run away and join the throng!"

She heard a sigh that was almost a groan, turned quickly and saw two slow tears running down her grandfather's face. He had been kicking against the pricks again and had hurt his foot.

With all the elaborate care of a Deerslayer, Joan got up, gave the boards that creaked a wide berth—she knew them all—and tiptoed to the door. The fact that she, at eighteen years of age, a full-grown woman in her own estimation, should be obliged to resort to such methods made her angry and humiliated. She was, however, rejoicing at one thing. Her grandfather had fallen asleep several pages of the paper earlier than usual, and she was to be spared from the utter boredom of wading through the leading articles which dealt with subways and Tammany and foreign politics and other matters for which she had a lofty contempt. She was never required to read the notices of new plays and operas and the doings of society, which alone were interesting to her and made her mouth water.

Just as she had maneuvered her way across the wide, long room and was within reach of the door, it opened and her grandmother hobbled in, leaning on her stick. There was a chuckle from the other end of the room. The blood flew to the girl's face. She knew without turning to look that the old man had been watching her careful escape and was enjoying the sight of her, caught at the moment when freedom was at hand.

Mrs. Ludlow was one of those busy little women who are thorns in the flesh of servants. Her eyes had always been like those of an inspecting general. No detail, however small, went unnoticed and unrectified.

She had been called by an uncountable number of housemaids and footmen "the little Madam"—the most sarcastic term of opprobrium contained in their dictionary. A leader of New York society, she had run charitable institutions and new movements with the same precision and efficiency that she had used in her houses. Every hour of her day had been filled. Not one moment had been wasted or frittered away. Her dinner parties had been famous, and she had had a spoke in the wheels of politics. Her witty sayings had been passed from mouth to mouth. Her little flirtations with prominent men and the ambitious tyros who had been drawn to her salon had given rise to much gossip. Not by any means a beauty, her pretty face and tiptilted nose, her perennial cheerfulness, birdlike vivacity and gift of repartee had made her the center of attraction for years.

But she, like Cumberland Ludlow, had refused to grow old gracefully and with resignation. She had put up an equally determined fight against age, and it was only when the remorseless calendar proved her to be sixty-five that she resigned from the struggle, washed the dye out of her hair and the make-up from her face and retired to that old house. Not even then, however, did she resign from all activity and remain contented to sit with her hands in her lap and prepare herself for the next world. This one still held a certain amount of joy, and she concentrated all the vitality that remained with her to the perfect running of her house. At eleven o'clock every morning the tap of her stick on the polished floors was the signal of her arrival, and if every man and woman of the menage was not actively at work, she knew the reason why. Her tongue was still as sharp as the blade of a razor, and for sloppiness she had no mercy. Careless maids trembled before her tirades, and strong men shook in their shoes under her biting phrases. At seventy, with her snowy hair, little face that had gone into as many lines as a dried pippin, bent, fragile body and tiny hands twisted by rheumatism, she looked like one of the old women in a Grimm's fairy tale who frightened children and scared animals and turned giants into cowards.

She drew up in front of the frustrated girl, stretched out her white hand lined with blue veins and began to tap her on the shoulder—announcing in that irritating manner that she had a complaint to make.

"My dear," she said, "when you write letters to your little friends or your sentimental mother, bear in mind that the place for ink is on the note paper and not on the carpet."

"Yes, Grandmother."

"Try to remember also that if you put your hand behind a candle you can blow it out without scattering hot grease on the wall paper."

"Yes, Grandmother"

"There is one other thing, if I may have your patience. You are not required to be a Columbus to discover that there is a basket for soiled linen in your bedroom. It is a large one and eager to fulfill its function. The floor of your clothes closet is intended for your shoes only. Will you be so good as to make a note of these things?"

"Yes, Grandmother."

Ink, candle grease, wash basket—what did they matter in the scheme of life, with spring tapping at the window? With a huge effort Joan forced back a wild burst of insurrection, and remained standing in what she hoped was the correct attitude of a properly repentant child. "How long can I stand it?" she cried inwardly. "How long before I smash things and make a dash for freedom?"

"Now go back and finish reading to your grand father."

And once more, trembling with anger and mortification, the girl picked her way over the limp and indifferent skins, took up the paper and sat down. Once more her clear, fresh voice, this time with a little quiver in it, fitted in to the regular tick of the querulous clock, the near-by chatter of birds' tongues and the hiss of burning logs.

The prim old lady, who had in her time borne a wonderful resemblance to the girl whom she watched so closely,—even to the chestnut-brown hair and the tip-tilted nose, the full lips, the round chin and the spirit that at any moment might urge her to break away from discipline,—retired to carry on her daily tour of inspection; and the old man stood again with his back to the fire to listen impatiently and with a futile jealousy to the deeds and misdeeds of an ever-young and ever-active world.

II

Joan was thankful when lunch was over, and murmured "Amen" to grace with a fervor that would have surprised an unimaginative and unobservant person. Like all the meals in that pompous dining-room, it was a form of torture to a young thing bubbling with health and high spirits, who was not supposed to speak unless directly addressed and was obliged to hold herself in check while her grandparents progressed slowly and deliberately through a menu of medically thought-out dishes. Both the old people were on a rigid diet, and mostly the conversation between them consisted of grumbles at having to dally with baby-food and reminiscences of the admirable dinners of the past. An aged butler and a footman in the sere and yellow only added to the general Rip van Winklism, and the presence of two very old dogs, one the grandfather's Airedale and the other Mrs. Ludlow's Irish terrier, with a white nose and rusty gray coat, did nothing to dispel the depression. The six full-length portraits in oils that hung on the walls represented men and women whose years, if added together, would have made a staggering grand total. Even the furniture was Colonial.

But when Joan had put on her hat, sweater and a pair of thick-soled country boots, and having taken care to see that no one was about, slid down the banisters into the hall on her way out for her usual lonely walk, she slipped into the garden with a queer sense of excitement, an odd and unaccountable premonition that something was going to happen. This queer thing had come to her in the middle of lunch and had made her heart suddenly begin to race. If she had been given to self analysis, which she was not, she might have told herself that she had received a wireless message from some one as lonely as herself, who had sent out the S.O.S. call in the hope of its being picked up and answered. As it was, it stirred her blood and made her restless and intensely eager to get into the open, to feel the sun and smell the sweetness in the air and listen to the cheery note of the birds.

It was with something of the excited interest which must have stirred Robinson Crusoe on seeing the foot-prints on the sand of what he had conceived to be a desert island that she ran up the hill, through the awakened woods whose thick carpet of brown leaves was alight with the green heads of young ferns, and out to the clearing from which she had so often gazed wist fully in the direction of the great city away in the distance.

She was surprised to find that she was alone as usual, bitterly disappointed to see no other sign of life than her friends the rabbits and the squirrels—the latter of which ambled toward her in the expectation of peanuts. She had no sort of concrete idea of what she had expected to find: nor had she any kind of explanation of the wave of sympathy that had come to her as clearly as though it had been sent over an electric wire. All she knew was that she was out of breath for no apparent reason, and on the verge of tears at seeing no one there to meet her. Once before, on her sixth birth day, the same call had been sent to her when she was playing alone with her dolls in the semitropical garden of a hired house in Florida, and she had started up and toddled round to the front and found a large-eyed little girl peering through the gate. It was the beginning of a close and blessed friendship.

This time, it seemed, the call had been meant for some other lonely soul, and so she stood and looked with blurred eyes over the wide valley that lay unrolled at her feet and, asked herself what she had ever done to deserve to be left out of all the joy of life. From somewhere near by the baying of hounds came, and from a farm to her left the crowing of a cock; and then a twig snapped behind her, and she turned eagerly.

"Oh, hello," said the boy.

"Oh, hello," she said.

He was not the hero of her dreams, by a long way. His hair didn't curl; his nose was not particularly straight; nor were his eyes large and magnetic. He was not something over six feet two; nor was he dressed in wonderful clothes into which he might have been poured in liquid form. He was a cheery, square-shouldered, good-natured looking fellow with laughter in his gray eyes and a little quizzical smile playing round a good firm mouth. He looked like a man who ought to have been in the navy and who, instead, gave the impression of having been born among horses. His small, dark head was bare; his skin had already caught the sun, and as he stood in his brown sweater with his hands thrust into the pockets of his riding breeches, he seemed to her to be just exactly like the brother that she ought to have had if she had had any luck at all, and she held out a friendly hand with a comfortable feeling of absolute security.

With some self-consciousness he took it and bowed with a nice touch of deference. He tried to hide the catch in his breath and the admiration in his eyes. "I'm glad it's spring," he said, not knowing quite what he was saying.

"So am I," said Joan. "Just look at those violets and the way the leaves are bursting."

"I know. Great, isn't it? Are you going anywhere?"

"No. I've nowhere to go."

"Same here. Let's go together."

And they both laughed, and the squirrel that had come to meet Joan darted off with a sour look. He had anticipated a fat meal of peanuts. He was out of it now, he saw, and muttered whatever was the squirrel equivalent for a swear-word.

The boy and girl took the path that ran round the outskirts of the wood, swung into step and chimed into the cantata of spring with talk and laughter.

There had been rather a long silence.

Joan was sitting with her back against the trunk of a fallen tree, with her hands clasped round her knees. She had tossed her hat aside, and the sunlight made her thick brown hair gleam like copper. They had come out at another aerie on the hill, from which a great stretch of open country could be seen. Her eyes were turned as usual in the direction of New York, but there was an expression of contentment in them that would have startled all the old people and things at home.

Martin Gray was lying full stretch on the turf with his elbows up and his chin on his left fist. He had eyes for nothing but the vivid girl whom he had found so unexpectedly and who was the most alive thing that he had ever seen.

During this walk their chatter had been of everything under the sun except themselves. Both were so frankly and unaffectedly glad to be able to talk at all that they broke into each other's laughing and childish comments on obvious things and forgot themselves in the pleasure of meeting. But now the time had come for mutual confidences, and both, in the inevitable young way, felt the desire to paint the picture of their own particular grievance against life which should make them out to be the two genuine martyrs of the century. It was now a question of which of them got the first look-in. The silence was deliberate and came out of the fine sense of sportsmanship that belonged to each. Although bursting to pour out her troubles, Joan wanted to be fair and give Martin the first turn, and Martin, equally keen to prove himself the champion of badly treated men, held himself in, in order that Joan, being a woman, should step into the limelight. It was, of course, the male member of the duet who began. A man's ego is naturally more aggressive than a woman's.

"Do you know," said Martin, arranging himself in a more comfortable attitude, "that it's over two months since I spoke to any one of about my own age?"

Joan settled herself to listen. With the uncanny intuition that makes women so disconcerting, she realized that she had missed her chance and must let the boy have his head.

Not until he had unburdened his soul would she be able, she knew, to focus his complete attention upon herself.

"Tell me about it," she said.

He gave her a grateful look. "You know the house with the kennels over there—the hounds don't let you miss it. I've been wandering about the place without seeing anybody since Father died."

"Oh, then, you're Martin Gray!"

"Yes."

"I was awfully sorry about your father."

"Thanks." The boy's mouth trembled a little, and he worked his thumb into the soft earth. "He was one of the very best, and it was not right. He was too young and too much missed. I don't understand it. He had twenty-five years to his credit, and I wanted to show him what I was going to do.

It's all a puzzle to me. There's something frightfully wrong about it all, and it's been worrying me awfully."

Joan couldn't find anything to say. Years before, when she was four years old, Death had come to her house and taken her own father away, and she had a dim remembrance of dark rooms and of her mother crying as though she had been very badly hurt. It was a vague figure now, and the boy's queer way of talking about it so personally made the conventional expressions that she had heard seem out of place. It was the little shake in his voice that touched her.

"He had just bought a couple of new hunters and was going to run the hunt this fall. I wanted him to live forever. He died in New York, and I came here to try and get used to being without him. I thought I should stay all alone for the rest of my life, but—this morning when I was moping about, everything looked so young and busy that I got a sort of longing to be young and busy again myself. I don't know how to explain it, but everything shouted at me to get up and shake myself together, and on the almanac in Father's room I read a thing that seemed to be a sort of message from him."

"Did you? What was it?"

"'We count it death to falter, not to die.' It was under to-day's date, and it was the first thing I saw when I went to the desk where Father used to sit, and it was his voice that read it to me. It was very wonderful and queer. It sort of made me ashamed of the way I was taking it, and I went out to begin again,—that's how it seemed to me,—and I woke everybody up and set things going and saw that the horses were all right, and then I climbed over the wall, and as I walked away, out again for the first time after all those bad weeks, I wanted to find some one young to talk to. I don't know how it was, but I went straight up the hill and wasn't a bit surprised when I saw you standing there."

"That's funny," said Joan.

"Funny—how?"

"I don't know. But if you hadn't found me after the feeling that came to me at lunch—"

"Well?"

"Well, I'm sure I should have turned bitter and never believed any more in fairies and all that. I don't think I mean fairies, and I can't explain what 'all that' stands for, but I know I should have been warped if I hadn't turned round and seen you."

And she laughed and set him laughing, and the reason of their having met was waved aside. The fact remained that there they were—youth with youth, and that was good enough.

III

There was a touch of idealism hidden away somewhere in Martin's character. A more than usually keen-eyed boy had once called him "the poet" at school. In order that this dubious nickname should be strangled at birth, there had been an epoch-making fight. Both lads came out of it in a more or less unrecognizable condition, but Martin reestablished his reputation and presently entered Yale free from the suspicion of being anything but a first-rate sportsman and an indisputable man.

There Martin had played football with all the desired bullishness. He had hammered ragtime on the piano like the best ordinary man in the University. With his father he rode to hounds hell for leather, and he wrote comic stuff in a Yale magazine which made him admiringly regarded as a sort of junior George Ade. It was only in secret, and then with a sneaking sense of shame, that he allowed his idealistic side to feed on Browning and Ruskin, Maeterlinck and Barrie, and only when alone on vacation that he bathed in the beauty of French cathedrals, sat thrilled and stirred by the waves of melody of the great composers, drew up curiously touched and awed at the sight of the places in the famous cities of Europe that echoed with the footsteps of history.

If the ideality of that boy had been seized upon and developed by a sympathetic hand, if his lively imagination and passion for the beautiful had been put through a proper educational course, he might have used the latent creative power with which nature had endowed him and taken a high place among artists, writers or composers. As it was, his machinelike, matter-of-fact training and his own self-conscious anxiety not to be different from the average good sportsman had made him conform admirably to type. He was a fine specimen of the eager, naive, quick-witted, clean-minded young American, free from "side," devoid of mannerisms, determined to make the utmost of life and its possibilities.

It is true that when death seized upon the man who was brother and pal as well as father to Martin, all the stucco beneath which he had so carefully hidden his spiritual and imaginative side cracked and broke. Under the indescribable shock of what seemed to him to be wanton and meaningless cruelty, the boy gave way to a grief that was angry and agonized by turns. He had left a fit, high-spirited father to drive to a golf shop to buy a new mashie, returned to take him out to Sleepy Hollow for a couple of rounds—and found him stretched out on the floor of the library, dead. Was it any wonder that he tortured himself with unanswerable questions, sat for hours in the dark trying with the most pitiful futility to fathom the riddle of life, or that he wandered aimlessly about the place, which was stamped with his father's fine and kindly personality,—like a stick suddenly swept out of the current of the main stream into a tideless backwater, untouched by the sun? And when finally, still deaf to the call of spring, his father's message of courage, "We count it death to falter, not to die," rang out and straightened him up and set him on the rails of action once again, it was not quite the same Martin Gray who uttered the silent cry for companionship that found an answer in Joan's lonely and rebellious heart. Sorrow had strengthened him. Out of the silent manliness of grief he went out again on the great main road with a wistful desire to love and be loved, to find some one with whom to link an arm in an empty world all crowded with strangers—and there stood Joan.

It was natural that he should believe, under those circumstances, that he and she did not meet by mere accident, that they had been brought together by design—all the more natural when he listened to her story of mental and physical imprisonment and came to see, during their daily stolen meetings, that he was as necessary to her as she was to him. Every time he left her and watched her run back to that old house of old people, it was borne in upon him more definitely that he was appointed in the cosmic scheme to rescue Joan from her peculiar cage and help her to try her wings. All about that young fresh, eager creature whose eyes were always turned so ardently toward the city, his imagination and superstition built a bower of love.

He had never met a girl in any way like her—one who wanted so much and would give so little in return for it, who had an eel-like way of dodging hard-and-fast facts and who had made up her mind with all the zest and thoughtlessness of youth to mold life, when finally she could prove how much alive she was, into no other shape than the one which most appealed to her. She surprised and delighted him with her quick mental turns and twists, and although she sometimes made him catch his breath at her astoundingly frank expression of individualism, he told himself that she was still in the chrysalis stage and could only get a true and normal hang of things after rubbing shoulders with what she called life with a capital L.

Two weeks slipped away more quickly than these two young things had ever known them to go, and the daily meetings, utterly guileless and free from flirtation, were the best part of the day; but there was a new note in Joan's laugh as she swung out of the wood and went toward Martin one afternoon.

He caught it and looked anxiously at her. "Is anything wrong?"

"There will be," she said. "I just caught sight of Gleave among the trees. He was spying!"

"Why do you think so?"

"Oh, he never walks a yard unless he has to. I thought I saw him eying me rather queerly at lunch. I've been looking happy lately, and that's made him suspicious."

"But what can he do?"

"What can't he do! Grandmother's one of the old-fashioned sort who thinks that a girl must never speak to a man without a chaperon. They must have been a lively lot of young women in her time! Gleave will tell her that I've been coming here to meet you, and then there'll be a pretty considerable row."

Martin was incredulous. He was in America in the twentieth century. Young people did as they liked, and parents hardly ventured to remonstrate. He showed his teeth in the silent laugh that was characteristic of him. "Oh, no! I'll be all right. Your grandfather knew my father."

"That won't make any difference. I believe that in a sort of way he's jealous of my having a good time. Queer, isn't it? Are all old people like that? And as to Grandmother, this will give her one of the finest chances to let herself go that she's had since I set a curtain on fire with a candle; and when she does that, well, things fly, I assure you."

"Are you worried about it?"

Joan gave a gesture of the most eloquent impatience. "I have to be," she said. "You can't understand it, but I'm treated just as if I were a little girl in short frocks. It's simply appalling. Everything I say and do and look is criticized from the point of view of 1850. Can't you imagine what will be thought of my sneaking out every afternoon to talk to a dangerous young man who has only just left Yale and lives among horses?"

That was too much for Martin. His laugh echoed among the trees.

But Joan didn't make it a duet. "It wouldn't be so funny to you if you stood in my shoes, Martin," she said. "If I had gone to Grandmother and asked her if I might meet you,—and just think of my having to do that,—she would have been utterly scandalized. Now, having done this perfectly dreadful thing without permission, I shall be hauled up on two charges,—deceit and unbecoming behavior,—and I shall be punished."

The boy wheeled around in amazement. "You don't mean that?"

"Of course I mean it. Haven't I told you over and over again that these two dear but irritating old people look down at me from their awful pile of years and only see me as a child?"

"But what will they do to you?"

Joan shrugged her shoulders. "Anything they like. I'm completely at their mercy. For Mother's sake I try to be patient and put up with it all. It's the only home I've got, and when you're dependent and haven't a cent to bless yourself with, you can't pack up and telephone for a cab and get out, can you? But it can't go on forever. Some day I shall answer back, and sparks will fly, and I shall borrow money from the coachman, who's my only friend, and go to Alice Palgrave and ask her to put me up until Mother comes back. I'm a queer case, Martin—that's the truth of it. In a book the other day I came across an exact description of myself. I could have laughed if it hadn't hit me so hard. It said: 'She was a super-modern in an early-Victorian frame, a pint of champagne in a little old cut-glass bottle, a gnome engine attached to a coach and pair.'" She picked up a stone and flung it down the hill.

One eager wild thought rushed through Martin's brain. It had made his blood race several times before, but he had thrown it aside because, during all their talks and walks, Joan had never once looked at him with anything but the eyes of a sister. As his wife he could free her, lift her out of her anomalous atmosphere and take her to the city to which her face was always turned. But he lacked the courage to speak and continued to hope that some day, by some miracle, she might become less superlatively neutral, less almost boyish in her way of treating him. He threw it aside again, tempted as he was to take advantage of a chance to bribe her into becoming his wife with an offer of life. Then too, she was only eighteen, and although he was twenty-four and in the habit of thinking of himself as a man of ripe years, he had to confess that the mere idea of marriage made him feel awfully young and scared. And so he said nothing and went on hoping.

Joan broke the silence. "Everything will be different when Mother comes back," she said. "I shall live with her then, and I give you my word I'll make up for lost time. So who cares? There are three good hours before I face Grandmother. Let's enjoy ourselves."

IV

Martin couldn't settle down after his solitary dinner that night. Several times he had jumped out of his father's reading chair and stood listening at the window. It seemed to him that some one had called his name. But the only sounds that broke the exquisite quietude of the night were the distant barking of a dog, the whirl of an automobile on the road or the pompous crowing of a master of a barnyard, taken up and answered by others near and far.

Each time the boy had stood at the open window and peered out eagerly and wistfully, but nothing had moved across the moon-bathed lawn or disturbed the sleeping flowers. Under the cold light of the stars the earth appeared to be more than usually peaceful and drowsy. All was well.

But the boy's blood tingled, and he was filled with an unexplainable sense of excitement. Some one needed him, and he wanted urgently to be needed. He turned from the window and ran his eyes over the long, wide, low-ceilinged masculine room, every single thing in which spelled Father to him; then he went back to the chair the right to sit in which had been given to him by death, persuaded that over the unseen wires that stretch from heart to heart a signal had been sent, certain that he was to hold himself in readiness to do something for Joan.

He had written out the words, "We count it death to falter, not to die" on a long strip of card in big bold letters. They faced him as he sat and read over and over again what he regarded as his father's message. It was a call to service, an inspiration to activity, and it had already filled him with the determination to fall into step with the movement of the world, to put the money of which he was now the most reluctant owner to some use as soon as the necessary legal steps of proving his father's Will had been taken. He had made up his mind to leave the countryside at the end of the week and meet his father's lawyers and take advice as to how he could hitch himself to some vigorous and operative pursuit. He was going, please God, to build up a workmanlike monument to the memory of his father.

Ten o'clock struck, and uninterested in his book, he would have gone to bed but for the growing feeling that he was not his own master, that he might be required at any moment. The feeling became so strong that finally he got up and went into the hall. He couldn't wait any longer. He must go out, slip into the garden of the Ludlow house and search the windows for a sight of Joan.

He unbolted the front door, gave a little gasp and found himself face to face with the girl who was in his thoughts.

There was a ripple of excited laughter; a bag was thrust into his hand, and like a bird escaped from a cage, Joan darted past him into the hall.

"I've done it," she cried, "I've done it!" And she broke into a dance.

Martin shut the door, put the bulging suit-case on a chair and watched the girl as she whirled about the hall, as graceful as a water sprite, with eyes alight with mischief and animation. The sight of her was so bewitching, the fact that she had come to him for help so good, that his curiosity to know what it was that she had done fell away.

Suddenly she came to a breathless stop and caught hold of his arm. "Bolt the door, Marty," she said, "quickly, quickly! They may send after me when they find I've got away. I'll never go back, never, never!"

All the spirit of romance in the boy's nature flamed. This was a great adventure. He had become a knight errant, the rescuer of a damsel in distress. He shot the bolts back, turned out the lights, took Joan's hand and led her into his father's room.

"Turn these lights out too," she said. "Make it look as if everybody had gone to bed."

He did so, with a sort of solemn sense of responsibility; and it was in a room lighted only by a shaft of pale moonlight that fell in a pool upon the polished floor that these two utterly inexperienced children sat knee to knee, the one to pour out her story, the other to listen and hold his breath.

"I was right about Gleave. He was spying. It turns out that he's been watching us for two or three days. When I went back this afternoon, I got a look from Mrs. Nye that told me there was a row in the air. I was later than usual and rushed up to my room to change for dinner. The whole house seemed awfully quiet and ominous, like the air before a thunderstorm. I expected to be sent for at once to stand like a criminal before Grandfather and Grandmother—but nothing happened. All through dinner, while Gleave tottered about, they sat facing each other at the long table, conducting,—that's the only word to describe it,—a polite conversation. Neither of them took any notice of me or even once looked my way. Even Gleave put things in front of me as though he didn't see me, and when I caught the watery eyes of the old dogs, they both seemed to make faces and go 'Yah!'"

"It was weird, and would have been frightfully funny if I hadn't known that sooner or later I should have to stand up and take my dose. Phew, it was a ghastly meal. I'm certain I shall dream it all over again every time I eat something that doesn't agree with me! It was a great relief when at last Grandmother turned at the door and looking at my feet as though they were curiosities, said: 'Joan, you will follow us to the drawing-room.' Her voice was cold enough to freeze the sea."

"Then she went out, her stick rapping the floor, Grandfather after her with his shoulders bent and a piece of bread on the back of his dinner jacket. The two dogs followed, and I made up the tail of that queer procession. I hate that stiff, cheerless drawing room anyhow, with all its shiny cases of china and a collection of all the uncomfortable chairs ever designed since Adam. I wanted to laugh and cry, and when I saw myself in the glass, I couldn't believe that I wasn't a little shivering girl with a ribbon in my hair and white socks."

Some one whistled outside. The girl seized the boy's arm in a sudden panic of fright.

"It's all right," he said. "It's only the gardener going to his cottage."

Joan laughed, and her grip relaxed. "I'm jumpy," she said. "My nerves are all over the place. Do you wonder?"

"No, tell me the rest."

Joan's voice took on a little deeper note like that of a child who has come to the really creepy bit of his story. "Marty," she went on, "I wish you could have heard the way in which Grandmother let herself go! She held me by the scruff of my neck and hit me right and left with the sort of sarcasm that made me crinkle. According to her, I was on the downward path. I had done something quite hopeless and unforgivable. She didn't know how she could bring herself to report the affair—think of calling it an affair, Marty!—to my poor mother. Mother, who'd never say a word to me, whatever I did! She might have out-of-date views, she said, of how young girls should behave, but they were the right views, and so long as I was under her roof and in her care, she would see that I conformed to them. She went on making a mountain out of our little molehill, till even Grandfather broke in with a word; and then she snapped at him, got into her second wind and went off again. I didn't listen half the time. I just stood and watched her as you'd watch one of those weird old women in one of Dickens' books come to life. What I remember of it all is that I am deceitful and fast, ungrateful, irresponsible, with no sense of decency, and when at last she pronounced sentence, what do you think it was? Confinement to the house for a week and if after that, I ever meet you again, to be packed off to a finishing-school in Massachusetts. She rapped her stick on the floor by way of a full stop, and waved her hand toward the door. I never said a word, not a single one. What was the use? I gave her a little bow and went. Just as I was going to rush upstairs and think over what I could do, Grandfather came out and told me to go to his room to read something to him. And there, for the first time, he let me see what a fine old fellow he really is. He agreed with Grandmother that I ought not to have met you on the sly. It was dangerous, he said, though perfectly natural. He was afraid I found it very trying to live among a lot of old grouches with their best feet in the grave, but he begged me to put up with it because he would miss me so. He liked having me about, not only to read to him but to look at. I reminded him of Grandmother when she was young, and life was worth living.

"I cried then. I couldn't help it—more for his sake than mine. He spoke with such a funny sort of sadness. 'Be patient, my dear,' he said. 'Treat us both with a little kindness. You're top dog. You have all your life before you. Make allowances for two old people entering second childhood. You'll be old some day, you know.' And he said this with such a twisted sort of smile that I felt awfully sorry for him, and he saw it and opened out and told me how appalling it was to become feeble when the heart is as young as ever. I had no idea he felt like that."

"When I left him I tried hard to be as patient as he asked me to be and wait till Mother comes back and make the allowances he spoke about and give up seeing you and all that. But when I got up to my room with the echo of Grandmother's rasping voice in my ears, the thought of being shut up in the house for a week and treated like a lunatic was too much for me. What had I done that every other healthy girl doesn't do every day without a question? How COULD I go on living there, watched and suspected? How could I put up any longer with the tyranny of an old lady who made me feel artificial and foolish and humiliated—a kind of doll stuffed with saw dust?

"Marty, I couldn't do it. I simply couldn't. Something went snap, and I just flung a few things into a suit-case, dropped it out the window, climbed down the creeper and made a dash for freedom. Nothing on earth will ever take me back to that house again, nothing, nothing!"

All this had been said with a mixture of humor and emotion that carried the boy before it. He saw and heard everything as she described it. His own relations with his father, which had been so free and friendly, made Joan's with those two old people seem fantastic and impossible. All his sympathy went out to her. To help her to get away appealed to him as being as humane as releasing a squirrel from a trap. No thought of the fact that she was a girl who had rushed impulsively into a most awkward position struck him. Into his healthy mind no sex question thrust itself. She was his friend, and as such, her claim upon him was overwhelming and unarguable.

"What do you want me to do?" he asked. "Have you thought of anything?"

"Of course I have. In the morning, early, before they find out that I've bolted, you must drive me to New York and take me to Alice Palgrave. She'll put me up, and I can telegraph to Mother for money to buy clothes with. Does it occur to you, Marty, that you're the cause of all this? If I hadn't turned and found you that afternoon, I should still be eating my soul away and having my young life crushed. As it is, you've forced my hand. So you're going to take me to the magic city, and if you want to see how a country cousin makes up for lost time and sets things humming, watch me!"

So they talked and talked, sitting in that room which was made the very sanctum of romance by young blood and moonlight. Eleven o'clock slipped by, and twelve and one; and while the earth slept, watched by a million glistening eyes, and nature moved imperceptibly one step nearer to maturity, this boy and girl made plans for the discovery of a world out of which so many similar explorers have crept with wounds and bitterness.

They were wonderful and memorable hours, not ever to be lived again. They were the hours that all youth enjoys and delights in once—when, like gold-diggers arrived in sight of El Dorado, they halt and peer at the chimera that lies at their feet—

"I'm going to make my mark," Martin said. "I'm going to make something that will last. My father's name was Martin Gray, and I'll make it MEAN some thing out there for his sake."

"And I," said Joan, springing to her feet and throwing up her chin, "will go joy-riding in the huge round-about. I've seen what it is to be old and useless, and so I shall make the most of every day and hour while I'm young. I can live only once, and so I shall make life spin whatever way I want it to go. If I can get anybody to pay my whack, good. If not, I'll pay it myself—whatever it costs. My motto's going to be a good time as long as I can get it, and who cares for the price?"

The boy followed her to the window, and the moonlight fell upon them both. "Yes," he said, "you'll get a bill, all right. How did you know that?"

"I haven't lived with all those old people so long for nothing," she answered. "But you won't catch me grumbling if I get half as much as I'm going out for. Listen to my creed, Martin, and take notes, if you want to keep up with me."

"Go ahead," he said, watching the sparkle in her eyes.

She squared her shoulders and folded her arms in a half-defiant way. "I shall open the door of every known Blue Room—hurrying out again if there are ugly things inside, staying to enjoy them if they're good to look at. I shall taste a little of every known bottle, feel everything there is to feel except the thing that hurts, laugh with any one whose laugh is catching, do everything there is to do, go into every booth in the big Bazaar; and when I'm tired out and there's nothing left, I shall slip out of the endless procession with a thousand things stored away in my memory. Isn't that the way to live?"

From the superior height of twenty-four, Martin looked down on Joan indulgently. He didn't take her frank and unblushing individualism seriously. She was just a kid, he told himself. She was a girl who had been caged up and held in. It was natural for her to say all those wild things. She would alter her point of view as soon as the first surprise of being free had worn off—and then he would speak; then he would ask her to throw in her lot with his and walk in step with him along the street of adventure.

"I sha'n't see the sun rise on this great day," she said, letting a yawn have full play. "I'm sleepy, Marty. I must lie down this very instant, even if the floor's the only place you can offer me. Quick! What else is there?" Before he could answer, she had caught sight of a low, long, enticing divan, and onto this, with a gurgle of pleasure, she made a dive, placed two cushions for her head, put one little hand under her face, snuggled into an attitude of perfect comfort and deliberately went to sleep. It was masterly.

Martin, not believing that she could turn off so suddenly at a complete tangent, spoke to her once or twice but got no other answer than a long, contented sigh. He stood for a little while trying to make out her outline in the dim corner of the room. Then he tiptoed out to the hall, possessed himself of a warm motor-rug, returned with it and laid it gently and tenderly over the unconscious girl.

He didn't intend to let sleep rob him of the first sight of a day that was to mean so much to him, and he went over to the open window, caught the scent of lilac and listened, with all his imagination and sense of beauty stirred, to the deep breathing of the night.... Yes, he had cut through the bars which had kept this girl from taking her place among the crowd. He was responsible for the fact that she was about to play her part in the comedy of life. He was glad to be responsible. He had passionately desired a cause to which to attach himself; and was there, in all the world, a better than Joan?

Spring had come again, and all things were young, and the call to mate rang in his ears and set his heart beating and his thoughts racing ahead. He loved her, this girl that he had come upon standing out in all her freshness against a blue sky. He would serve her as the great lovers had served, and please God, she would some day return his love. They would build up a home and bring up a family and go together up the inevitable hill.

And as he stood sentinel, in a waking dream, waiting for the finger of dawn to rub the night away, sleep tapped him on the shoulder, and he turned and went to the divan and sat down with his back to it, touched one of Joan's placid hands with his lips and drifted into further dreams with a smile around his mouth.

V

It was ten o'clock in the morning when Martin brought his car to a stop and looked up at the heavy Gothic decorations of a pompous house in East Fifty-fifth Street. "Is this it?"

"Yes," said Joan, getting out of the leather-lined coat that he had wrapped her in. "It really is a house, isn't it; and luckily, all the gargoyles are on the outside." She held out her hand and gave Martin the sort of smile for which any genuine man would sell his soul. "Marty," she added, "you've been far more than a brother to me. You've been a cousin. I shall never be able to thank you. And I adored the drive with our noses turned to the city. I shan't be able to be seen on the streets until I've got some frocks, so please come and see me every day. As soon as Alice has got over her shock at the sight of me, I'm going to compose an historical letter to Grandmother."

"Let her down lightly," said Martin, climbing out with the suit-case. "You've won."

"Yes, that's true; but I shouldn't be a woman if I didn't get in the last word."

"You're not a woman," said Martin. "You're a kid, and you're in New York, and you're light-headed; so look out."

Joan laughed at his sudden gravity and ran up the wide steps and put her finger on the bell. "I've written down your telephone number," she said, "and memorized your address. I'll call you up at three o'clock this afternoon, and if you've nothing else to do, you may take me for a walk in the Park."

"I sha'n't have anything else to do."

The door was opened. The footman was obviously English, with the art of footmanism in his blood.

"Is Mrs. Gilbert Palgrave at home?" asked Joan as if the question were entirely superfluous.

"No, miss."

"Are you sure?"

"Quite sure, miss. Mrs. Palgrave left for Boston yesterday on account of hillness in the family, miss."

There was an awkward and appalled silence. Little did the man suspect the kind of blow that his statement contained.

Joan darted an agonized look at Martin.

"But Mr. Palgrave is at 'ome, miss."

And that galvanized the boy into action. He had met Gilbert Palgrave out hunting. He had seen the impertinent, cocksure way in which he ran his eyes over women. He clutched the handle of the case and said: "That's all right, thanks. Miss Ludlow will write to Mrs. Palgrave." Then he turned and went down the steps to the car.

Trying to look unconcerned, Joan followed.

"Get in, quick," said Martin. "We'll talk as we go."

"But why? If I don't stay here, where am I to stay?"

"I don't know. Please get in."

Joan stood firm. The color had come back to her face, and a look of something like anger had taken the place of fright. "I didn't tell you to march off like that. Gilbert's here."

"That's why we're going," Said Martin.

"I don't understand." Her eyes were blazing.

"I know you don't. You can't stay in that house. It isn't done."

"I can do it, and I must do it. Do you suppose I'm going back with my tail between my legs?"

"If we argue here, we shall collect a crowd." He got into the car and held out his hand.

Joan ignored it but followed him in. She was angry, puzzled, disappointed, nonplussed. Alice had no right to be away on such an occasion. Everything had looked so easy and smooth-sailing. Even Martin had changed into a different man, and was ordering her about. If he thought he could drive her back to that prison again, he was considerably wrong. She would never go back, never.

The car was running slowly. "Have you any other friends in town?" asked Martin, who seemed to be trying to hide an odd kind of excitement.

"No," said Joan. "Alice is my only friend here. Drive to some place where I can call up Gilbert Palgrave and explain the whole thing. What does it matter about my being alone? If I don't mind, who should? Please do as I say. There's no other place for me to go to, and wild horses sha'n't drag me back."

"You sha'n't go back," said Martin. He turned the car up Madison Avenue and drove without another word to East Sixty-seventh Street and stopped in front of a small house that was sandwiched between a mansion and a twelve-story apartment-house. "This is mine," he said simply. "Will you come in?"

A smile of huge relief came into Joan's eyes. "Why worry?" she said. "How foolish of us not to have thought of this before!"

But there was no smile on Martin's face. His eyes were amazingly bright and his mouth set firmly. His chin looked squarer than ever. Once more he carried out the suit-case, put a latchkey into the lock and threw back the door. Joan went in and stood looking about the cheery hall with its old oak, and sporting prints, white wood and red carpet. "Oh, but this is perfectly charming, Marty," she cried out. "Why did we bother our heads about Alice when there is this haven of refuge?"

Martin marched up to her and stood eye to eye. "Because I'm alone," he said, "and you're a girl. That's why."

Joan made a face. "I see. The conventions again. Isn't there any sort of woman here?"

"Yes, the cook."

She laughed. There was a comic side to this tragedy, after all, it seemed. "Well, perhaps she'll give us some scrambled eggs and coffee. I could eat a horse."

Martin opened the door of the sitting room. Like the one in which she had slept so soundly the previous night, it was stamped with the character and personality of the other Martin Gray. Books, warm and friendly, lined the walls. Mounted on wood, fish of different sizes and breeds hung above the cases, and over the fireplace there was a full-length oil painting of a man in a red coat and riding breeches. His kind eyes greeted Joan.

For several minutes she stood beneath it, smiling back. Then she turned and put her hand involuntarily on the boy's shoulder. "Oh, Marty!" she said. "I AM sorry."

The boy gave one quick upward glance, and cleared his throat. "I told you that this house is mine. It isn't. It's yours. It's the only way, if you're to remain in the city. Is it good enough? Do you want to stay as much as all that?"

The puzzled look came back. For a moment Joan was silent, worrying out the meaning of Martin's abrupt and rather cryptic words. There seemed to be a tremendous amount of fuss because she happened to be a girl.

Martin spoke again before she had emerged from the thicket of inward questions. She was only eighteen, after all.

"I mean, you can marry me if you like." he said, "and then no one can take you back." He was amazed at his courage and hideously afraid that she would laugh at him. He had never dared to say how much he loved her.

She did laugh, but with a ring of so much pleasure and relief that the blood flew to his head. "Why, Marty, what a brain! What organization! Of course I'll marry you. Why ever didn't we think of that last night?"

But before he could pull himself together a man-servant entered with an air of extreme surprise. "I didn't know you'd come home, sir," he said, "until I saw the suit-case." He saw Joan, and his eyes rounded.

"I was just going to ring," said Martin. "We want some breakfast. Will you see to it, please?" Alone again, Martin held out his hand to Joan, in an odd, boyish way. And she took it, boyishly too. "Thank you, Marty, dear," she said. "You've found the magic carpet. My troubles are over; and oh, what a pretty little bomb I shall have for Grandmamma! And now let's explore my house. If it's all like this, I shall simply love it!" And away she darted into the hall.

"And now," said Joan, "being duly married,—and you certainly do make things move when you start, Marty,—to send a telegram to Grandmother! Lead me to the nearest place."

Certain that every person in that crowded street saw in them a newly married couple, Martin tried to hide his joy under a mask of extreme callousness and universal indifference. With the challenging antagonism of an English husband,—whose national habit it is invariably to stalk ahead of his women-kind while they scramble along at his heels,—he led the way well in advance of his unblushing bride. But his eyes were black with emotion. He saw rainbows all over the sky, and rings of bright light round the square heads of all the buildings which competed in an endeavor to touch the clouds; and there was a song in his heart.

They sat down side by side in a Western Union office, dallied for a moment or two with the tied pencils the points of which are always blunt, and to the incessant longs and shorts of a dozen telegraph instruments they put their epoch-making news on the neat blanks. Martin did not intend to be left out of it. His best pal was off the map, and so he chose a second-best friend and wrote triumphantly: "Have been married to-day. Staying in New York for honeymoon. How are you?" He was sorry that he couldn't remember the addresses of a hundred other men. He felt in the mood to pelt the earth with such telegrams as that.

"Listen," said Joan, her eyes dancing with mischief. "I think this is a pretty good effort: 'Blessings and congratulations on her marriage to-day may be sent to Mrs. Martin Gray, at 26 East Sixty-seventh Street, New York.—Joan.' How's that?"

It was the first time the boy had seen that name, and he blinked and smiled and got very red. "Terse and literary," he said, dying to put his arms round her and kiss her before all mankind. "They'll have something to talk about at dinner to-night. A nice whack in the eye for Gleave."

He managed to achieve a supremely blase air while the words were being counted, but it crumbled instantly when the telegraphist shot a quick look at Joan and gave Martin a grin of cordial congratulation.

As soon as he saw a taxi, Martin hailed it and told the chauffeur to drive to the corner of Forty-second Street and Fifth Avenue. "We'll walk from there," he said to Joan, "—if you'd like to, that is."

"I would like to. I want to peer into the shop windows and look at hats and dresses. I've got absolutely nothing to wear. Marty, tell me, are we well off?"

Martin laughed. She reminded him of a youngster going for a picnic and pooling pocket money. "Yes," he said, "—quite."

She sat back with her hands crossed in her lap. "I'm so glad. It simplifies everything to have plenty to spend." But for her exquisite slightness and freshness, no one would have imagined that she was an only just-fledged bird, flying for the first time. Her equability and poise were those of a completely sophisticated woman. Nothing seemed to surprise her. Whatever happened was all part and parcel of the great adventure. Yesterday she was an overwatched girl, looking yearningly at a city that appeared to be unattainable. To-day she was a married woman who, a moment ago, had been standing before a minister, binding herself for good or ill to a man who was delightfully a boy and of whom she knew next to nothing. What did it matter—what did anything matter—so long as she achieved her long-dreamed-of ambition to live and see life?

"Then I can go ahead," she added, "and dress as becomes the wife of a man of one of our best families. I've never been able to dress before. Trust

"You're not thinking about that already, surely!"

"Oh, no. But information is always useful, isn't it?"

Just for a moment the boy's heart went down into his boots. She didn't love him yet; he knew that He intended to earn her love as an honest man earns his living. What hurt was the note of flippancy in her voice in talking of an event that was to him so momentous and wonderful. It seemed to mean no more to her to have entered into a lifelong tie than the buying of a mere hat—not so much, not nearly so much, as to have found a way of not going back to those two old people in the country. She was young, awfully young, he told himself again. Presently her feet would touch the earth, and she would understand.

As they walked up Fifth Avenue and with little gurgles of enthusiasm Joan halted at every other shop to look at hats that appealed to Martin as absurdly, willfully freakish, and evening dresses which seemed deliberately to have been handed over to a cat to be torn to ribbons, it came back to him that one just such soft spring evening, the year before, he had walked home from the Grand Central Station and been seized suddenly with an almost painful longing to be asked by some precious person who belonged wholly to him to share her delight in all the things which then stood for nothing in his life. Then and there he fulfilled an ambition long cherished and hidden away; he touched Joan on the arm and opened the elaborate door of a famous jeweler. He was known to the shop from the fact that he and his father had always dealt there for wedding and Christmas presents. He was welcomed by a man in the clothes of a concert singer and with the bedside manner of a family doctor.

He was desperately self-conscious, and his collar felt two sizes too small, but he managed to get into his voice a tone that was sufficiently matter-of-fact to blunt the edge of the man's rather roguish smile. "Let me see your latest gold-mesh bags," he said as ordinary, everyday people ask to see collar studs.

"Marty!" whispered Joan. "What are you going to do?"

"Oh, that's all right," said Martin. "You can't get along without a bag, you see."

Half a dozen yellow, insinuating things were laid out on the shining glass, and with a wonderful smile that was worth all the gold the earth contained to Martin, Joan made a choice—but not hastily, and not before she had inspected every other gold bag in the shop. Even at eighteen she was woman enough to want to be quite certain that she possessed herself of the very best thing of its kind and would never have, in future, to feel jealous of one that might lie alluringly in the window.

"This one," she said finally. "I'm quite sure."

Martin didn't ask the price. It was for his bride. He picked it up and hung it over her wrist, said "The old address," nodded to the man,—who was just about to call attention to a tray of diamond brooches,—and led the way out, feeling at least six feet two.

And as Joan regained the street, she passed another milestone in her life. To be the proprietor of precisely just such a gold bag had been one of her steady dreams.

"Marty," she said, "what a darling you are!"

The boy's eyes filled with tears.

VI

It was an evening Martin would never forget.

His suggestion that they should dine at Delmonico's and go to the Empire to see Ethel Barrymore, accepted with avidity, had stirred Joan to immediate action. She had hailed a taxi, said, "You'll see me in an hour,

Marty," and disappeared with a quick injunction to have whatever she bought sent home C.O.D.

It was actually two hours before he saw her again. He thanked his stars that he had enough money in the bank to meet the checks that he was required to make out in quick succession. Joan had not wasted time, and as she got into the car to drive away from that sandwich house of excited servants, two other milestones had been left behind. She was in a real evening frock, and all the other things she had bought were silk.

They drove straight home from the theater. Joan was tired. The day had been long and filled with amazements. She was out in the world at last. Realization had exceeded expectation for the first time in history.

The sand-man had been busy with Martin's eyes too, but he led the way into the dining room with shoulders square and chin high and spring in his blood. This was home indeed.

"What a tempting little supper!" said Joan. "And just look at all these flowers."

They were everywhere, lilacs and narcissi, daffodils, violets and hothouse roses. Hours ago he had sent out the almost unbelieving footman for them. Joan and flowers—they were synonymous.

She put her pretty face into a great bowl of violets. "You remembered all my little friends, Marty," she said.

They sat opposite each other at the long table. Martin's father looked down at Martin's wife, and his mother at the boy from whom she had been taken when his eager eyes came up to the level of her pillow. And there was much tenderness on both their faces.

Martin caught the manservant's eyes. "Don't wait," he said. "We'll look after ourselves."

Presently Joan gave a little laugh. "Please have something yourself. You're better than a footman. You're a butler."

His smile as he took his place would have lighted up a tunnel.

"I like Delmonico's," said Joan. "We'll often dine there. And the play was perfectly splendid. What a lot of others there are to see! I don't think we'll let the grass grow under our feet, Marty. And presently we'll have some very proper little dinner parties in this room, won't we? Interesting, vital people, who must all be good-looking and young. It will be a long time before I shall want to see anyone old again. Think what Alice Palgrave will say when she comes back! She'll underline every word if she can find any words. She wasn't married till she was twenty."

And presently, having pecked at an admirable fruit salad, just sipped a glass of wine and made close-fitting plans that covered at least a month, Joan rose. "I shall go up now, Marty," she said. "It's twelve o'clock."

He watched her go upstairs with his heart in his throat. Surely this was all a dream, and in a moment he would find himself rudely and coldly awake, standing in the middle of a crowded, lonely world? But she stopped on the landing, turned, smiled at him and waved her hand. He drew in a deep breath, went back into the dining room, put his lips to the violets that had been touched by her face, and switched off the lights. The scent of spring was in the air.

"Come in," she said, when presently, after a long pause, he knocked at her door.

She was sitting at a gleaming dressing table in something white and clinging, doing her hair that was so soft and brown and electrical.

He dared not trust himself to speak. He sat down on the edge of a sofa at the foot of the bed and watched her.

She went on brushing but with her unoccupied hand gathered her gown about her. "What is it, Marty?" she asked quietly.

"Nothing," he said, finding something that sounded curiously unlike his voice.

She could see his young, eager face and broad shoulders in the looking-glass. His hands were clasped tightly round one knee.

"I've been listening to the sound of traffic," she said. "That's the sort of music that appeals to me. It seems a year since I did my hair in that great, prim room and heard the owls cry and watched myself grow old. Just think! It's really only a few hours ago that I dropped my suit-case out of a window and climbed down the creeper. We said we'd make things move, didn't we?"

"I shall write to your grandfather in the morning," said Martin, with almost comical gravity and an unconscious touch of patronage. How childlike the old are to the very young!

"That will be nice of you," answered Joan. "We'll be very kind to him, won't we? There'll be no one to read the papers to him now."

"He was a great chap once," said Martin. "My father liked him awfully."

She swung her hair free and turned her chair a little. "You must tell me what he said about him, in the morning. Heigh-ho, I'm so sleepy."

Martin got up and went to see if the windows were all open. "They'll call us at eight," he said, "unless you'd like it to be later."

Joan went to the door and opened it and held out her hand. "Eight's good," she said. "Good night, Marty."

The boy looked at the little open hand with its long fingers, and at his wife, who seemed so cool and sweet and friendly. What did she mean?

He asked her, with an odd catch in his voice.

And she gave him the smile of a tired child. "Just that, old boy. Good night."

"But—but we're married," he said with a little stammer.

"Do you think I can forget that, in this room, with that sound in the street?"

"Well, then, why say good night to me like this?"

"How else, Marty dear?"

An icy chill ran over Martin and struck at his heart. Was it really true that she could stand there and hold out her hand and with the beginning of impatience expect him to leave a room the right to which had been made over to him by law and agreement?

He asked her that, as well as he could, in steadier, kinder words than he need have used.

And she dropped her hand and sighed a little. "Don't spoil everything by arguing with me, Marty. I really am only a kid, you know. Be good and run along now. Look—it's almost one."

The blood rushed to his head, and he held out his hands to her. "But I love you. I love you, Joany. You can't—you CAN'T tell me to go." It was a boy's cry, a boy profoundly, terribly hurt and puzzled.

"Well, if we've got to go into all this now I may as well sit down," she said, and did. "That air's rather chilly, too." She folded her arms over her breast.

It was enough. All the chivalry in Martin came up and choked his anger and bitterness and untranslatable disappointment. He went out and shut the door and stumbled downstairs into the dark sitting room and stood there for a long time all among chaos and ruin. He loved her to adoration, and the spring was in his blood; and if she was young, she was not so young as all that; and where was her side of the bargain? And at last, through the riot and jumble of his thoughts, her creed of life came back to him, word for word: she took all she could get and gave nothing in return; and "Who cares?" was her motto.

And after that he stood like a man balanced on the edge of a precipice. In cold blood he could go back and like a brute demand his price. And if he went forward and let her off because he loved her so and was a gentleman, down he must go, like a stone.

He was very white, and his lips were set when he went up to his room. With curious deliberation he got back into his clothes and saw that he had money, returned to the hall, put on his coat and hat, shut the door behind him and walked out under the stars.

"All right, then, who cares?" he said, facing toward the "Great White Way." "Who the devil cares?"

And up in her room, with her hand under her cheek like a child, Joan had left the world with sleep.

PART TWO

THE ROUND-ABOUT

I

Alice Palgrave's partner had dealt, and having gone three in "no trumps" and found seven to the ace, king, queen in hearts lying before her in dummy, she wore a smile of beatific satisfaction. So also did Alice—for two reasons. The deal obviously spelled money, and Vere Millet could be trusted to get every trick out of it. There were four bridge tables fully occupied in the charming drawing-room, and as she caught the hostess' eye and smiled, she felt just a little bit like a fairy godmother in having surrounded Joan with so many of the smartest members of the younger set barely three weeks after her astonishing arrival in a city in which she had only one friend.

Alice didn't blind herself to the fact that in order to gamble, most of the girls in the room would go, without the smallest discrimination, to anybody's house; but there were others,—notably Mrs. Alan Hosack, Mrs.

Cooper Jekyll and Enid Ouchterlony,—whose pride it was to draw a hard, relentless line between themselves and every one, however wealthy, who did not belong to families of the same, or almost the same, unquestionable standing as their own. Their presence in the little house in East Sixty-seventh Street gave it, they were well aware, a most enviable cachet and placed Joan safely within the inner circle of New York society—the democratic royal inclosure. It was something to have achieved so soon—little as Joan appeared, in her astonishing coolness, to appreciate it. The Ludlows, as Joan had told Alice with one of her frequent laughs, might have come over in the only staterooms on the ship which towed the heavily laden Mayflower, but that didn't alter the fact that the Hosacks, the Jekylls and the Ouchterlonys were the three most consistently exclusive and difficult families in the country, to know whom all social climbers would joyously mortgage their chances of eternity. Alice placed a feather in her cap accordingly.

Joan's table was the first to break up. She was a loser to the tune of seventy dollars, and while she wrote her check to Marie Littlejohn, a tiny blond exotic not much older than herself,—who laid down the law with the ripe authority of a Cabinet Minister and kept to a daily time-table with the unalterable effrontery of a fashionable doctor,—talked over her shoulder to Christine Hurley.

"Alice tells me that your brother has gone to France with the Canadian Flying Corps. Aren't you proud of him?"

"I suppose so, but it isn't our war, and they're awfully annoyed about it at Piping Rock. He was the crack man of the polo team, you know. I don't see that there was any need of his butting into this European fracas."

"I quite agree with you," said Miss Littlejohn, with her eyes on the clock. "I broke my engagement to Metcalfe Hussey because he insisted on going over to join the English regiment his grandfather used to belong to. I've no patience with sentimentality." She took the check and screwed it into a small gold case. "I'm dining with my bandage-rolling aunt and going on to the opera. Thank goodness, the music will drown her war talk. Good-by." She nodded here and there and left, to be driven home with her adipose chow in a Rolls-Royce.

Christine Hurley touched a photograph that stood on Joan's desk. "Who's this good-looking person?" she asked.

"My husband," said Joan.

"Oh, really! When are we to see something of him?"

"Oh, I don't know," said Joan. "He's about somewhere."

Miss Hurley laughed. "It's like that already, is it? Haven't you only just been married?"

"Yes," said Joan lightly, "but we've begun where most people leave off. It's a great saving of time and temper!"

The sophisticated Christine, no longer in the first flush of giddy youth, still unmarried after four enterprising years, was surprised into looking with very real interest at the girl who had been until that moment merely a hostess. Her extreme finish, her unself-conscious confidence and intrepidity, her unassumed lightness of temper were not often found in one so young and apparently virginal. She dismissed as unbelievable the story that this girl had been brought up in the country in an atmosphere of early Victorianism. She had obviously just come from one of those elaborate finishing schools in which the daughters of rich people are turned into hothouse plants by sycophants and parasites and sent out into the world the most perfect specimens of superautocracy, to patronize their parents, scoff at discipline, ignore duty and demand the sort of luxury that brought Rome to its fall. With admiration and amusement she watched her say good-by to one woman after another as the various tables broke up. It really gave her quite a moment to see the way in which Joan gave as careless and unawed a hand to Mrs. Alan Hosack and Mrs. Cooper Jekyll as to the Countess Palotta, who had nothing but pride to rattle in her little bag; and when finally she too drove away, it was with the uneasy sense of dissatisfaction that goes with the dramatic critic from a production in which he has honestly to confess that there is something new—and arresting.

Alice Palgrave stayed behind. She felt a natural proprietary interest in the success of the afternoon. "My dear," she said emotionally, "you're perfectly wonderful!"

"I am? Why?"

"To any other just-married girl this would have been an ordeal, a nerve-wrecking event. But you've been as cool as a fish—I've been watching you. You might have been brought up in a vice-regal lodge and hobnobbed all your life with ambassadors. How do you do it?"

Joan laughed and threw out her arms. "Oh, I don't know," she said, with her eyes dancing and her nostrils extended. "I don't stop to think how to do things. I just do them. These people are young and alive, and it's good to be among them. I work off some of my own vitality on them and get recharged at the sound of their chatter. People, people—give me people and the clash of tongues and the sense of movement. I don't much care who they are. I shall pick up all the little snobbish stuff sooner or later, of course, and talk about the right set and all that, as you do. I'm bound to. At present everything's new and exciting, and I'm whipping it up. You wait a little. I'll cut out some of the dull and pompous when I've got things going, and limit myself to red-blooded speed-breakers. Give me time, Alice."

She sat down at the piano and crashed out a fox-trot that was all over town. No one would have imagined from her freshness and vivacity that she had been dancing until daylight every night that week.

"Well," said Alice when she could be heard, "I see you making history, my dear; there's no doubt about that."

"None whatever," answered Joan. "I'm outside the walls at last, and I'll go the pace until the ambulance comes."

"With or without Martin Gray?"

"With, if he's quick enough—without, if not."

"Be careful," said Alice.

"Not I, my dear. I left care away back in the country with my little old frocks."

Alice held out her hand. "You bewilder me a little," she said. "You make me feel as if I were in a high wind. You did when we were at school, I remember. Well, don't bother to thank me for having got up this party." She added this a little dryly.

With a most winning smile Joan kissed her. "You're a good pal, Alice," she said, "and I'm very grateful."

Alice was compensated, although her shrewd knowledge of character told her how easily her friend won her points. "And I hope you're duly grateful to Martin Gray?"

"To dear old Marty? Rather! He and I are great pals."

But that was all Alice got. Her burning curiosity to know precisely how this young couple stood must go unsatisfied for the time being. She had only caught a few fleeting glimpses of the man who had given Joan the key to life, and every time had wondered, from something in his eyes, whether he found things wholly good. She was just a little suspicious of romances. Her own had worn thin so quickly. "Good-by, my dear," she said. "Don't forget you're dining with me to-morrow."

"Not likely."

"What are you doing to-night?"

"Going to bed at nine o'clock to sleep the clock round. I'm awfully tired."

She stood quite still for many minutes after Alice had gone, and shut her eyes. In a quick series of moving pictures she saw thousands of little lights and swaying people and clashing colors, and caught snatches of lilting music and laughter. She was tired, and something that seemed like a hand pressed her forehead tightly, but the near-by sound of incessant traffic sent her blood spinning, and she opened her eyes and gave a little laugh and went out.

Martin was on his way downstairs. He drew up abruptly. "Oh, hello!" he said.

"Oh, hello!" said Joan.

He was in evening clothes. His face had lost its tan and his eyes their clear country early-to-bed look. "You've had a tea-fight, I see. I peered into the drawing-room an hour ago and backed out, quick."

"Why? They were all consumed with curiosity about you. Alice has advertised our romantic story, you see." She clasped her hands together and adopted a pose in caricature of the play heroine in an ecstasy of egomania.

But Martin's laugh was short and hollow. He wasn't amused. "How did you get on?" he asked.

"Lost seventy dollars—that's all. Three-handed bridge with Grandfather and Grandmother was not a good apprenticeship. I must have a few lessons. D'you like my frock? Come up. You can't see it from there."

And he came up and looked at her as she turned this way and that. How slim she was, and alluring! The fire in him flamed up, and his eyes flickered. "Awful nice!" he said.

"You really like it?"

"Yes, really. You look beyond criticism in anything, always."

Joan stretched out her hand. "Thank you, Marty," she said. "You say and do the most charming things that have ever been said and done."

He bent over the long-fingered hand. His pride begged him not to let her see the hunger and pain that were in his eyes.

"Going out?" she asked.

Martin gave a careless glance at one of B. C. Koekkoek's inimitable Dutch interiors that hung between two pieces of Flemish tapestry. His voice showed some of his eagerness, though. "I was going to have dinner with some men at the University Club, but I can chuck that and take you to the Biltmore or somewhere else if you like."

Joan shook her head. "Not to-night, Marty. I'm going to bed early, for a change."

"Aren't you going to give me one evening, then?" His question was apparently as casual as his attitude. He stood with his hands in his pockets and his legs wide apart and his teeth showing. He might have been talking to a sister.

"Oh, lots, presently. I'm so tired to-night, old boy."

He would have given Parnassus for a different answer. "All right then," he said. "So long."

"So long, Marty! Don't be too late." She nodded and smiled and went upstairs.

And he nodded and smiled and went down—to the mental depths. "What am I to do?" he asked himself. "What am I to do?" And he put his arms into the coat that was held out and took his hat. In the street the soft April light was fading, and the scent of spring was blown to him from the Park. He turned into Fifth Avenue in company with a horde of questions that he couldn't shake off. He couldn't believe that any of all this was true. Was there no one in all this world of people who would help him and give him a few words of advice? "Oh, Father," he said from the bottom of his heart, "dear old Father, where are you?"

The telephone bell was ringing as Joan went into her room. Gilbert Palgrave spoke—lightly and fluently and with easy words of flattery.

She laughed and sat on the edge of the bed and crossed her legs and put the instrument on her knee. "You read all that in a book," she said. "I'm tired. Yesterday and the night before... No... No... All right, then. Fetch me in an hour." She put the receiver back.

"Why not?" she said to herself, ringing for her maid. "Bed's for old people. Thank God, I sha'n't be old for a century."

She presented her back to the deft-fingered girl and yawned. But the near-by clatter of traffic sounded in her ears.

II

Gilbert Palgrave turned back to his dressing table. An hour gave him ample time to get ready.

"Don't let that bath get cold," he said. "And look here. You may take those links out. I'll wear the pearls instead."

The small, eel-like Japanese murmured sibilantly and disappeared into the bathroom.

This virginal girl, who imagined herself able to play with fire without burning her fingers, was providing him with most welcome amusement. And he needed it. He had been considerably bored of late—always a dangerous mood for him to fall into. He was thirty-one. For ten years he had paid far more than there had been any necessity to keep constantly amused, constantly interested. Thanks to a shrewd ancestor who had bought large tracts of land in a part of Manhattan which had then been untouched by bricks and mortar, and to others, equally shrewd, who had held on and watched a city spreading up the Island like a mustard plant, he could afford whatever price he was asked to pay. Whole blocks were his where once the sheep had grazed.

Ingenuity to spend his income was required of Palgrave. He possessed that gift to an expert degree. But he was no easy mark, no mere degenerate who hacked off great chunks of a splendid fortune for the sake of violent exercise. He was too indolent for violence, too inherently fastidious for degeneracy. And deep down somewhere in a nature that had had no incentive to develop, there was the fag end of that family shrewdness which had made the early Palgraves envied and maligned. Tall and well built, with a handsome Anglo-Saxon type of face, small, soft, fair mustache, large, rather bovine gray eyes, and a deep cleft in his chin, he gave at first sight an impression of strength—which left him, however, when he spoke to pretty women. It was not so much the things he said,—light, jesting, personal things,—as the indications they gave of the overweening vanity of the spoiled boy and of a brain which occupied itself merely with the fluff and thistledown of life. He was, and he knew it and made no effort to disguise the fact, a typical specimen of the very small class of indolent bystanders made rich by the energy of other men who are to be found in every country. He was, in fact, the peculiar type of aristocrat only to be found in a democracy—the aristocrat not of blood and breeding or intellect, but of wealth. He was utterly without any ambition to shine either in social life or politics, or to achieve advertisement by the affectation of a half-genuine interest in any cause. On the contrary, he reveled in being idle and indifferent, and unlike the aristocrats of Europe he refused to catch that archaic habit, encouraged at Eton and Oxford, of relating everything in the universe to the standards and prejudices of a single class.

Palgrave was triumphantly one-eyed and selfish; but he waited, with a sort of satirical wistfulness, for the time when some one person should cause him to stand eager and startled in a chaos of individualism and indolence and shake him into a Great Emotion. He had looked for her at all times and places, though without any troublesome optimism or personal energy, and had almost come to believe that she was to him what the end of the rainbow is to the idealist. In marrying Alice he had followed the path of least resistance. She was young, pretty and charming, and had been very much in love with him. Also it pleased his mother, and she had been worth pleasing. He gave his wife all that she could possibly need, except very much of himself. She was a perfectly dear little soul.

Joan only kept him waiting about fifteen minutes. With perfect patience he stood in front of an Italian mirror in the drawing-room, smoking a cigarette through a long tortoise-shell holder. He regarded himself with keen and friendly interest, not in the least surprised that his wife's little friend from the country so evidently liked him. He found that he looked up to his best form, murmured a word of praise for the manner in which his evening coat was cut and smiled once or twice in order to have the satisfaction of getting a glimpse of his peculiarly good teeth. Then he laughed, called himself a conceited ass and went over to examine a rather virile sketch of a muscular, deep-chested young man in rowing costume which occupied an inconspicuous place among many well-chosen pictures. He recognized Martin, whom he had seen several times following the hounds, and tried to remember if Alice had told him whether Joan had run away with this strenuous young fellow or been run away with by him. There was much difference between the two methods.

He heard nothing, but caught the scent of Peau d'Espagne. It carried his mind back to a charming little suite in the Hotel de Crillon in Paris. He turned and found Joan standing in the doorway, watching him.

"Did you ever row?" she asked.

"No," he said, "never. Too much fag. I played squash and roulette. You look like a newly risen moon in her first quarter. Where would you like to go?"

"I don't know," said Joan. "Let's break away from the conventional places. I rather want to see queer people and taste different food. But don't let's discuss it. I leave it to you." She went downstairs. She might have been living in that house for years.

He followed, admiring the way her small, patrician head was set on her shoulders, and the rich brown note of her hair. Extraordinary little person, this! He told his chauffeur to drive to the Brevoort, and got into the car. It was possible at that hour to deal with the Avenue as a street and not as a rest-cure interrupted by short spurts.

"Would you rather the windows were up, Gehane?" he asked, looking at her through his long lashes.

"No. The air's full of new ferns. But why Gehane?"

"You remind me of her, and I'm pretty certain that you also could do your hair in the same two long braids. Given the chance, I can see you developing into some-thing like medievalism and joining the ranks of women who loved greatly."

They passed the Plaza with all its windows gleaming, like a giant's house in a fairy tale.

Joan shook her head. "No," she said. "No. I'm just the last word of this very minute. Everybody in America for a hundred and fifty years has worked to make me. I'm the reward of mighty effort. I'm the dream-child of the pioneers, as far removed from them as the chimney of the highest building from the rock on which it's rooted."

Palgrave laughed a little. "It appears that you did some thinking out there in your country cage."

"Thinking! That's all I had to do! I spent a lifetime standing on the hill with the woods behind me trying to catch the music of this street, the sound of this very car, and I thought it all out, every bit of it."

"Every bit of what?"

"Life and death and the great hereafter," she said, "principally life. That's why I'm going out to dinner with you instead of going early to bed."

The glare of a lamp silvered her profile and the young curve of her bosom. Somewhere, at some time, Palgrave had knelt humbly, with strange anguish and hunger, at the feet of a girl with just that young proud face and those unawakened eyes. The memory of it was like an echo of an echo.

"Why," said Joan, halting for a moment on her way to the steps of the old hotel, "this looks like a picture postcard of a bit of Paris."

"Yes, on the other side of the Seine, near the Odeon. Our grandfathers imagined that they were very smart when they stayed here. It's one of the few places in town that has atmosphere."

"I like it," said Joan.

The hall was alive with people, laughing and talking, and the walls with the rather bold designs of the posters. A band, which made up in vim and go what it lacked in numbers, was playing a selection from "The Chocolate Soldier." The place was full of the smell of garlic and cigarette smoke and coffee. There was a certain dramatic animation among the waiters, characteristically Latin. Few of the diners wore evening clothes. The walls were refreshingly free from the hideous gold decorations of the average hotel.

Men stared at Joan with undisguised interest and approbation. Her virginity was like the breath of spring in the room. Women looked after Palgrave in the same way. Into that semi-Bohemianism he struck a rather surprising note, like the sudden advent of caviar and champagne upon a table of beer and pickles.

They were given a table near the wall by the window, far too close to other tables for complete comfort. Waiters were required to be gymnasts to slide between them and avoid an accident. Palgrave ordered without any hesitation, like a newspaper man finding his way through a daily paper.

"How do you like it?" he said.

Joan looked about her. Mostly the tables were occupied by a man and a woman, but at a few were four and six of both in equal numbers, and here and there parties of men. At one or two, women with eccentric heads sat together in curious garments which had the appearance of being made at home on the spur of the moment. They smoked between mouthfuls and laughed without restraint. Some of the men wore longish hair and the double tie of those who wish to be mistaken for dramatists. Others affected a poetic disarrangement of collar, and fantastic beards. There were others who had wandered over the border of middle age and who were bald and strangely adipose, with mackerel eyes and unpleasant mouths. They were with young girls, gaudily but shabbily dressed, shopgirls perhaps, or artists' models or stenographers, who in dull and sordid lives grappled any chance to obtain a square meal, even if it had to be accessory to such companionship. The minority of men present was made up of honest, clean, commonplace citizens who were there for a good dinner in surroundings that offered a certain stimulus to the imagination.

"Who are they all?" asked Joan, beating time with a finger to the lilting tune which the little band had just begun, with obvious enjoyment. "Adventurers, mostly, I imagine," replied Palgrave, not unpleased to play Baedeker to a girl who was becoming more and more attractive to him. "I mean people who live by their wits—writers, illustrators, actors, newspaper men, with a smattering of Wall Street brokers seeking a little mild diversion as we are, and foreigners to whom this place has a sentimental interest because it reminds them of home. Sophisticated children, most of them, optimists with moments of hideous pessimism, enthusiasts at various stages of Parnassus, the peak of which is lighted with a huge dollar sign. A friendly, kindly lot, hard-working and temperamental, with some brilliance and a rather high level of cleverness—slaves of the magazine, probably, and therefore not able to throw stones farther into the future than the end of the month. This is not a country in which literature and art can ever grow big; the cost of living is too high. The modern Chatterton detests garrets and must drive something with an engine in it, whatever the name it goes by."

There was one electrical moment during the next hour which shook the complacency of every one in the larger room and forced the thoughts, even of those who deliberately turned their backs to the drama of Europe, out across the waters which they fondly and fatuously hoped cut off the United States from ever being singed by the blaze. The little band was playing one of those rather feeble descriptive pieces which begin with soft, peaceful music with the suggestion of the life of a farmyard, and the sound of church bells, swing into the approach of armed men with shrill bugle calls, become chaotic with the rush of fearful women and children, and the commencement of heavy artillery, and wind up with the broad triumphant strains of a national anthem. It happened, naturally enough, that the particular national anthem chosen by the energetic and patriotic man who led the band at the piano was "The Marseillaise."

The incessant chatter and laughter went on as usual. The music had no more effect upon the closely filled room than a hackneyed ragtime. Suddenly, as the first few notes of that immortal air rang out, a little old white-haired man, dining in a corner with a much-bosomed, elderly woman, sprang to his feet and in a voice vibrating with the fervor of emotion screamed "Vive la France—vive la patrie!" again and again.

Instantly, from here and there, other men, stout and middle-aged, lifted out of their chairs by this intense and beautiful burst of feeling, joined in that old heart-cry, and for two or three shattering minutes the air was rent with hoarse shouts of "Vive Joffre," "Vive la France," "Vive la patrie," to the louder and louder undercurrent of music. Indifference, complacency, neutrality, gave way. There was a general uprising and uproar; and America, as represented by that olla podrida of the professions, including the one which is the oldest in the world, paid homage and tribute and yelled sympathy to those few Frenchmen among them whose passionate love of country found almost hysterical vent at the sound of the hymn which had stirred all France to a height of bravery and sacrifice never before reached in the history of nations.

There were one or two hisses and several scoffing laughs, but these were instantly drowned by vigorous hand-clapping. The next moment the room resumed its normal appearance.

When Palgrave, who had been surprised to find himself on his feet, sat down again, he saw that Joan's lips were trembling and that there were tears in her eyes. He gave a little laugh, but before he could say any thing, her hand was on his arm. "No, don't," she said. "Let it go without a single word. It was too good for sarcasm."

"Oddly enough, I had no sarcasm ready," replied Palgrave. "When our time comes, I wonder whether we shall have an eightieth part of that enthusiasm for our little old tune. What do you think?"

"Our time? What time?"

"The time when we have to get into this melee or become the pariah dog among countries. I don't profess to any knowledge of international affairs, but any fool can see that our sham neutrality will be the most costly piece of political blundering ever perpetrated in history. Here we are in 1915. The war's nine months old. For every day we stand aside we shall eventually pay a year's bill."

"That's all too deep for me," said Joan. "And anyway, I shan't be asked to pay anything. What shall we do now?"

"What would you like to do? Go on to the Ritz and dance?" He had a sudden desire to hold this girl in his arms.

"Why not? I'm on the verge of getting fed up with this place. Let's give civilization a turn."

"I think so." He beckoned to his waiter. "The check," he said. "Sharp's the word, please."

The Crystal Room was not content with one band. Even musicians must sometimes pause for breath, and anything like a break in the jangle and noise might bring depression to the diners who had crowded in to dance. As soon, therefore, as the left band was exhausted, the one on the right sprang in with renewed and feverish energy. Whatever melody there might have been in the incessant ragtime and fox trots was lost beneath the bang and clang of drum and cymbals, to which had been added other more ingenious ear tortures in the shape of rattles and whistles. Broken-collared men and faded women struggled for elbow room like a mass of flies caught on sticky paper. There was something both heathenish and pathetic in the whole thing. The place was reekingly hot.

"Come on," said Joan, her blood stirred by the movement and sound.

Palgrave held her close and edged his way into the crowd between pointed bare elbows and tightly clasped hands.

"They call this dancing!" he said.

"What do you call it?"

"A bullfight in Hades." And he laughed and put his cheek against her hair and held her young slim body against his own. What did he care what it was or where they were? He had all the excuse that he needed to get the sense and scent of her. His utter distaste of being bruised and bumped, and of adding himself to a heterogeneous collection of people with no more individuality than sheep, who followed each other from place to place in flocks after the manner of sheep, left him. This girl was something more than a young, naive creature from the country, childishly keen to do everything and go everywhere at fever heat—something more than the very epitome of triumphant youth as clean and sweet as apple blossoms, with whom to flirt and pose as being the blase man of the world, the Mr. Know-All of civilization, a wild flower in a hot house. Attracted at once by her exquisite coloring and delicious profile, and amused by her imperative manner and intolerant point of view, he had now begun to be piqued and intrigued by her insurgent way of treating marriage and of ignoring her husband—by her assumption of sexlessness and the fact that she was unmoved by his compliments and looked at him with eyes in which there was no remote suggestion of physical interest.

And it was this attitude, new to him hitherto on his easy way, that began to challenge him, to stir in him a desire to bring her down to his own level, to make her fall in love and become what he called human. He had given her several evenings, and had put himself out to cater to her eager demand to see life and burn the night away in crowds and noise. He had treated her, this young, new thing, as he was in the habit of treating any beautiful woman with whom he was on the verge of an affair and who realized the art of give and take. But more than ever she conveyed the impression of sex detachment to which he was wholly unaccustomed. He might have been any inarticulate lad of her own age, useful as a companion, to be ordered to fetch and carry, dance or walk, go or come. At that moment there was no woman in the city for whom he would undergo the boredom and the bruising and the dementia of such a place as the one to which she had drawn him. He was not a provincial who imagined that it was the smart thing to attend this dull orgy and struggle on a polished floor packed as in a sardine tin. Years ago he had outgrown cabaret mania and recovered from the fascination of syncopation. And yet here he was, once more, against all his fastidiousness, playing the out-of-town lad to a girl who took everything and gave nothing in return. It was absurd, fantastic. He was Gilbert Palgrave, the man who picked and chose, for whose attentions many women would give their ears, who stood in satirical aloofness from the general ruck; and as he held Joan in his arms and made sporadic efforts to dance whenever there was a few inches of room in which to do so, using all his ingenuity to dodge the menace of the elbows and feet of people who pushed and forced as though they were in a subway crush, he told himself that he would make it his business from that moment onward to lay siege to Joan, apply to her all his well-proved gifts of attraction and eventually make her pay his price for services rendered.

He had just arrived at this cold-blooded determination when, to his complete astonishment and annoyance, a strong, muscular form thrust itself roughly between himself and Joan and swept her away.

III

"Marty!" cried Joan.

There was a curious glint in Martin's gray eyes, like the flash of steel in front of a window. His jaw was set, and his face strangely white.

"You said you were going to bed."

"I was going to bed, Marty dear."

"What are you doing here, then?"

"I changed my mind, old boy, and went out to dinner."

"Chucked me in favor of Palgrave."

"No, I didn't."

"What then?"

"He rang up after you'd gone; and going to bed like an old crock seemed silly and feeble, and so I dressed and went out."

"Why with that rotter Palgrave?"

"Why not? And why rotter?"

"You don't answer my question!"

"Have I got to answer your question?"

"You're my wife, although you don't seem to know it; and I object to Pargrave."

"I can't help that, Marty. I like him, you see, and humble little person as I am, I can't be expected to turn my back on every one except the men you choose for me."

"I don't choose any men for you. I want you for myself."

"Dear old Marty, but you've got me forever!"

"No, I haven't. You're less mine now than you were when I only saw you in dreams. But all the same you're my wife, and I tell you now, you sha'n't be handled by a man like Palgrave."

They were in the middle of the floor. There were people all round them, thickly. They were obliged to keep going in that lunatic movement or be run down. What a way and in what a place to bare a bleeding heart!

For the first time since he had answered to her call and found her standing clean-cut against the sky, Martin held Joan in his arms. His joy in doing so was mixed with rage and jealousy. It had been worse than a blow in the mouth suddenly to see her, of whom he had thought as fast asleep in what was only the mere husk of home, dancing with a man like Palgrave.

And her nearness maddened him. All the starved and pent-up passion that was in him flamed and blazed. It blinded him and buzzed in his ears. He held her so tight and so hungrily that she could hardly breathe. She was his, this girl. She had called him, and he had answered, and she was his wife. He had the right to her by law and nature. He adored her and had let her off and tried to be patient and win his way to her by love and gentleness. But with his lips within an inch of her sweet, impertinent face, and the scent of her hair in his brain, and the wound that she had opened again sapping his blood, he held her to his heart and charged the crowd to the beat of the music, like a man intoxicated, like a man heedless of his surroundings. He didn't give a curse who overheard what he said, or saw the look in his eyes. She had turned him down, this half-wife, on the plea of weariness; and as soon as he had left the house to go and eat his heart out in the hub of that swarming lonely city, she had darted out with this doll-man whom he wouldn't have her touch with the end of a pole. There was a limit to all things, and he had come to it.

"You're coming home," he said.

"Marty, but I can't. Gilbert Palgrave—"

"Gilbert Palgrave be damned. You're coming home, I tell you, if I have to carry you out."

She laughed. This was a new Marty, a high-handed, fiery Marty—one who must not be encouraged. "Are you often like this?" she asked.

"Be careful. I've had enough, and if you don't want me to smash this place up and cause a riot, you'll do what I tell you."

Her eyes flashed back at him, and two angry spots of color came into her cheeks. He was out of control. She realized that. She had never in her life seen any one so out of control—unaccountable as she found it. That he would smash up the place and cause a riot she knew instinctively. She put up no further opposition. If anything were to be avoided, it was a scene, and in her mind's eye she could see herself being carried out by this plunging boy, with a yard of stocking showing and the laughter of every one ringing in her ears. No, no, not that! She began to look for Palgrave, with her mind all alert and full of a mischievous desire to turn the tables on Martin. He must be shown quickly that if any one gave orders, she did.

He danced her to the edge of the floor, led her panting through the tables to the foot of the stairs and with his hand grasping her arm like a vice, guided her up to the place where ladies left their wraps.

"We're going home," he said, "to have things out. I'll wait here." Then he called a boy and told him to get his hat and coat and gave him his check.

Five minutes later, in pulsating silence, both of them angry and inarticulate, they stood in the street waiting for a taxi. The soft air touched their hot faces with a refreshing finger. Hardly any one who saw that slip of a girl and that square-shouldered boy with his unlined face would have imagined that they could be anything but brother and sister. The marriage of babies! Was there no single apostle of common sense in all the country—a country so gloriously free that it granted licenses to every foolishness without a qualm?

Palgrave was standing on the curb, scowling. His car moved up, and the porter went forward to open the door. As quick as lightning, Joan saw her chance to put Martin into his place and evade an argument. Wasn't she out of that old country cage at last? Couldn't she revel in free flight without being called to order and treated like a school-girl, at last? What fun to use Palgrave to show Martin her spirit!

She touched him on the arm and looked up at him with dancing eyes and a teasing smile. "Not this time, Marty," she said, and was across the sidewalk in a bound. "Quick," she said to Palgrave. "Quick!" And he, catching the idea with something more than amusement, sprang into the car after her, and away they went.

A duet of laughter hung briefly in the air.

With all the blood in his head, Martin, coming out of utter surprise, made a dash for the retreating car, collided with the porter and stood ruefully and self-consciously over the burly figure that had gone down with a crash upon the pavement.

It was no use. Joan had been one too many for him. What, in any case, was the good of trying to follow? She preferred Palgrave. She had no use, at that moment, for home. She was bored at the mere idea of talking things over. She was not serious. She refused to be faced up with seriousness. She was like a precocious child who snapped her fingers at authority and pursued the policy of the eel at the approach of discipline. What had she cried out that night in the dark with her chin tilted up and her arms thrown out? "I shall go joy-riding in that huge round-about. If I can get anybody to pay my score, good. If not, I'll pay it myself, whatever it costs. My motto's going to be 'A good time as long as I can get it, and who cares for the price!'"

Martin helped the porter to his feet, stanched his flow of County Kerry reproaches with a ten-dollar bill and went back into the Crystal Room. He had gone there half an hour ago with a party of young people to kill loneliness and forget a bad hour of despair. His friend, Howard Oldershaw, who had breezed him out of the reading room of the Yale Club, was one of the party. He was in the first flush of speed-breaking and knew the town and its midnight haunts. He had offered to show Martin the way to get rid of depression. Right! He should be put to the test. Two could play the "Who cares?" game; and Martin, cut to the quick, angry and resisted, would enter his name. Not again would he put himself in the way of being laughed at and ridiculed and turned down, teased and tantalized and made a fool of.

Patience and gentleness—to what end? He loved a will-o'-the-wisp; he had married a butterfly. Why continue to play the martyr and follow the fruitless path of rectitude? Hadn't she said, "I can only live once, and so I shall make life spin whichever way I want it to go?" He could only live once, and if life was not to spin with her, let it spin without her. "Who cares?" he said to himself. "Who the devil cares?" He gave up his coat and hat, and went back into that room of false joy and syncopation.

It was one o'clock when he stood in the street once more, hot and wined and careless. "Let's hit it up," he said to Oldershaw as the car moved away with the sisters and cousins of the other two men. "I haven't started yet."

The red-haired, roistering Oldershaw, newly injected with the virus of the Great White Way, clapped him on the back. "Bully for you, old son," he said. "I'm in the mood to paint the little old town. I left my car round the corner in charge of a down-at-heel night-bird. Come on. Let's go and see if he's pinched it."

It was one of those Italian semi-racing cars with a body which gave it the naked appearance of a muscular Russian dancer dressed in a skin and a pair of bangles. The night-bird, one of the large army of city gypsies who hang on to life by the skin of their teeth, was sitting on the running board with his arms folded across his shirtless chest, smoking a salvaged cigar, dreaming, probably, of hot sausages and coffee. He afforded a striking illustration of the under dog cringing contentedly at the knees of wealth.

"Good man," said Oldershaw, paying him generously. "Slip aboard, Martin, and I'll introduce you to one of the choicest dives I know."

But the introduction was not to be effected that night, at any rate. Driving the car as though it were a monoplane in a clear sky, with an open throttle that awoke the echoes, Oldershaw charged into Fifth Avenue and caught the bonnet of a taxicab that was going uptown. There was a crash, a scream, a rending of metal. And when Martin picked himself up with a bruised elbow and a curious sensation of having stopped a punching bag with his face, he saw Oldershaw bending over the crumpled body of the taxi driver and heard a girl with red lips and a small white hat calling on Heaven for retribution.

"Some men oughtn't to be trusted with machinery," said Oldershaw with his inevitable grin. "If I can yank my little pet out of this buckled-up lump of stuff, I'll drive that poor chap to the nearest hospital. Look after the angel, Martin, and give my name and address to the policeman. As this is my third attempt to kill myself this month, things ought to settle down into humdrum monotony for a bit now."

Martin went over to the girl. "I hope you're not hurt?" he asked.

"Hurt?" she cried out hysterically, feeling herself all over. "Of course I'm hurt. I'm crippled for life. My backbone's broken; I shall have water on both knees, a glass eye and a mouth full of store teeth. But you don't care, you Hun. You like it."

And on she went, at the top of her voice, in an endless flow of farce and tragedy, crying and laughing, examining herself with eager hands, disbelieving more and more in the fact that she was still in the only world that mattered to her.

Having succeeded in backing his dented car out of the debris, Oldershaw leaped out. His face had been cut by the glass of the broken windshield. Blood was trickling down his fat, good-natured face. His hat was smashed and looked like that of the tramp cyclist of the vaudeville stage. "All my fault, old man," he said in his best irrepressible manner, as a policeman bore down upon him. "Help me to hike our prostrate friend into my car, and I'll whip him off to a hospital. He's only had the stuffing knocked out of him. It's no worse than that.... That's fine. Big chap, isn't he—weighs a ton. I'll get off right away, and my friend there will give you all you want to know. So long." And off he went, one of his front wheels wabbling foolishly.

The policeman was not Irish or German-American. He was therefore neither loud nor browbeating. He was dry, quiet and accurate, and it seemed to Martin that either he didn't enjoy being dressed in a little brief authority or was a misanthrope, eager to return to his noiseless and solitary tramp under the April stars. Martin gave him Oldershaw's full name and address and his own; and the girl, still shrill and shattered, gave hers, after protesting that all automobiles ought to be put in a gigantic pile and scrapped, that all harum-scarum young men should be clapped in bed at ten o'clock and that all policemen should be locked up in their stations to play dominoes. "If it'll do you any good to know it," she said finally, "it's Susie Capper, commonly called 'Tootles.' And I tell you what it is. If you come snooping round my place to get me before the beak, I'll scream and kick, so help me Bob, I will." There was an English cockney twang in her voice.

The policeman left her in the middle of a paean, with the wounded taxi and Martin, and the light of a lamp-post throwing up the unnatural red of her lips on a pretty little white face. He had probably gone to call up the taxicab company.

Then she turned to Martin. "The decent thing for you to do, Mr. Nut, is to see me home," she said. "I'm blowed if I'm going to face any more attempts at murder alone. My word, what a life!"

"Come along, then," said Martin, and he put his hand under her elbow. That amazing avenue, which had the appearance of a great, deep cut down the middle of an uneven mountain, was almost deserted. From the long line of street lamps intermittent patches of light were reflected as though in glass. The night and the absence of thickly crawling motors and swarming crowds gave it dignity. A strange, incongruous Oriental note was struck by the deep red of velvet hangings thrown up by the lights in a furniture dealer's shop on the second floor of a white building.

"Look for a row of women's ugly wooden heads painted by some one suffering from delirium tremens," said Miss Susie Capper as they turned down West Forty-sixth Street. "It's a dressmaker's, although you might think it was an asylum for dope fiends. I've got a bedroom, sitter and bath on the top floor. The house is a rabbit warren of bedrooms, sitters and baths, and in every one of them there's some poor devil trying to squeeze a little kindness out of fate. That wretched taxi driver! He may have a wife waiting for him. Do you think that red-haired feller's got to the hospital yet? He had a nice cut on his own silly face—and serve him right! I hope it'll teach him that he hasn't bought the blooming world—but of course it won't. He's the sort that never gets taught anything, worse luck! Nobody spanked him when he was young and soft. Come on up, and you shall taste my scrambled eggs. I'll show you what a forgiving little soul I am."

She laughed, ran her eyes quickly over Martin, and opened the door with a latchkey. Half a dozen small letter boxes were fastened to the wall, with cards in their slots.

"Who the devil cares?" said Martin to himself, and he followed the girl up the narrow, ill-lighted staircase covered with shabby carpet. Two or three inches of white stockings gleamed above the drab uppers of her high-heeled boots. Outside the open door of a room on the first floor there was a line of milk bottles, and Martin sighted a man in shirt sleeves, cooking sausages on a small gas jet in a cubby-hole. He looked up, and a cheery smile broke out on his clean-shaven face. There was brown grease paint on his collar. "Hello, Tootles," he called out.

"Hello, Laddy," she said. "How'd it go to-night?"

"Fine. Best second night in the history of the theater. Come in and have a bite."

"Can't. Got company."

And up they went, the aroma following.

A young woman in a sky-blue peignoir scuttled across the next landing, carrying a bottle of beer in each hand. There was a smell of onions and hot cheese. "What ho, Tootles," she said.

"What ho, Irene. Is it true they've put your notice up?"

"Yep, the dirty dogs! Twelve weeks' rehearsals and eight nights' playing! Me for the novelties at Gimbel's, if this goes on."

A phonograph in another room ground out an air from "Boheme."

They mounted again. "Here's me," said Miss Capper, waving her hand to a man in a dirty dressing gown who was standing on the threshold of the front apartment, probably to achieve air. The room behind him was foggy with tobacco smoke which rose from four men playing cards. He himself was conspicuously drunk and would have spoken if he had been able. As it was, he nodded owlishly and waggled his fingers.

The girl threw open her door and turned up the light. "England, Home and Beauty," she said. "Excuse me while I dress the ship."

Seizing a pair of corsets that sprawled loosely on the center table, she rammed them under a not very pristine cushion on the sofa.

Martin burst out laughing. The Crystal Room wine was still in his head. "Very nippy!" he said.

"Have to be nippy in this life, believe me. Give me a minute to powder my nose and murmur a prayer of thanksgivin', and then I'll set the festive board and show you how we used to scramble eggs in Shaftesbury Avenue."

"Right," said Martin, getting out of his overcoat. How about it? Was this one way of making the little old earth spin?

Susie Capper went into a bedroom even smaller than the sitting room, turned up the light over her dressing table and took off her little white hat. From where Martin stood, he could see in the looking-glass the girl's golden bobbed hair, pretty oval face with too red lips and round white neck. There, it was obvious, stood a little person feminine from the curls around her ears to the hole in one of her stockings, and as highly and gladly sexed as a purring cat.

"Buck up, Tootles," cried Martin. "Where do you keep the frying pan?"

She turned and gave him another searching look, this time of marked approval. "My word, what a kid you look in the light!" she said. "No one would take you for a blooming road-hog. Well, who knows? You and I may have been brought together like this to work out one of Fate's little games. This may be the beginning of a side-street romance, eh?"

And she chuckled at the word and turned her nose into a small snow-capped hill.

IV

Pagliacci was to be followed as usual by "Cavalleria." It was the swan song of the opera season.

In a part that he acted as well as he sang, Caruso had been permitted finally to retire, wringing wet, to his dressing room. With all the dignity of a man of genuine feeling and sensitiveness he had taken call after call on the fall of the curtain and stood bent almost double before the increasing breakers of applause. Once more he had done his best in a role which demanded everything that he had of voice and passion, comedy and tragedy. Once more, although his soul was with his comrades in battle, he had played the fool and broken his heart for the benefit of his good friends in front.

In her box on the first tier Mrs. Cooper Jekyll, in a dress imaginatively designed to display a considerable quantity of her figure, was surrounded by a party which attracted many glasses. Alice Palgrave was there, pretty and scrupulously neat, even perhaps a little prim, her pearls as big as marbles. Mrs. Alan Hosack made a most effective picture with her black hair and white skin in a geranium-colored frock—a Van Beers study to the life. Mrs. Noel d'Oyly lent an air of opulence to the box, being one of those lovely but all too ample women who, while compelling admiration, dispel intimacy. Joan, a young daffodil, sat bolt upright among them, with diamonds glistening in her hair like dew. Of the four men, Gilbert Palgrave, standing where he could be seen, might have been an illustration by Du Maurier of one of Ouida's impossible guardsmen. He made the other three, all of the extraordinary ordinary type, appear fifty per cent, more manly than they really were—the young old Hosack with his groomlike face and immaculate clothes, the burly Howard Cannon, who retained a walrus mustache in the face of persistent chaff, and Noel d'Oyly, who when seen with his Junoesque wife made the gravest naturalists laugh at the thought of the love manners of the male and female spider.

Turning her chair round, Alice touched Joan's arm. "Will you do something for me?" she asked.

Joan looked at her with a smile of disturbing frankness. "It all depends whether it will upset any of my plans," she said.

"I wouldn't have asked you if I had thought that."

Joan laughed. "You've been studying my character, Alice."

"I did that at school, my dear." Mrs. Palgrave spoke lightly, but it was plain to see that there was something on her mind. "Don't go out to supper with Howard Cannon. Come back with me. I want to talk to you. Will you?"

Joan had recently danced in Cannon's huge studio-apartment and been oppressed by its Gulliveresque atmosphere, and she had just come from the Fifth Avenue house of the Hosack family, where a characteristically dignified dinner had got on her nerves. Gilbert, she knew, was engaged to play roulette at the club, and none of her other new men friends was available for dancing. She hadn't seen anything of Martin for several days. She could easily oblige Alice under the circumstances.

So she said: "Yes, of course I will—just to prove how very little you really know about me."

"Thank you," said Alice. "I'll say that I have a headache and that you're coming home with me. Don't be talked out of it."

A puzzled expression came into Joan's eyes, and she turned her shoulder to Palgrave, who was giving her his most amorous glances. "It doesn't matter," she said, "but I notice that you are all beginning to treat me like a sort of moral weathercock. I wonder why?" She gave no more thought to the matter which just for the most fleeting moment had rather piqued her, but sat drinking in the music of Mascagni's immortal opera entirely ignoring the fact that Palgrave's face was within an inch of her shoulder and that Alan Hosack, on her other side, was whispering heavy compliments.

Alice sat back and looked anxiously from the face of the girl who had been her closest friend at school to that of the man to whom she had given all her heart. In spite of the fact that she had been married a year and had taken her place in the comparatively small set which made up New York society, Mrs. Palgrave was an optimist. As a fiction-fed girl she had expected, with a thrill of excitement, that after marriage she would find herself in a whirlpool of careless and extravagant people who made their own elastic code of morals and played ducks and drakes with the Commandments. She had accepted as a fact the novelist-playwright contention that society was synonymous with flippancy, selfishness and unchastity, and that the possession of money and leisure necessarily undermined all that was excellent in human nature. Perhaps a little to her disappointment, she had soon discovered how grotesque and ignorant this play-and-book idea was. She had returned from her honeymoon in November of the first year of the war and had been astonished to find that nearly all the well-known women whose names, in the public imagination, were associated with decadence and irresponsibility, were as a matter of fact devoted to Red Cross work and allied war charities; that the majority of the men who were popularly supposed to be killing time with ingenious wickedness worked as hard as the average downtown merchant, and that even the debutantes newly burst upon the world had, for the most part, banded themselves together as a junior war-relief society and were turning out weekly an immense number of bandages for the wounded soldiers of France and England. Young men of high and gallant spirit, who bore the old names of New York, had disappeared without a line of publicity—to be heard of later as members of the already famous Escadrille or as ambulance workers on the Western front. Beautiful girls had slipped quietly away from their usual haunts, touched by a deep and rare emotion, to work in Allied hospitals three thousand miles and more away—if not as full-blown nurses, then as scullery maids or motor drivers.

There were, of course, the Oldershaws and the Marie Littlejohns and the Christine Hurleys and the rest. Alice had met and watched them throwing themselves against any bright light like all silly moths. And there were the girls like Joan, newly released from the exotic atmosphere of those fashionable finishing schools which no sane country should permit. But even these wild and unbroken colts and fillies, she believed, had excuses. They were the natural results of a complete lack of parental discipline and school training. They ran amuck, advertised by the press and applauded by the hawks who pounced upon their wallets. They were more to be pitied than condemned, far more foolish and ridiculous than decadent. They were not unique, either, or peculiar to their own country. Every nation possessed its "smart set," its little group of men and women who were ripe for the lunatic asylum, and even the war and its iron tonic had failed to shock them into sanity. In her particularly sane way of looking at things, Alice saw all this, was proud to know that the majority of the people who formed American society were fine and sound and generous, and kept as much as possible out of the way of those others whose one object in life was to outrage the conventions. It was only when people began to tell her of seeing her husband and her friend about together night after night that she found herself wondering, with jealousy in her heart, how long her optimism would endure, because Gilbert had already shown her a foot of clay, and Joan was deliberately flying wild.

It was, at any rate, all to the good that Joan kept her promise and utterly refused to be turned by the pleadings and blandishments of Cannon and Hosack. They drove together to Palgrave's elaborate house, a faithful replica of one of the famous Paris mansions in the Avenue Wagram and sat down to a little supper in Alice's boudoir.

They made a curious picture, these two children, one just over twenty, the other under nineteen; and as they sat in that lofty room hung with French tapestries and furnished with the spindle-legged gilt chairs and tables of Louis XIV, they might have been playing, with all the gravity and imitative genius of little girls in a nursery, at being grown up.

While the servants moved discreetly about, Joan kept up a rattle of impersonalities, laughing at Cannon's amazing mustache and Gargantuan furniture, enthusing wildly over Caruso's once-in-a-century voice, throwing satire at Mrs. Cooper Jekyll's confirmed belief in her divine right to queen it, and saying things that made Alice chuckle about the d'Oylys—that apparently ill-matched pair. She drank a glass of champagne with the air of a connoisseur and finally, having displayed an excellent appetite, mounted a cigarette into a long thin mother-of-pearl holder, lighted it and sank with a sigh into the room's one comfortable chair.

"Gilbert gave me a cigarette holder like that," said Alice.

"Yes? I think this comes from him," said Joan. "A thoughtful person!"

That Joan was not quite sure from whom she received it annoyed Alice far more than if she had boasted of it as one of Gilbert's numerous gifts. She needed no screwing up now to say what she had rather timidly brought this cool young slip of a thing there to discuss.

"Will you tell me about yourself and Gilbert?" she asked quietly. There was no need for Joan to act complete composure. She felt it. "What is there to tell, my dear?"

"I hope there isn't anything—I mean anything that matters. But perhaps you don't know that people have begun to talk about you, and I think you owe it to me to be perfectly frank."

Even then it didn't occur to Joan that there was anything serious in the business. "I'll be as frank as the front page of The Times—'All the news that's fit to print,'" she said. "What do you want to know?"

Alice proved her courage. She drew up a chair, bent forward and came straight to the point. "Be honest with me, Joan, even if you have to hurt me. Gilbert is very handsome, and women throw themselves at him. I did, I suppose; but having won him and being still in my first year of marriage, I'm naturally jealous when he lets himself be drawn off by them. The women who have tried to take Gilbert away from me I didn't know, and they owed me no friendship. But you're different, and I can't believe that you—"

Joan broke in with a peal of laughter. "Can't you? Why not? I haven't got wings on my shoulders. Isn't everything fair in love and war?"

Alice drew back. She had many times been called prim and old-fashioned, especially at school, by Joan and others when men were talked about, and the glittering life that lay beyond the walls. Sophistication, to put it mildly, had been the order of the day in that temporary home of the young idea. But this calm declaration of disloyalty took her color away, and her breath. Here was honesty with a vengeance!

"Joan!" she cried. "Joan!" And she put up her hand as though to ward off an unbelievable thought.

In an instant Joan was on her feet with her arms around the shoulders of the best friend she had, whose face had gone as white as stone. "Oh, my dear," she said, "I'm sorry. Forgive me. I didn't mean that in the least, not in the very least. It was only one of my cheap flippancies, said just to amuse myself and shock you. Don't you believe me?"

Tears came to Alice. She had had at least one utterly sleepless night and several days of mental anguish. She was one of the women who love too well. She confessed to these things, brokenly, and it came as a kind of shock to Joan to find some one taking things seriously and allowing herself to suffer.

"Why, Alice," she said, "Gilbert means nothing to me. He's a dear old thing; he's awfully nice to look at; he sums things up in a way that makes me laugh; and he dances like a streak. But as to flirting with him or anything of that sort—why, my dear, he looks on me as a little boob from the country, and in my eyes he's simply a man who carries a latchkey to amusement and can give me a good time. That's true. I swear it."

It was true, and Alice realized it, with immense relief. She dried her eyes and held Joan away from her at arm's length and looked at her young, frank, intrepid face with puzzled admiration. It didn't go with her determined trifling. "I shall always believe what you tell me, Joan," she said. "You've taken a bigger load than you imagine off my heart—which is Gilbert's. And now sit down again and be comfortable and let's do what we used to do at school at night and talk about ourselves. We've both changed since those days, haven't we?"

"Have we? I don't think I have." Joan took another cigarette and went back to her chair. Her small round shoulders looked very white against the black of a velvet cushion. If there was nothing boyish or unfeminine about her, there was certainly an indefinable appearance of being untouched, unawakened. She was the same girl who had been found by Martin that afternoon clean-cut against the sky—the determined individualist.

Alice sat in front of her on a low stool with her hands clasped round a knee. "What a queer mixture you are of—of town and country, Joany. You're like a piece of honeysuckle playing at being an orchid."

"That's because I'm a kid," said Joan. "The horrible hour will come when I shall be an orchid and try and palm myself off as honeysuckle, never fear."

"Don't you think marriage has changed you a little?" asked Alice. "It usually does. It changed me from an empty-headed little fool to a woman with oh, such a tremendous desire to be worthy of it."

"Yes, but then you married for love."

"Didn't you, Joany?"

"I? Marry for love?" Joan waved her arm for joy at the idea.

Alice knew the story of the escape from old age. She also knew from the way in which Martin looked at Joan why he had given her his name and house. Here was her chance to get to the bottom of a constant puzzle. "You may not have married for love," she said, "but of course you're fond of Martin."

Joan considered the matter. It might be a good thing to go into it now that there was an unexpected lull in the wild rush that she had made to get into life. There had been something rather erratic about Martin's comings and goings during the last week. She hadn't spoken to him since the night at the Ritz.

"Yes, I am fond of him," she said. "That's the word. As fond as I might be of a very nice, sound boy whom I'd known all my life."

"Is that all?"

Joan made a series of smoke rings and watched them curl into the air. "Yes, that's all," she said.

Alice became even more interested and curious and puzzled. She held very serious views about marriage. "And are you happy with him?"

"I don't know that I can be said to be happy with him," said Joan. "I'm perfectly happy as things are."

"Tell me how they are." There was obviously something here that was far from right.

Joan was amused at her friend's gravity. She had always been a responsible little person with very definite and old-fashioned views. "Well," she said, "it's a charming little story, really. I was the maiden who had to be rescued from the ugly castle, and Martin was the knight who performed the deed. And being a knight with a tremendous sense of convention and a castle of his own full of well-trained servants, it didn't seem to him that he could give me the run of his house in the Paul and Virginia manner, which isn't being done now; and so, like a little gentleman, he married me, or as I suppose you would put it, went through the form of marriage. It's all part of the adventure that we started one afternoon on the edge of the woods. I call it the cool and common-sense romance of two very modern and civilized people."

"I don't think there's any place in romance for such things as coolness and common sense," said Alice warmly. "And as to there being two very modern and civilized people in your adventure, as you call it, that I doubt."

Joan's large brown eyes grew a little larger, and she looked at the enthusiastic girl in front of her with more interest. "Do you?" she asked. "Why?"

Alice got up. She was disturbed and worried. She had a great affection for Joan, and that boy was indeed a knight. "I saw Martin walking away from your house the night you dined with Gilbert at the Brevoort—I was told about that!—and there was something in his eyes that wasn't the least bit cool. Also I rode in the Park with him one morning a week ago, and I thought he looked ill and haggard and—if you must know—starved. No one would say that you aren't modern and civilized,—and those are tame words, —but if Martin were to come in now and make a clean breast of it, you'd be surprised to find how little he is of either of those things, if I know anything about him."

"Then, my dear," replied Joan, making a very special ring of smoke, "you know more about him than I do."

Alice began to walk about. A form of marriage—that was the phrase that stuck in her mind. And here was a girl who was without a genuine friend in all that heartless town except herself, and a fine boy who needed one, she began to see, very badly. She, at any rate, and she thanked God for it, was properly married, and she owed it to friendship to make a try to put things right with these two.

"Joan, I believe I do," she said. "I really believe I do, although I've only had one real talk with him. You're terribly and awfully young, I know. You had a bad year with your grandfather and grandmother, and the reaction has made you wild and careless. But you're not a girl who has been brought up behind a screen in a room lighted with one candle. You know what marriage means. There isn't a book you haven't read or a thing you haven't talked over. And if you imagine that Martin is content to play Paul to your imitation Virginia, you're wrong. Oh, Joan, you're dangerously wrong."

Settling into her chair and working her shoulders more comfortably into the cushion, Joan crossed one leg over the other and lighted another cigarette. "Go on," she said with a tantalizing smile. "I love to hear you talk. It's far more interesting than listening to Howard Cannon's dark prophecies about the day after to-morrow and his gloomy rumblings about the writing on the wall. You stand for the unemancipated married woman. Don't you?"

"Yes, I do," said Alice quickly, her eyes gleaming. "I consider that a girl who lets a man marry her under false pretenses is a cheat."

"A strong word, my dear!"

"But not too strong."

"Wait a minute. Suppose she doesn't love him. What then?"

"Then she oughtn't to have married him."

"Yes, but it may have suited her to marry him."

"Then she should fulfill the bargain honestly and play the game according to the rules. However modern and civilized people are, they do that."

Joan shrugged her round white shoulders and flicked her cigarette ash expertly into the china tray on the spindle-legged table at her elbow. She was quite unmoved. Alice had always taken it upon herself to lecture her about individualism—the enthusiastic little thing. "Dear old girl," she said, "don't you remember that I always make my own rules?"

"I know you do, but you can't tell me that Martin wants to go by them—or that he'll be able to remain a knight long, while you're going by one set and he's keen to go by another? Where will it end?"

"End? But why drag in the end when Martin and I are only at the beginning?"

Alice sat down again and bent forward and caught up Joan's unoccupied hand. "Listen, dear," she said with more than characteristic earnestness. "Last night I went with the Merrills to the Ziegfeld Follies, and I saw Martin there with a little white-faced girl with red lips and the golden hair that comes out of a bottle."

"Good old Martin!" said Joan. "The devil you did!"

"Doesn't that give you a jar?"

"Good heavens, no! If you'd peeked into the One-o'clock Club this morning at half past two, you would have seen me with a white-faced man with a red mustache and a kink in his hair that comes from a hot iron. Martin and I are young and giddy, and we're on the round-about, and we're hitting it up. Who cares?"

There was a little silence—and then Alice drew back, shaking her pretty neat head. "It won't do, Joany," she said, "it won't do. I've heard you say 'Who cares?' loads of times and never seen anybody take you by the shoulders and shake you into caring. That's why you go on saying it. But somebody always cares, Joany dear, and there's not one thing that any of us can say or do that doesn't react on some one else, either to hurt or bless. Martin Gray's your knight. You said so. Don't you be the one to turn his gleaming armor into common broadcloth—please, please don't."

Joan gave a little laugh and a little yawn and stretched herself like a boy and got up. "Who'd have thought it? It's half-past twelve, and we're both losing our much needed beauty sleep. I must really tear myself away." She put her arm around Alice and kissed her. "The same dear little wise, responsible Alice who would like to put the earth into woolens with a mustard plaster on its chest. But it takes all sorts to make up a world, you know, and it would be rather drab without a few butterflies. Don't throw bricks at me until I've fluttered a bit more, Ally. My colors won't last long, and I know what old age means, better than most. If I were in love as you are, my man's rules would be the ones I'd go by all the time; but I'm not in love, and I don't want to be—yet; and I'm only a kid, and I think I have the right to my fling. This marriage of mine is just a part of the adventure that Martin and I plunged into as a great joke, and he knows it and he's one of the best, and I'm grateful to him, believe me. Good night. God bless you!"

She stood for a moment on the top step to taste the air that was filled with the essence of youth. Across a sky as clear as crystal a series of young clouds were chasing each other, putting out the stars for a moment as they scurried playfully along. It was a joy to be alive and fit and careless. Summer was lying in wait for spring, and autumn would lay a withering hand upon summer, and winter with its crooked limbs and lack-luster eyes was waiting its inevitable turn.

"A short life and a merry one!" whispered Joan to the moon, throwing it a kiss.

A footman, sullen for want of sleep, opened the door of the limousine. Some one was sitting in the corner with his arms crossed over his chest.

"Marty! Is that you?"

"It's all right," said Gilbert Palgrave. "I've been playing patience for half an hour. I'm going to see you home."

V

"You are going home?"

"Yes," said Joan, "without the shadow of a doubt."

"Which means that I'd better tell the chauffeur to drive round to the One-o'clock, eh?"

"I'll drop you there if you like. I'm really truly going home."

"All right."

Joan began to sing as the car bowled up Fifth Avenue. Movement always made her sing, and the effect of things slipping behind her. But she stopped suddenly as an expression of Alice's flicked across her memory. "You'll catch Alice up, if you go straight back," she said.

"Alice-Sit-by-the-Fire! I wonder why it is the really good woman is never appreciated by a man until he's obliged to sit on the other side of the fireplace? I wish we were driving away out into the country. I have an unusual hankering to stand on the bank of a huge lake and watch the moonlight on the water."

Joan was singing again. The trees in the Park were bespattered with young leaves.

Palgrave controlled an ardent desire to touch with his lips that cool white shoulder from which the cloak had slipped. It was extraordinary how this mere girl inflamed him. Alice—Alice-Sit-by-the-Fire! She seemed oddly like some other man's wife, these days.

"Suppose I tell your man to drive out of the city beyond this rabble of bricks and mortar?"

But Joan went on singing. Spring was in her blood. How fast the car was moving, and those young clouds.

Palgrave helped her out with a hot hand.

She opened the door with her latch-key. "Thank you, Gilbert," she said. "Good night."

But Palgrave followed her in. "Don't you think I've earned the right to one cigarette?" He threw his coat into a chair in the hall and hung his hat on the longest point of an antler. It was a new thing for this much flattered man to ask for favors. This young thing's exultant youth made him feel old and rather humble.

"There are sandwiches in the dining room and various things to drink," said Joan, waving her hand toward it.

"No, no. Let's go up to the drawing-room—that is, unless you—"

But Joan was already on the stairs, with the chorus of her song. She didn't feel in the least like sleep with its escape from life. It was so good to be awake, to be vital, to be tingling with the current of electricity like a telegraph wire. She flung back the curtains, raised all the windows, opened her arms to the air, spilled her cloak on the floor, sat at the piano and ragged "The Spring Song."

"I am a kid," she said, speaking above the sound, and going on with her argument to Alice. "I am and I will be, I will be. And I'll play the fool and revel in it as long as I can—so there!"

Palgrave had picked up the cloak and was holding it unconsciously against his immaculate shirt. It was the sentimental act of a virtuoso in the art of pleasing women—who are so easily pleased. At the moment he had achieved forgetfulness of boudoir trickery and so retained almost all his usual assumption of dignity. Even Joan, with her quick eye for the ridiculous, failed to detect the bathos of his attitude, and merely thought that he was trying to be funny and not succeeding.

It so happened that over Palgrave's shoulder she could see the bold crayon drawing of Martin, brown and healthy and muscular, without an ounce of affectation, an unmistakable man with his nice irregular features and clean, merry eyes. There was strength and capability stamped all over him, and there was, as well, a pleasing sense of reliability which gained immediate confidence. With the sort of shock one gets on going into the fresh air from a steam-heated room, she realized the contrast between these two.

There is always something as unreal about handsome men as there is about Japanese gardens. Palgrave's hair was so scrupulously sleek and wiglike, his features so well-balanced and well-chosen, his wide-set eyes so large and long-lashed, and his fair, soft mustache so miraculously precise. His clothes, too, were a degree more than perfect. They were so right as to be a little freakish because they attracted as much attention as if they were badly cut. He was born for tea fights and winter resorts, to listen with a distrait half-smile to the gushing adulation of the oh-my-dear type of women.

He attracted Joan. She admired his assurance and polish and manners. With these three things even a man with a broken nose and a head bald as an egg can carry a beautiful woman to the altar. He was something new to her, too, and she found much to amuse her in his way of expressing himself. He observed, and sometimes crystallized his observations with a certain neatness. Also, and she made no bones about owning to it, his obvious attention flattered her. All the same, she was in the mood just then for Martin. He went better with the time of year, and there was something awfully companionable about his sudden laugh. She would have hailed his appearance at that moment with an outdoor cry.

It was bad luck for Palgrave, because he now knew definitely that in Joan he had found the girl who was to give him the great emotion.

She broke away from "The Spring Song" and swung into "D'ye Ken John Peel with His Coat So Gay?" It was Martin's favorite air. How often she had heard him shout it among the trees on his way to meet her out there on the edge of the woods where they had found each other. It was curious how her thoughts turned to Martin that night.

She left the piano in the middle of a bar. "One cigarette," she said, and held out a silver box.

Palgrave's hand closed tightly over her slim white arm. In his throat his heart was pumping. He spoke incoherently, like a man. "God," he said, "you—you take my breath away. You make my brain whirl. Why didn't you come out of your garden a year ago?"

He was acting, she thought, and she laughed. "My arm, I think," she said.

"No, mine. It's got to be mine. What's the good of beating about the bush?" He spoke with a queer hoarseness, and his hand shook.

She laughed again. He was trying his parlor tricks, as Hosack had called them one night at the Crystal Room, watching him greet a woman with both hands. What a joke to see what he would do if she pretended to be carried away. He might as well be made to pay for keeping her up. "Oh, Gilbert," she said, "what are you saying!" Her shyness and fright were admirable.

They added fuel to his fire. "What I've been waiting to say for years and never thought I should. I love you. You've just got me."

How often had he said those very words to other women! He did it surpassingly well. She continued to act. "Oh, Gilbert," she said in a low voice, "you mustn't. There's Alice." Two could play at his pet game.

"Yes, there is Alice. But what does that matter? I don't care, and you don't. Your motto is not to care. You're always saying so. I'm no more married to Alice than you are to Gray. They're accidents, both of them. I love you, I tell you." And he ran his hand up to her shoulder and bore down upon her. Where were his manners and polish and assurance? It was amazing to see the change in the man.

But she dodged away and took up a stand behind the piano and laughed at him. "You're an artist, Gilbert," she said. "It's all very well for you to practice on women of your own age, but I'm an unsophisticated girl. You might turn my head, you know."

Her sarcasm threw him up short. She was mocking. He was profoundly hurt. "But you've chosen me. You've picked me out. You've used me to take you to places night after night! Don't fool with me, Joan. I'm in dead earnest."

And she saw with astonishment that he was. His face was white, and he stood in a curious attitude of supplication, with his hands out. She was amazed, and for a moment thrilled. Gilbert Palgrave, the woman's man, in love with her. Think of it!

"But Gilbert," she said, "there's Alice. She's my friend." That seemed to matter more than the fact that she was his wife.

"That hasn't mattered to you all along. Why drag it in now? Night after night you've danced with me; I've been at your beck and call; you used me to rescue you from Gray that time. What are you? What are you made of? Unsophisticated! You!" He wasn't angry. He was fumbling at reasons in order to try and get at her point of view. "You know well enough that a man doesn't put himself out to that extent for nothing. What becomes of give and take? Do you conceive that you are going to sail through life taking everything and giving nothing?"

Martin had asked her this, and Alice, and now here was Gilbert Palgrave putting it to her as though it were an indictment! "But I'm a kid," she cried out. "What do you all mean? Can't I be allowed to have any fun without paying for it? I'm only just out of the shell. I've only been living for a few weeks. Can't you see that I'm a kid? I have the right to take all I can get for nothing,—the right of youth. What do you mean—all of you?"

She came out from behind the piano and stood in front of him, as erect as a silver birch, and as slim and young. There was a great indignation all about her.

His eager hands went out, and fell. He was not a brute. It would be cowardly to touch this amazing child. She was armed with fearlessness and virginity—and he had mistaken these things for callousness.

"I don't know what to say," he said. "You stagger me. How long are you going to hide behind this youthfulness? When are you going to be old enough to be honest? Men have patience only up to a point. At any rate, you didn't claim youth when Gray asked you to marry him—though you may have done so afterward. Did you?"

She kept silent. But her eyes ran over him with contempt. According to her, she had given him no right to put such questions.

He ignored it. It was undeserved. It was she who deserved contempt, not he. And he threw it back at her in a strange incoherent outburst in which, all the same, there was a vibrating note of gladness and relief. And all the while, unmoved by the passion into which he broke, she stood watching with a curious gravity his no longer immobile face. She was thinking about Martin. She was redeveloping Martin's expression when she had opened the door of her bedroom the night of her marriage and let him out. What about her creed, then? Was she hiding behind youthfulness? Were there, after all, certain things that must be paid for? Was she already old enough to be what Alice and this man called honest? Was every man made of the stuff that only gave for what he hoped to get in return?

His words trailed off. He was wasting them, he saw. She was looking through his head. But he rejoiced as to one thing like a potter who opens the door of his oven and finds his masterpiece unbroken. And silence fell upon them, interrupted only by the intermittent humming of passing cars.

Finally Palgrave took the cigarette box out of Joan's hand and put it down on a little table and stood looking more of a man than might have been expected.

"I've always hoped that one day I should meet you—just you," he said quietly; "and when I did, I knew that it would be to love. Well, I've told you. Do what you can for me until you decide that you're grown up. I'll wait."

And he turned and went away, and presently she heard a door shut and echo, and slow footsteps in the street below.

Where was Martin?

VI

She wanted Martin. Everything that had happened that night made her want Martin. He knew that she was a kid, and treated her as such. He didn't stand up and try and force her forward into being a woman—although, of all men, he had the right. He was big and generous and had given her his name and house and the run of the world, but not from his lips ever came the hard words that she had heard that night. How extraordinary that they should have come from Alice as well as from Gilbert.

She wanted Martin. Where was Martin? She felt more like a bird, at that moment, than a butterfly—like a bird that had flown too far from its nest and couldn't find its way back. She had been honest with Martin, all along. Why, the night before they had started on the street of adventure, she had told him her creed, in that dark, quiet room with the moonlight on the floor in a little pool, and had frankly cried out, "Who cares?" for the first time. And later, upstairs in her room, in his house, she had asked him to leave her; and he had gone, because he understood that she wanted to remain irresponsible for a time and must not be taken by the shoulders and shaken into caring until she had had her fling. He understood everything—especially as to what she meant by saying that she would go joy-riding, that she would make life spin whichever way she wanted it to go. It was the right of youth, and what was she but just a kid? He had never stood over her and demanded payment, and yet he had given her everything. He understood that she was new to the careless and carefree, and had never flung the word honest at her head, because, being so young, she considered that she could be let off from making payments for a time.

She wanted Martin. She wanted the comforting sight of his clean eyes and deep chest and square shoulders. She wanted to sit down knee to knee with him as they had done so often on the edge of the woods, and talk and talk. She wanted to hear his man's voice and see the laughter-lines come and go round his eyes. He was her pal and was as reliable as the calendar.

He would wipe out the effect of the reproaches that she had been made to listen to by Alice and Gilbert. They might be justified; they were justified; but they showed a lack of understanding of her present mood that was to her inconceivable. She was a kid. Couldn't they see that she was a kid? Why should they both throw bricks at her as though she were a hawk and not a mere butterfly?

Where was Martin? Why hadn't she seen him for several days? Why had he stayed away from home without saying where he was and what he was doing? And what was all this about a girl with a white face and red lips? Martin must have friends, of course. She had hers—Gilbert and Hosack and the others, if they could be called friends. But why a girl with a white face and red lips and hair that came out of a bottle? That didn't sound much like Martin.

All these thoughts ran through Joan's mind as she walked about the drawing-room with its open windows, in the first hour of the morning, sending out an S. O. S. to Martin. She ought to be in bed and asleep—not thinking and going over everything as if she were a woman. She wasn't a woman yet, and could only be a kid once. It was too bad of Alice to try and force her to take things seriously so soon. Seriousness was for older people, and even then something to avoid if possible. And as for Gilbert—well, she didn't for one instant deny the fact that it was rather exciting and exhilarating for him to be in love with her, although she was awfully sorry for Alice. She had done nothing to encourage him, and it was really a matter of absolute indifference to her whether he loved her or not, so long as he was at hand to take her about. And she didn't intend to encourage him, either. Love meant ties and responsibility—Alice proved that clearly enough. There was plenty of time for love. Let her flit first. Let her remain young as long as she could, careless and care-free. The fact that she was married was just an accident, an item in her adventure. It didn't make her less young to be married, and she didn't see why it should. Martin understood, and that was why it was so far-fetched of Alice to suggest that her attitude could turn Martin's armor into broadcloth, and hint at his having ceased to be a knight because he had been seen with a girl—never mind whether her face was white and her lips red, and her hair too golden.

"I'm a kid, I tell you," she said aloud, throwing out her justification to the whole world. "I am and I will be, I will be. I'll play the fool and revel in it as long as I can—so there. Who cares?" And she laughed once more, and ran her hand over her hair as though waving all these thoughts away, and shut the windows and turned out the lights and went upstairs to her bedroom. "I'm a selfish, self-willed little devil, crazy about myself, thinking of nothing but having a good time," she added inwardly. "I know it, all of you, as well as you do, but give me time. Give me my head for a bit. When I must begin to pay, I'll pay with all I've got."

But presently, all ready for bed, she put on a dressing gown and left her room and padded along the passage in heelless slippers to Martin's room. He might have been asleep all this time. How silly not to have thought of that! She would wake him for one of their talks. It seemed an age since they had sat on the hill together among the young buds, and she had conjured up the high-reaching buildings of New York against the blue sky, like a mirage.

She had begun to think again. Alice and Gilbert between them had set her brain working—and she couldn't stop it. What if the time had come already when she must pull herself together and face facts and play what everybody called the game? Well, if it had, and she simply couldn't hide behind youthfulness any longer, as Gilbert had said, she would show that she could change her tune of "Who cares?" to "I care" with the best of them! "I'm only a little over eighteen. I don't know quite what it is, but I'm something more than pretty. I'm still not much more than a flapper—an irritating, empty-headed, fashionable-school-fed, undisciplined, sophisticated kid. I know all about that as well as they do. I'm making no pretense to be anything different. Heaven knows, I'm frank enough about it—even to myself. But it's only a phase. Why not let me get over it and live it down? If there's anything good in me, and there is, it will come out sooner or later. Why not let me go through it my own way? A few months to play the fool in—it isn't much to ask, and don't I know what it means to be old?"

She hadn't been along that passage before. It was Martin's side of the house. She hadn't given much thought to Martin's side of anything. She tried a door and opened it, fumbled for the button that would turn the light on and found it. It was a large and usefully fitted dressing room with a hanging cupboard that ran all along one wall, with several doors. Two old shiny-faced English tallboys were separated by a boot rack. Between the two windows was a shaving glass over a basin. There was a bookcase on each side of the fire-place and a table conveniently near a deep armchair with a tobacco jar, pipes and a box of cigarettes. Every available space of wall was crammed with framed photographs of college groups, some showing men with the whiskered faces and the strange garments of the early Victorian period, others of the clean-shaven men of the day, but all of them fit and eager and care-free, caught in their happiest hours. It was a man's room, arranged by one, now used by another.

Joan went through into the bedroom. The light followed her. There was no Martin. It was all strangely tidy. Its owner might have been away for weeks.

With a sense of chill and a feeling of queer loneliness, she went back to the dressing room. She wanted Martin. If Martin had been there, she would have had it all out with him, freely and frankly. Somehow she couldn't wave away the idea any longer that the time had come for her to cross another bridge. Thank God she would still be young, but the kid of her would be left on the other side. If Martin had been there, she would have told him some of the things that Alice had said about being honest and paying up, and left it to him to say whether the girlhood which she had wanted to spin out was over and must be put away among her toys.

Alice and Gilbert Palgrave,—curious that it should have been those two, —had shaken her individualism, as well as something else, vague and untranslatable, that she couldn't quite grasp, that eluded her hand. She sat down in the deep chair and with a little smile took up one of Martin's pipes and looked at it. The good tobaccoey scent of it took her back to the hill on the edge of the woods, and in her mind's eye there was a picture of two clean eyes with laughter-lines coming and going, a strong young face that had already caught the sun, square shoulders and a broad chest, and a pair of reliable hands with spatulate fingers clasped round a knee. She could hear birds calling. Spring was in the air.

Where was Martin?

VII

It was the first dress rehearsal of "The Ukelele Girl," to be produced "under the personal direction of Stanwood Mosely." The piece had been in rehearsal for eleven weeks.

The curtain had been up on the second act for an hour. Scene designers, scene painters and scene shifters were standing about with a stage director, whose raucous voice cut the fuggy atmosphere incessantly in what was intended to represent the exterior of a hotel at Monte Carlo. It more nearly resembled the materialization of a dope fiend's dream of an opium factory. What might have been a bank building in Utopia, an old Spanish galleon in drydock, or the exterior of a German beer garden according to the cover of Vogue occupied the center of the scene. The bricks were violet and old gold, sprayed with tomato juice and marked by the indeterminate silver tracks of snails. Pillars, modeled on the sugar-stick posts that advertise barber's shops, ran up and lost themselves among the flies. A number of wide stairs, all over wine stains, wandered aimlessly about, coming to a conclusion between gigantic urns filled with unnatural flowers of all the colors of a diseased rainbow. Jotted about here and there on the stage were octopus-limbed trees with magenta leaves growing in flower pots all covered with bilious blobs. Stan Mosely didn't profess to understand it, but having been assured by the designer that it was art nouveau, which also he didn't understand, he was wholly satisfied.

Not so the stage director, whose language in describing the effect it had upon him would have done credit to a gunman under the influence of cheap brandy and fright. The rehearsal, which had commenced at eight o'clock, had been hung up for a time considerable enough to allow him to give vent to his sentiments. The pause enabled Mosely, squatting frog-wise in the middle of the orchestra stalls, to surround himself with several women whose gigantic proportions were horribly exposed to the eye. The rumble of his voice and the high squeals of their laughter clashed with the sounds of the vitriolic argument on the stage, and the noises of a bored band, in which an oboe was giving a remarkable imitation of a gobbling turkey cock, and a cornet of a man blowing his nose. The leader of the band was pacing up and down the musicians' room, saying to himself: "Zis is ze last timer. Zis is ze last timer," well knowing that it wasn't. The poor devil had a wife and children to feed.

Bevies of weary and spirit-broken chorus girls in costume were sprawling on the chairs in the lower boxes, some sleeping, some too tired to sleep, and some eating ravenously from paper bags. Chorus men and costumers, wig makers and lyric writers, authors and friends of the company, sat about singly and in pairs in the orchestra seats. They were mostly bored so far beyond mere impatience by all this super-inefficiency and chaos as to have arrived at a state of intellectual coma. The various men out of whose brains had originally come the book and lyrics no longer hated each other and themselves; they lusted for the blood of the stage director or saw gorgeous mental pictures of a little fat oozy corpse surrounded by the gleeful faces of the army of people who had been impotent to protest against the lash of his whip, the impertinence of his tongue or the gross dishonesty of his methods.

One other man in addition to the raucous, self-advertising stage director, Jackrack, commonly called "Jack-in-office," showed distinct signs of life—a short, overdressed, perky person with piano fingers and baldish head much too big for his body, who flitted about among the chorus girls, followed by a pale, drab woman with pins, and touched their dresses and sniggered and made remarks with a certain touch of literary excellence in a slightly guttural voice. This was Poppy Shemalitz, the frock expert, the man milliner of the firm, who was required to make bricks out of straw, or as he frequently said to the friends of his "bosom," "make fifteen dollars look like fifty." Self-preservation and a sense of humor encouraged him through the abusive days of a dog's life.

Sitting in the last row of the orchestra, wearing the expression of interest and astonishment of a man who had fallen suddenly into another world, was Martin. He had been there since eight o'clock. For over six hours he had watched banality emerge from chaos and had listened to the blasphemy and insults of Jackrack. He would have continued to watch and listen until daylight peered upbraidingly through the chinks in the exit doors but for the sudden appearance of Susie Capper, dressed for the street.

"Hello, Tootles! But you're not through, are you?"

"Absobloominlootely," she said emphatically.

"I thought you said your best bit was in the second act?"

"'Was' is right. Come on outer here. I can't stand the place a minute longer. It'll give me apoplexy."

Martin followed her into the foyer. The tragic rage on the girl's little, pretty, usually good-natured face worried him. He knew that she had looked forward to this production to make her name on Broadway.

"My dear Tootles, what's happened?"

She turned to him and clutched his arm. Tears welled up into her eyes, and her red lips began to tremble. "What did I look like?" she demanded.

"Splendid!"

"Didn't I get every ounce of comedy out of my two scenes in Act One?"

"Every ounce."

"I know I did. Even the stage hands laughed, and if you can do that there's no argument. And didn't my number go over fine? Wasn't it the best thing in the act? I don't care what you say. I know it was. Even the orchestra wanted it over again."

"But it was," said Martin, "and I heard one of the authors say that it would be the hit of the piece."

"Oh, Martin, I've been sweating blood for this chance for five years, and I'm not going to get it. I'm not going to get it. I wish I was dead." She put her arms against the wall and her face down on her arms and burst into an agony of tears.

Martin was moved. This plucky, struggling, hardworking atom of a remorseless world deserved a little luck for a change. Hitherto it had eluded her eager hands, although she had paid for it in advance with something more than blood and energy. "Dear old Tootles," he said, "what's happened? Try and tell me what's happened? I don't understand."

"You don't understand, because you don't know the tricks of this rotten theater. For eleven weeks I've been rehearsing. For eleven weeks—time enough to produce a couple of Shakespeare's bally plays in Latin,—I've put up with the brow-beating of that mad dog Jackrack. For eleven weeks, without touching one dirty little Mosely cent, I've worked at my part and numbers, morning, noon and night; and now, on the edge of production, he cuts me out and puts in a simpering cow with a fifteen-thousand-dollar necklace and a snapping little Pekinese to oblige one of his angels, and I'm reduced to the chorus. I wish I was dead, I tell you—I wish I was dead and buried and at peace. I wish I could creep home and get into bed and never see another day of this cruel life. Oh, I'm just whipped and broke and out. Take me away, take me away, Martin. I'm through."

Martin put his arm round the slight, shaking form, led her to one of the doors and out into a narrow passage that ran up into the deserted street. To have gone down into the stalls and hit that oily martinet in the mouth would have been to lay himself open to a charge of cruelty to animals. He was so puny and fat and soft. Poor little Tootles, who had had a tardy and elusive recognition torn from her grasp! It was a tragedy.

It was not much more than a stone's-throw from the theater to the rabbit warren in West Forty-sixth Street, but Martin gave a shout at a prowling taxi. Not even policemen and newspaper boys and street cleaners must see this girl as she was then, in a collapse of smashed hopes, sobbing dreadfully, completely broken down. It wasn't fair. In all that city of courageous under-dogs and fate-fighters, there was not one who pretended to careless contentment with a chin so high as Tootles. He half carried her into the cab, trying with a queer blundering sympathy to soothe and quiet her. And he had almost succeeded by the time they reached the brownstone house of sitters, bedrooms and baths, gas stoves, cubby-holes, the persistent reek of onions, cigarettes and hot cheese. The hysteria of the artistic temperament, or the natural exaggeration of an artificial life, had worn itself out for the time being. Rather pathetic little sobs had taken its place, it was with a face streaked with the black stuff from her eyelashes that Tootles turned quickly to Martin at the foot of the narrow, dirty staircase.

"Let's go up quiet," she said. "If any of the others are about, I don't want 'em to know tonight. See?"

"I see," said Martin.

And it was good to watch the way in which she took hold of herself with a grip of iron, scrubbed her face with his handkerchief, dabbed it thickly with powder from a small silver box, threw back her head and went up two stairs at a time. On the second floor there was a cackle of laughter, but doors were shut. On the third all was quiet. But on the fourth the tall, thin, Raphael-headed man was drunk again, arguing thickly in the usual cloud of smoke, which drifted sullenly into the passage through the open door.

With deft fingers Tootles used her latchkey, and they slipped into the apartment like thieves. And then Martin took the pins out of her little once-white hat, drew her coat off, picked her up as if she were a child and put her on the sofa.

"There you are, Tootles," he said, without aggressive cheerfulness, but still cheerful. "You lie there, young 'un, and I'll get you something to eat. It's nearly a day since you saw food."

And after a little while, humanized by the honest kindness of this obvious man, she sat up and leaned on an elbow and watched him through the gap in the curtains that hid her domestic arrangements. He was scrambling some eggs. He had made a pile of chicken sandwiches and laid the table. He had put some flowers that he had brought for her earlier in the evening in the middle of it, stuck into an empty milk bottle. In her excitement and joy about the play, she had forgotten to put them in water. They were distinctly sad.

"Me word!" she said to herself, through the aftermath of her emotion. "That's some boy. Gee, that's some good boy." Even her thoughts were conducted in a mixture of Brixton and Broadway.

"Now, then," he said, "all ready, marm," and put his handiwork in what he hoped was an appetizing manner on the table. The hot eggs were on a cold plate, but did that really matter?

Not to Tootles, who was glad to get anything, anyhow. That room was the Ritz Hotel in comparison with the slatterly tenement in which she had won through the first unsoaped years of a sordid life. And Martin—well, Martin was something out of a fairy tale.

Between them they made a clean sweep of everything, falling back finally on a huge round box of candies contributed the previous day by Martin.

They made short work of several bottles of beer, also contributed by Martin. He knew that Tootles was not paid a penny during rehearsals. She laughed several times and cracked one or two feeble jokes—poor little soul with the swollen eyes and powder-dabbed face! Her bobbed hair glistened under the light like the dome of the Palace of Cooch Behar under the Indian sun.

"Boy," she said presently, putting her hand on his knees and closing her tired eyes, "where's that magic carpet? If I could sit on it with you and be taken to where the air's clean and the trees are whisperin' and all the young things hoppin' about—I'd give twenty-five years of me life, s'elp me Bob, I would."

"Would you, Tootles?" A sudden thought struck Martin. Make use of that house in the country, make use of it, lying idle and neglected!

"Oh," she said, "to get away from all this for a bit—to shake Broadway and grease paint and slang and electric light, if only for a week. I'm fed up, boy. I'm all out, like an empty gasoline tin. I want to see something clean and sweet."

Martin had made up his mind. Look at that poor little bruised soul, as much in need of water as those sad flowers in the milk bottle. "Tootles," he said, "pack up your troubles in your old kit-bag, and be ready for me in the morning."

"What d'yer mean, boy?"

"What I say. At eleven o'clock to-morrow—to-day, I'll have a car here and drive you away to woods and birds and all clean things. I'll give you a holiday in a big cathedral, and you shall lie and listen to God's own choir."

"Go on—ye're pullin' me leg!"

She waved her hand to stop him. It was all too good to joke about.

"No, I'm not. I've got a house away in the country. It was my father's. We shall both be proud to welcome you there, Tootles."

She sprang up, put her hands on his face and tilted it back and looked into his eyes. It was true! It was true! She saw it there. And she kissed him and gave a great sobbing sigh and went into her bedroom and began to undress. Was there anything like life, after all?

Martin cleared the table and drew the curtains over the domestic arrangements. He didn't like domestic arrangements. Then he sat down and lighted a cigarette. His head was all blurred with sleep.

And presently a tired voice, called "Boy!" and he went in. The all-too-golden head was deep into the pillow and long lashes made fans on that powdered face.

"Where did you pinch the magic carpet?" she asked, and smiled, and fell into sleep as a stone disappears into water.

As Martin drew the clothes over her thinly clad shoulder, something touched him. It was like a tap on the heart. Before he knew what he was doing, he had turned out the light, gone into the sitting room, the passage, down the stairs and into the silent street. At top speed he ran into Sixth

Avenue, yelled to a cab that was slipping along the trolley lines and told the driver to go to East Sixty-seventh Street for all that he was worth.

Joan wanted him.

Joan!

Joan heard the cab drive up and stop, heard Martin sing out "That's all right," open and shut the front door and mount the stairs; heard him go quickly to her room and knock.

She went out and called "Marty, Marty," and stood on the threshold of his dressing room, smiling a welcome. She was glad, beyond words glad, and surprised. There had seemed to be no chance of seeing him that morning.

Martin came along the passage with his characteristic light tread and drew up short. He looked anxious.

"You wanted me?" he said.

And Joan held out her hand. "I did and do, Marty. But how did you guess?"

"I didn't guess; I knew." And he held her hand nervously.

She looked younger and sweeter than ever in her blue silk dressing gown and shorter in her heelless slippers. What a kid she was, after all, he thought.

"How amazing!" she said. "I wonder how?"

He shook his head. "I dunno—just as I did the first time, when I tore through the woods and found you on the hill."

"Isn't that wonderful! Do you suppose I shall always be able to get you when I want you very much?"

"Yes, always."

"Why?"

She had gone back into the dressing room. The light was on her face. Her usual expression of elfish impertinence was not there. She was the girl of the stolen meetings once more, the girl whose eyes reflected the open beauty of what Martin had called the big cathedral. For all that, she was the girl who had hurt him to the soul, shown him her door, played that trick upon him at the Ritz and sent him adrift full of the spirit of "Who cares?" which was her fetish. It was in his heart to say: "Because I adore you! Because I am so much yours that you have only to think my name for me to hear it across the world as if you had shouted it through a giant megaphone! Because whatever I do and whatever you do, I shall love you!" But she had hurt him twice. She had cut him to the very core. He couldn't forget. He was too proud to lay himself open to yet another of her laughing snubs.

So he shook his head again. "I dunno," he said. "It's like that. It's something that can't be explained."

She sat on the arm of the chair with her hands round a knee. A little of her pink ankle showed. The pipe that she had dropped when his voice had come up from the street lay on the floor.

His answer had disappointed her; she didn't quite know why. The old Marty would have been franker and more spontaneous. The old Marty might have made her laugh with his boyish ingenuousness, but he would have warmed her and made her feel delightfully vain. Could it be that she was responsible for this new Marty? Was Alice too terribly right when she had talked about armor turning into broadcloth because of her selfish desire to remain a kid a little longer? She was afraid to ask him where he was when he had felt that she wanted him, and she hated herself for that.

There was a short silence.

These two young things had lost the complete confidence that had been theirs before they had come to that great town. What a pity!

"Well," he asked, standing straight like a man ready to take orders, "why did you call?"

And then an overwhelming shyness seized her. It had seemed easy enough in thought to tell Martin that she was ready to cross the bridge and be, as Alice had called it, honest, and as Gilbert had said, to play the game. But it was far from easy when he stood in the middle of the room in the glare of the light, with something all about him that froze her words and made her self-conscious and timid. And yet a clear, unmistakable voice urged her to have courage and make her confession, say that she was sorry for having been a feather-brained little fool and ask him to forgive—to win him back, if—if she hadn't already lost him.

But she blundered into an answer and spoke flippantly from nervousness. "Because it's rather soon to become a grass widow, and I want you to be seen with me somewhere to-morrow."

That was all, then. She was only amusing herself. It was a case of "Horse, horse, play with me!"—the other horses being otherwise occupied. She wasn't serious. He needn't have come. "I can't," he said. "I'm sorry, but I'm going out of town."

She saw him look at the clock on the mantelshelf and crinkle up his forehead. Day must be stretching itself somewhere. She got up, quickly. How could she say it? She was losing him.

"Are you angry with me, Marty?" she asked, trying to fumble her way to honesty.

"No, Joan. But it's very late. You ought to be in bed."

"Didn't you think that I should miss you while you've been away?"

"No, Joan. Look. It's half-past two. A kid like you ought to have been asleep hours ago." He went over to the door.

"I'm not a kid—I'm not" she burst out.

He was too tired to be surprised. He had not forgotten how she had hidden behind her youth. He couldn't understand her mood. "I must get to bed," he said, "if you don't mind. I must be up pretty early. Run along, Joany."

He couldn't have hurt her more awfully whatever he had said. To be treated like a naughty girl! But it served her right, and she knew it. Her plea had come back like a boomerang.

"Well, have a good time," she said, with her chin high. "I shall see you again some day, I suppose," and she went out.

It was no use. She had lost him—she had lost him, just as she had discovered that she wanted him. There was a girl with a white face and red lips and hair that came out of a bottle. Martin watched her go and shut the door, and stood with his hands over his face.

VIII

Mr. and Mrs. George Harley had made an appointment to meet at half-past eleven sharp on the doorstep of the little house in Sixty-seventh Street. Business had interrupted their honeymoon and brought them unexpectedly to New York. Harley had come by subway from Wall Street to the Grand Central and taken a taxicab. It was twelve o'clock before he arrived. Nevertheless he wore a smile of placid ease of mind. His little wife had only to walk from the Plaza, it was true, but he knew, although a newly married man, that to be half an hour late was to be ten minutes early.

At exactly five minutes past twelve he saw her turn off the Avenue, and as he strolled along to meet her, charmed and delighted by her daintiness, proud and happy at his possession of her, he did a thing that all wise and tactful husbands do—he forced back an irresistible desire to be humorous at her expense and so won an entry of approval from the Recording Angel.

If they had both been punctual they would have seen Martin go off in his car to drive the girl who had had no luck to the trees and the wild flowers and the good green earth.

Joan's mother, all agog to see the young couple who had taken life into their own hands with the sublime faith of youth, had made it her first duty to call, however awkward and unusual the hour. Her choice of hats in which to do so had been a matter of the utmost importance.

They were told that Mr. Gray had gone out of town, that Mrs. Gray was not yet awake and followed the butler upstairs to the drawing-room with a distinct sense of disappointment. The room still quivered under the emotion of Gilbert Palgrave.

Rather awkwardly they waited to be alone. Butlers always appear to resent the untimely visitation of relations. Sunlight poured in through the windows. It was a gorgeous morning.

"Well," said George Harley, "I've seen my brokers and can do nothing more to-day. Let the child have her sleep out. I'm just as happy to be here with you, Lil, as anywhere else." And he bent over his wife as if he were her lover, as indeed he was, and kissed her pretty ear. His clothes were very new and his collar the shade of an inch too high for comfort and his patent leather shoes something on the tight side, but the spirits of the great lovers had welcomed him and were unafraid.

He won a most affectionate and grateful smile from the neat little lady whose brown hair was honestly tinged with white, and whose unlined face was innocent of make-up. Mrs. Harley had not yet recovered from her astonishment at having been swept to the altar after fifteen years of widowhood by this most simple and admirable man. Even then she was not quite sure that she was not dreaming all this. She patted his big hand and would have put her head against his chest if the brim of her hat had permitted her to do so.

"That's very sweet of you, Geordie," she said. "How good you are to me."

He echoed the word "Good!" and laughed and waved his hands. It was the gesture of a man whose choice of ready words was not large enough to describe all that he longed and tried to be to her. And then he stood back with his long legs wide apart and his large hands thrust into his pockets and his rather untidy gray head stuck on one side and studied her as if she were a picture in a gallery. He looked like a great big faithful St. Bernard dog.

Mrs. Harley didn't think so. He seemed to her to be the boy of whom she had dreamed in her first half-budding dreams and who had gone wandering and come under the hand of Time, but remained a boy in his heart. She was glad that she had made him change his tie. She loved those deep cuts in his face.

"Very well, then," she said. "Although it is twelve o'clock I'll let her sleep another half an hour." And then she stopped with a little cry of dismay, "Let her! ... I'm forgetting that it's no longer in my power to say what she's to do or not to do!"

"How's that?"

"She's no longer the young, big-eyed, watchful child who startled us by saying uncanny things. She's no longer the slip of a thing that I left with her grandparents, with her wistful eyes on the horizon. She's a married woman, Geordie, with a house of her own, and it isn't for me to 'let' her do anything or tell her or even ask her. She can do what she likes now. I've lost her, Geordie."

"Why, how's that, Lil?" There was surprise as well as sympathy in Harley's voice. He had only known other people's children.

She went on quickly, with a queer touch of emotion. "The inevitable change has come before I've had time to realize it. It's a shock. It takes my breath away. I feel as if I had been set adrift from an anchor. Instead of being my little girl she's my daughter now. I'm no longer 'mammy.' I'm mother. Isn't it,—isn't it wonderful? It's like standing under a mountain that's always seemed to be a little hill miles and miles away. From now on I shall be the one to be told to do things, I shall be the child to be kept in order. It's a queer moment in the life of a mother, Geordie."

She laughed, but she didn't catch her tears before they were halfway down her cheeks. "I'm an old lady, my dear."

Harley gave one of his hearty, incredulous laughs. "You, old. You're one of the everlasting young ones, you are, Lil," and he stood and beamed with love and admiration.

"But I've got you, Geordie," she added, and her surprised heart that had suddenly felt so empty warmed again and was soothed when he took her hand eagerly and pressed it to his lips.

Grandfather and Grandmother Ludlow, Joan and many others who had formed the habit of believing that Christopher Ludlow's widow would remain true to his memory, failed utterly to understand the reason for her sudden breakaway from a settled and steady routine, to plunge into belated matrimony with a self-made man of fifty-five who seemed to them to be not only devoid of all attractiveness but bourgeois and rather ridiculous. But why? A little sympathy, a little knowledge of human nature,—that's all that was necessary to make this romance understandable. Because it was romance, in the best sense of that much abused word. It was not the romance defined in the dictionary as an action or adventure of an unusual or wonderful character, soaring beyond the limits of fact and real life and often of probability, but the result of loneliness and middle age, and of two hearts starving for love and the expression of love, for sympathy, companionship and the natural desire for something that would feed vanity, which, if it is permitted to die, is replaced by bitterness and a very warped point of view.

Christopher Ludlow, a wild, harum-scarum fellow who had risked his life many times during his hunting trips, came to his death in a prosaic street accident. For fifteen years his widow, then twenty-five, lived in the country with his parents and his little daughter. She was at their mercy, because Christopher had left no money. He had been dependent on an allowance from his father. Either she lived with them and bore cheerfully and tactfully with their increasing crotchetiness and impatience of old age, or left them to eke out a purposely small income in a second-rate hotel or a six by six apartment barely on the edge of the map. A timid woman, all for peace, without the grit and courage that goes with self-direction, she pursued the easy policy of least resistance, sacrificed her youth on the altar of Comfort and dwindled with only a few secret pangs into middle age. From time to time, with Joan, she left the safe waters of Lethe and put an almost frightened foot into the swift main stream. As time went on and Spring went out of her and Summer ripened to maturity, she was more and more glad to return from these brief excursions to the quiet country and the safe monotonous round. Then the day came when her no longer little girl came finally out of school, urgent and rebellious, kicking against the pricks, electrically alive and eager, autocrat and individualist rolled into one. Catching something of this youthfulness and shocked to wake to a realization of her lost years, she made a frantic and despairing effort to grasp at the tail-end of Summer and with a daughter far more worldly than herself escaped as frequently as possible into town to taste the pleasures that she had almost forgotten, and revive under the influence of the theater and the roar of life. It was during one of these excursions, while Joan was lunching with Alice Palgrave, that she caught an arrow shot at random by that mischievous little devil Cupid, which landed plum in the middle of a heart that had been placid so long. In getting out of a taxicab she had slipped and fallen, was raised deferentially to her feet, and looked up to catch the lonely and bewildered eyes of George Harley. They were outside their mutual hotel. What more natural and courteous than that he should escort her into the hotel with many expressions of anxious regret, ascend with her in the elevator to their mutual floor, linger with her for a polite few minutes in the sunlight that poured through the passage windows and leave her to hurry finally to her room thrilling under the recollection of two admiring eyes and a lingering handshake? She, even she, then, at her time of life, plump and partridge-like as she was, could inspire the interest and approval of a man. It was wonderful. It was absurd. It was ... altogether too good to be true! Later, after she had spent a half-amused, half-wistful quarter of an hour in front of her glass, seeing inescapable white hairs and an irremediable double chin, she had gone down to the dining room for lunch. All the tables being occupied, what more natural or disconcerting than for this modern Raleigh to rise and rather clumsily and eagerly beg that she would share the one just allotted to himself.

To the elderly man, whose nose had been too close to the grindstone to permit of dalliance, and who now, monied and retired, found himself terribly alone in the pale sun of St. Martin's Summer, and to the little charming woman of forty, led back to life by an ardent and impetuous girl, this quite ordinary everyday incident, which seemed to them to be touched by romance, came at a moment when both were pathetically receptive. They arranged to meet again, they met again, and one fine afternoon while Joan was at a theater with Alice, he spoke and she listened. It was in the more than usually hotel-like drawing-room of their mutual hotel. People were having tea, and the band was playing. There was a jangle of voices, the jingle of a musical comedy, the movement of waiters. Under the leaves of a tame palm which once had known the gorgeous freedom of a semi-tropical forest he stumbled over a proposal, the honest, fearful, pulsating proposal of a man who conceived that he was trying hopelessly to hitch his wagon to a star, and she, tremulous, amazed, and on the verge of tears, accepted him. Hers presumably the dreadful ordeal of facing an incredulous daughter and two sarcastic parents-in-law and his of standing for judgment before them, —argument, discussion, satire, irony, abuse even,—a quiet and determined marriage and a new and beautiful life.

"What a delightful room," said Mrs. Harley. "It looks so comfortable for a drawing-room that it must have been furnished by a man."

"We'll have a house in town by October, around here, and I'll bet it won't be uncomfortable when you've finished with it."

The raucous shouts of men crying an "extra" took Harley quickly to the open window. He watched one scare-monger edge his way up one side of the street and another, whose voice was like the jagged edge of a rusty saw, bandy leg his way up the other side. "Sounds like big sea battle," he said, after listening carefully. "Six German warships sunk, five British. Horrible loss of life. But I may be wrong. These men do their best not to be quite understood. Only six German ships! I wish the whole fleet of those dirty dogs could be sunk to the bottom."

There was nothing neutral or blind-eyed about George Harley. He had followed all the moves that had forced the war upon the nations whose spineless and inefficient governments had so long been playing the policy of the ostrich. He had nothing but detestation for the vile and ruthless methods of the German war party and nation and nothing but contempt for the allied politicians who had made such methods possible. He had followed the course of the war with pain, anguish and bated breath, thrilling at the supreme bravery of the Belgians and the French, and the First Hundred Thousand, thanking God for the miracle that saved Paris from desecration, and paying honest tribute to the giant effort of the British to wipe out the stain of a scandalous and criminal unpreparedness. He had squirmed with humiliation at the attempts of the little, dreadful clever people of his own country,—professors, parsons, pacifists and pro-Germans,—to prove that it was the duty of the United States to stand aloof and unmoved in the face of a menace which affected herself in no less a degree than it affected the nations then fighting for their lives, and had watched with increasing alarm the fatuous complacency of Congress which continued to deceive itself into believing that a great stretch of mere water rendered the country immune from taking its honest part in its own war. "Oh, my God," he had said in his heart, as all clear-sighted Americans had been saying, "has commercialism eaten into our very vitals? Has the good red blood of the early pioneers turned to water? Are we without the nerve any longer to read the writing on the wall?" And the only times that his national pride had been able to raise its head beneath the weight of shame and foreboding were those when he passed the windows of Red Cross Depots and caught sight of a roomful of good and noble women feverishly at work on bandages; when he read of the keen and splendid training voluntarily undergone by the far-sighted men who were making Plattsburg the nucleus of an officers' training corps, when he was told how many of his young and red-blooded fellow-countrymen had taken up arms with the Canadian contingents or had slipped over to France as ambulance men. What would he not have given to be young again!

He heaved a great sigh and turned back to the precious little woman who had placed her life into his hands for love. The hoarse alarming voices receded into the distance, leaving their curious echo behind.

"What were we talking about?" he asked. "Oh, ah, yes. The house. Lil, during the few days that I have to be in the city, let's find the house, let's nose around and choose the roof under which you and I will spend all the rest of our honeymoon. What do you say, dear?"

"I'd love it, Geordie; I'd just love it. A little house, smaller than this, with windows that catch the sun, quite near the Park, so that we can toddle across and watch the children playing. Wouldn't that be nice? And now I think I'll ring for some one to show me Joan's room and creep in and suggest that she gets up."

But there was no need. The door opened, and Joan came in, with eyes like stars.

IX

Three o'clock that afternoon found the Harleys still in Martin's house, with Mrs. Harley fidgetting to get George out for a walk in order that she might enjoy an intimate, mother-talk with Joan, and Joan deliberately using all her gifts to keep him there in order to avoid it.

Lunch had been a simple enough affair as lunches go, lifted above the ordinary ruck of such meals by the 1906 Chateau Latour and the Courvoisier Cognac from the cellar carefully stocked by Martin's father. From the psychological side of it, however, nothing could well have been more complicated. George had not forgotten his reception by the Ludlows that day of his ever-to-be-remembered visit of inspection—the cold, satirical eyes of Grandmother, the freezing courtesy of Grandfather, and the silent, eloquent resentment of the girl who saw herself on the verge of desertion by the one person who made life worth living in intermittent spots. He was nervous and overanxious to appear to advantage. The young thoroughbred at the head of the table who had given him a swift all-embracing look, an enigmatical smile and a light laughing question as to whether he would like to be called "Father, papa, Uncle George or what" awed him. He couldn't help feeling like a clumsy piece of modern pottery in the presence of an exquisite specimen of porcelain. His hands and feet multiplied themselves, and his vocabulary seemed to contain no more than a dozen slang phrases. He was conscious of the fact that his collar was too high and his clothes a little too bold in pattern, and he was definitely certain for the first time in his life, that he had not yet discovered a barber who knew how to cut hair.

Overeager to emphasize her realization of the change in her relationship to Joan, overanxious to let it be seen at once that she was merely an affectionate and interested visitor and not a mother with a budget of suggestions and corrections and rearrangements, Mrs. Harley added to the complication. Usually the most natural woman in the world with a soft infectious laugh, a rather shrewd humor and a neat gift of comment, she assumed a metallic artificiality that distressed herself and surprised Joan. She babbled about absolutely nothing by the yard, talked over George's halting but gallant attempts to make things easy like any Clubwoman, and in an ultra-scrupulous endeavor to treat Joan as if she were a woman of the world, long emancipated from maternal apron strings, said things to her, inane, insincere things, that she would not have said to a complete stranger on the veranda of a summer hotel or the sun deck of a transatlantic liner. She hated herself and was terrified.

For two reasons this unexpected lunch was an ordeal so far as Joan was concerned. She remembered how antagonistic she had been to Harley under the first rough shock of her mother's startling and what then had appeared to be disloyal aberration, and wanted to make up for it to the big, simple, uncomfortable man who was so obviously in love. Also she was still all alone in the mental chaos into which everything that had happened last night had conspired to plunge her and was trying, with every atom of courage that she possessed, to hide the fact from her mother's quick solicitous eyes. SHE of all people must not know that Martin had gone away or find the loose end of her married life!

It was one of those painful hours that crop up from time to time in life and seem to leave a little scratch upon the soul.

But when quarter past three came Mrs. Harley pulled herself together. She had already dropped hints of every known and well-recognized kind to George, without success. She had even invented appointments for him at the dentist's and the tailor's. But George was basking in Joan's favor and was too dazzled to be able to catch and concentrate upon his wife's insinuations as to things and people that didn't exist. And Joan held him with her smile and led him from one anecdote to another. Finally, with no one realized how supreme an effort, Mrs. Harley came to the point. As a rule she never came to points.

"Geordie," she said, seizing a pause, "you may run along now, dear, and take a walk. It will do you good to get a little exercise before dinner. I want to be alone with Joan for a while."

And before Joan could swing the conversation off at a tangent the faithful and obedient St. Bernard was on his feet, ready and willing to ramble whichever way he was told to go. With unconscious dignity and a guilelessness utterly unknown to drawing-rooms he bent over Joan's reluctant hand and said, "Thank you for being so kind to me," laid a hearty kiss on his wife's cheek and went.

"And now, darling," said Mrs. Harley, settling into her chair with an air of natural triumph, "tell me where Martin is and how long he's going to be away and all about everything."

These were precisely the questions that Joan had worked so hard and skilfully to dodge. "Well, first of all, Mummy," she said, with filial artfulness, "you must come and see the house."

And Mrs. Harley, who had been consumed with the usual feminine curiosity to examine every corner and cranny of it, rose with alacrity. "What I've already seen is all charming," she said. "I knew Martin's father, you know. He spent a great deal of time at his house near your grandfather's, and was nearly always in the saddle. He was not a bit like one's idea of a horsey man. He was, in fact, a gentleman who was fond of horses. There is a world of difference. He had a most delightful smile and was the only man I ever met, except your grandfather, who could drink too much wine without showing it. Who's this good-looking boy with the trustworthy eyes?"

"Martin," said Joan. "Martin," she added inwardly, "who treated me like a kid last night."

Mrs. Harley looked up at the portrait. An involuntary smiled played round her mouth. "Yes, of course. I remember him. What a dear boy! No wonder you fell in love with him, darling. You must be very happy."

Joan followed her mother out of the room. She was glad of the chance to control her expression. She went upstairs with a curious lack of the spirit of proprietorship. It hurt her to feel as if she were showing a house taken furnished for the season in which she had no rights, no pride and no personal interest. Martin had treated her like a kid last night and gone away in the morning without a word. Alice and Gilbert had taunted her with not being a wife. She wasn't, and this was Martin's house, not hers and Martin's ... it hurt.

"Ah," said Mrs. Harley softly as she went into Joan's bedroom. "Ah. Very nice. You both have room to move here." But the mass of little filet lace pillows puzzled her, and she darted a quick look at the tall young thing with the inscrutable face who had ceased to be her little girl and had become her daughter.

"The sun pours in," said Joan, turning away.

Mrs. Harley noticed a door and brightened up.

"Martin's dressing room?" she asked. "No. My maid's room!" Joan said.

Mrs. Harley shook her head ever so little. She was not in sympathy with what she called new-fashioned ideas. It was on the tip of her tongue to say so and to forget, just this once, the inevitable change in their relationship and speak like mammy once more. But she was a timid, sensitive little woman, and the indefinable barrier that had suddenly sprung up held her back. Joan made no attempt to meet her halfway. The moment passed.

They went along the passage. "There are Martin's rooms," said Joan.

Mrs. Harley went halfway in. "Like a bachelor's rooms, aren't they?" she said, without guile. And while she glanced at the pictures and the crowded bootrack and the old tallboys, Joan's sudden color went away again.... He was a bachelor. He had left her on the other side of the bridge. He had hurt her last night. How awfully she must have hurt him!

"When will Martin be back?"

"I don't know," said Joan. "Probably to-morrow. I'm not sure." She stumbled a little, realized that she was giving herself away,—because if a bride is not to know her husband's movements, who is?—and made a desperate effort to recover her position. "It all depends on how long he's kept. But he needed exercise, and golf's such a good game, isn't it? I sha'n't hurry him back."

She looked straight into her mother's anxious eyes, saw them clear, saw a smile come—and took a deep breath of relief. If there was one thing that she had to put up the most strenuous fight to avoid, in her present chaotic state of mind, it was a direct question as to her life with Martin. Of all people, her mother must be left in the belief that she was happy. Pride demanded that, even to the extent of lying. It was hard luck to be caught by her mother, at the very moment when she was standing among all the debris of her kid's ideas, among all the broken beams of carelessness, and the shattered panes of high spirits.

She was thankful that her mother was not one of those aggressive, close-questioning women, utterly devoid of sensitiveness and delicacy who are not satisfied until they have forced open all the secret drawers of the mind and stuck the contents on a bill file,—one of those hard-bosomed women who stump into church as they stump into a department store with an air of "Now then, what can you show me that's new," who go about with a metaphorical set of burglar's tools in a large bag with which to break open confidences and who have no faith in human nature.

And with a sudden sense of gratitude she turned to the woman whom she had always accepted as a fact, an institution, and looked at her with new eyes, a new estimate and a new emotion. The little, loving, gentle, anxious woman with the capacity of receiving impressions from external objects that amounted to a gift but with a reticence of so fine and tender a quality that she seemed always to stand on tiptoes on the delicate ground of people's feelings, was HERS, was her mother. The word burst into a new meaning, blossomed into a new truth. She had been accepted all these years, —loved, in a sort of way; obeyed, perhaps, expected to do things and provide things and make things easy, and here she stood more needed, at the moment when she imagined that the need of her had passed, than at any other time of her motherhood.

In a flash Joan understood all this and its paradox, looked all the way back along the faithful, unappreciated years, and being no longer a child was stirred with a strange maternal fellow feeling that started her tears. Nature is merciless. Everything is sacrificed to youth. Birds build their nests and rear their young and are left as soon as wings are ready. Women marry and bear children and bring them up with love and sacrifice, only to be relegated to a second place at the first moment of independence. Joan saw this then. Her mother's altered attitude, and her own feeling of having grown out of maternal possession brought it before her. She saw the underlying drama of this small inevitable scene in the divine comedy of life and was touched by a great sympathy and made sorry and ashamed.

But pride came between her and a desire to go down on her knees at her mother's side, make a clean breast of everything and beg for advice and help.

And so these two, between whom there should have been complete confidence, were like people speaking to each other from opposite banks of a stream, conscious of being overheard.

X

Day after day went by with not a word from Martin. April was slipping off the calendar. A consistent blue sky hung over a teeming city that grew warm and dry beneath a radiant sun. Winter forgotten, spring an overgrown boy, the whole town underwent a subtle change. Its rather sullen winter expression melted into a smile, and all its foreign characteristics and color broke out once more under the influence of sun and blue sky. Alone among the great cities of the world stands New York for contrariety and contrast. Its architecture is as various as its citizenship, its manners are as dissimilar as its accents, its moods as diverse as its climate. Awnings appeared, straw hats peppered the streets like daisies in long fields, shadows moved, days lengthened, and the call of the country fell on city ears like the thin wistful notes of the pipes of Pan.

Brought up against a black wall Joan left the Roundabout, desisted from joy-riding, and, spending most of her time with her mother, tried secretly and without any outward sign, to regain her equilibrium. She saw nothing of Alice and the set, now beginning to scatter, in which Alice had placed her. She was consistently out to Gilbert Palgrave and the other men who had been gathering hotly at her heels. Her policy of "who cares?" had received a shock and left her reluctantly and impatiently serious. She had withdrawn temporarily into a backwater in order to think things over and wait for Martin to reappear. It seemed to her that her future way of life was in his hands. If Martin came back soon and caught her in her present mood she would play the game according to the rules. If he stayed away or, coming back, persisted in considering her as a kid and treating her as such, away would go seriousness, life being short, and youth but a small part of it, and back she would go to the Merry-go-round, and once more, at twice the pace, with twice the carelessness, the joy-ride would continue. It was all up to Martin, little as he knew it.

And where was Martin?

There was no letter, no message, no sign as day followed day. Without allowing herself to send out an S. O. S. to him, which she well knew that she had the power to do, she waited, as one waits at crossroads, to go either one way or the other. Although tempted many times to tap the invisible wire which stretched between them, and to put an end to a state of uncertainty which was indescribably irksome to her impulsive and imperative nature, she held her hand. Pride steeled her, and vanity gave her temporary patience. She even went so far as to think of him under another name so that no influence of hers might bring him back. She wanted him to return naturally, on his own account, because he was unable to keep away. She wanted him, wherever he was and whatever he was doing, to want her, not to come in cold blood from a sense of duty, in the spirit of martyrdom. She wanted him, for her pride's sake, to be again the old eager Marty, the burning-eyed, inarticulate Marty, who had brought her to his house and laid it at her feet with all that was his. In no other way was she prepared to cross what she thought of as the bridge.

And so, seeing only her mother and George Harley, she waited, saying to herself confidently "If he doesn't come to-day, he will come to-morrow. I told him that I was a kid, and he understood. I've hurt him awfully, but he loves me. He will come to-morrow."

But to-morrow came and where was Martin?

It was a curious time for this girl-woman to go through alone, hiding her crisis from her mother behind smiling eyes, disguising her anxiety under a cloak of high spirits, herself hurt but realizing that she had committed a hurt. It made her feel like an aeroplane voluntarily landed in perfect condition at the start of a race, waiting for the pilot to get aboard. That he would return at any moment and take her up again she never doubted. Why should she? She knew Martin. His eyes won confidence, and there was a heart of gold behind his smile. She didn't believe that she could have lost him so soon. He would come back because he loved her. Hadn't he agreed that she was a kid? And when he did come back she would take her courage in both hands and tell him that she wanted to play the game. And then, having been honest, she would hitch on to life again with a light heart, and neither Alice nor Gilbert could stand up and flick her conscience. Martin would be happy.

To-morrow and to-morrow, and no Martin.

At the end of a week a letter was received by her mother from Grandmother Ludlow, in which, with a tinge of sarcasm, she asked that she might be honored by a visit of a few days, always supposing that trains still ran between New York and Peapack and gasolene could still be procured for privately owned cars. And there was a postscript in these words. "Perhaps you have the necessary eloquence to induce the athletic Mrs. Martin Gray to join you."

The letter was handed to Joan across the luncheon table at the Plaza. She read the characteristic effusion with keen amusement. She could hear the old lady's incisive voice in every word and the tap of her stick across the hall as she laid the letter in the box. How good to see the country again and go through the woods to the old high place where she had turned and found Martin. How good to go back to that old prison house as an independent person, with the right to respect and even consideration. It would serve Martin right to find her away when he came back. She would leave a little note on his dressing table.

"No wonder the old lady asks if the trains have broken down," said Mrs. Harley. "Of course, we ought to have gone out to see her, Geordie."

"Of course," said George, "of course"—but he darted a glance at Joan which very plainly conveyed the hope that she would find some reason why the visit should not be made. Would he ever forget standing in that stiff drawing-room before that contemptuous old dame, feeling exactly like a very small worm?

The strain of waiting for Martin day after day had told on Joan. She longed for a change of atmosphere, a change of scene. And what a joke it would be to be able to face her grandfather and grandmother without shaking in her shoes! "Of course," said Joan. "Let's drive out to-day in time for dinner, and send a telegram at once. Nothing like striking while the iron's hot. Papa Geordie, tell the waiter to bring a blank, and we'll concoct a message between us. Is that all right for you, Mother?"

Mrs. Harley looked rather like a woman being asked to run a quarter of a mile to catch a train, but she gave a little laugh and said, "Yes, dear. I think so, although, perhaps, to-morrow—"

"To-day is a much better word," said Joan. She was sick of to-morrow and to-morrow. "Packing won't take any time. I'll go home directly after lunch and set things moving and be here in the car at three thirty. We can see the trees and smell the ferns and watch the sun set before we have to change for dinner. I'm dying to do that."

No arguments or objections were put forward.

This impetuous young thing must have her way.

And when the car drove away from the Plaza a few minutes after the appointed time Joan was as excited as a child, Mrs. Harley quite certain that she had forgotten her sponge bag and her bedroom slippers, and George Harley betting on a time that would put more lines on his face.

There was certainly more than a touch of irony in Joan's gladness to go back so soon to the cage from which she had escaped with such eagerness.

There had been no word and no sign of Martin.

But as Joan had run upstairs Gilbert Palgrave had come out from the drawing-room and put himself deliberately in her way.

"I can't stay now, Gilbert," she had said. "I'm going into the country, and I haven't half a second to spare. I'm so sorry."

He had held his place. "You've got to give me five minutes. You've got to," and something in his eyes had made her take hold of her impatience.

"You don't know what you're doing to me," he had said, with no sign of his usual style and self-consciousness, but simply, like a man who had sat in the dark and suffered. "Or if you do know your cruelty is inhuman. I've tried to see you every day—not to talk about myself or bore you with my love, but just to look at you. You've had me turned away as if I were a poor relation. You've sent your maid to lie to me over the telephone as if I were a West Point cadet in a primitive state of sloppy sentiment. Don't do it. It isn't fair. I hauled down my fourth wall to you, and however much you may scorn what you saw there you must respect it. Love must always be respected. It's the rarest thing on earth. I'm here to tell you that you must let me see you, just see you. I've waited for many years for this. I'm all upheaved. You've exploded me. I'm different. I'm remade. I'm beginning again. I shall ask for nothing but kindness until I've made you love me, and then I shall not have to ask. You will come to me. I can wait. That's all I want you to know. When you come back ring me up. I'll be patient."

With that he had stood aside with a curious humbleness, had gripped the hand that she had given him and had gone downstairs and away.

The country round Peapack was in its first glorious flush of young beauty. The green of everything dazzled under the sun. The woods were full of the echo of fairy laughter. Wild flowers ran riot among the fields. Delicate-footed May was following on the heels of April with its slight fingers full of added glory for the earth.

There was something soft and English in the look of the trees and fields as they came nearer to the old house. They might have been driving through the kind garden of Kent.

Framed in the fine Colonial doorway stood the tall old man with his white head and fireless eyes, the little distinguished woman still charged with electricity and the two veteran dogs with their hollow barks.

"Not one blushing bride, but two," said Grandmother Ludlow. "How romantic." She presented her cheek to the nervous Mrs. Harley. "You look years younger, my dear. Quite fluttery and foolish. How do you do, Mr. Harley? You are very welcome, Sir." She passed them both on to the old man and turned to Joan with the kind of smile that one sees on the faces of Chinese gods. "And here is our little girl in whose marvellous happiness we have all rejoiced."

Joan stood up bravely to the little old lady whose sarcasm went home like the sharp point of a rapier.

"How do you do, dear Grandmamma," she said.

"No better than can be expected, my love, but no worse." The queer smile broadened. "But surely you haven't torn yourself away from the young husband from whom, I hear, you have never been parted for a moment? That I can't believe. People tell me that there has never been such a devoted and love-sick couple. Martin Gray is driving another car, of course."

Joan never flicked an eyelash. She would rather die than let this cunning old lady have the satisfaction of seeing that she had drawn blood. "No, Grandmamma," she said. "Martin needed exercise and is playing golf at Shinnecock. He rang me up this morning and asked me to say how sorry he was not to have the pleasure of seeing you this time." She went over to her grandfather and held up a marvellously equable face.

The old dame watched her with reluctant admiration. The child had all the thoroughbred points of a Ludlow. All the same she should be shown that, even in the twentieth century, young girls could not break away from discipline and flout authority without punishment. The smile became almost gleeful at the thought of the little surprise that was in store for her.

The old sportsman took Joan in his arms and held her tight for a moment. "I've missed you, my dear," he said. "The house has been like a mausoleum without you. But I've no reproaches. Youth to youth,—it's right and proper." And he led her into the lofty hall with his arm round her shoulder.

There was a sinister grin on Gleave's poacher-like face when Joan gave him a friendly nod. And it was with a momentary spasm of uneasiness that she asked herself what he and her grandmother knew. It was evident that they had something up their sleeves. But when, after a tea during which she continued to fence and play the part of happy bride, she went out into the scented garden that was like an old and loving friend, this premonition of something evil left her. With every step she felt herself greeted and welcomed. Young flowers as guileless as children waved their green hands. Heads nodded as she passed. The old trees that had watched her grow up rustled their leaves in affectionate excitement. She had not understood until that very moment how many true friends she had or how warm a place in her heart that old house had taken. It was with a curious maternal emotion that clouded her eyes with tears that she stood for a moment and kissed her hands to the right and left like a young queen to her subjects. Then she ran along the familiar path through the woods to the spot where she had been found by Martin and stood once more facing the sweep of open country and the distant horizon beyond which lay the Eldorado of her girl's dreams. She was still a girl, but she had come back hurt and sorry and ashamed. Martin might have lost his faith in her. He had gone away without a word or sign. Gilbert Palgrave held her in such small respect that he waited with patience for her to come, although married, into his arms. And there was not a man or a woman on the Round-about, except Alice, who really cared whether she ever went back again. The greedy squirrel peeked at her from behind a fern, recognized his old playmate, and came forward in a series of runs and leaps. With a little cry Joan bent down and held out her hand. And away in the distance there was the baying of Martin's hounds. But where was Martin?

XI

"Rather beg than work, wouldn't he? I call him Micawber because he's always waiting for something to turn up."

Joan wheeled round. To hear a stranger's voice in a place that was peculiarly hers and Martin's amazed and offended her. It was unbelievable.

A girl was sitting in the long grass, hatless, with her hands clasped round her knees. The sun lit up her bobbed hair that shone like brass and had touched her white skin with a warm finger. Wistful and elfish, sitting like Puck on a toadstool, she might have slipped out of some mossy corner of the woods to taste the breeze and speculate about life. She wore a butter-colored sport shirt wide open at the neck and brown cord riding breeches and puttees. Slight and small boned and rather thin she could easily have passed for a delicate boy or, except for something at the back of her eyes that showed that she had not always lived among trees, for Peter Pan's brother of whom the world had never heard.

Few people would have recognized in this spring maid the Tootles of Broadway and that rabbit warren in West Forty-sixth Street. The dew of the country had washed her face and lips, and the choir voices of Martin's big cathedral had put peace and gentleness into her expression.

She ran her eyes with frank admiration over the unself-consciously patrician Joan in her immaculate town clothes and let them rest finally on a face that seemed to her to be the most attractive that she had ever seen, for all that its expression made her want to scramble to her feet and take to her heels. But she controlled herself and sat tight, summoned her native impertinence to the rescue and gave a friendly nod. After all, it was a free country. There were no princesses knocking about.

"You don't look as if you were a pal of squirrels," she said.

Joan's resentment at the unexpected presence of this interloper only lasted a moment. It gave way almost immediately before interest and curiosity and liking,—even, for a vague reason, sympathy.

"I've known this one all his life," she said. "His father and mother were among my most intimate friends and, what's more, his grandfather and grandmother relied on me to help them out in bad times."

The duet of laughter echoed among the trees.

With a total lack of dignity the squirrel retired and stood, with erect tail, behind a tuft of coarse grass, wondering what had happened.

"It's a gift to be country and look town," said Tootles, with unconcealed flattery. "It's having as many ancestors as the squirrels, I suppose. According to the rules I ought to feel awkward, oughtn't I?"

"Why?"

"Well, I'm trespassing. I saw it in your eyes. 'Pon my soul it never occurred to me before. Shall I try and make a conventional exit or may I stay if I promise not to pinch the hill? This view is better than face massage. It rubs out all the lines. My word, but it's good to be alive up here!"

The mixture of cool cheek and ecstasy, given forth in the patois of the London suburbs, amused Joan. Here was a funny, whimsical, pathetic, pretty little thing, she thought—queerly wise, too, and with all about her a curious appeal for friendship and kindness. "Stay, of course," she said. "I'm very glad you like my hill. Use it as often as you can." She sat down on the flat-topped piece of rock that she had so often shared with Martin. There was a sense of humanity about this girl that had the effect of a magnet. She inspired confidence, as Martin did.

"Thanks most awfully," said Tootles. "You're kinder than you think to let me stay here. And I'm glad you're going to sit down for a bit. I like you, and I don't mind who knows it."

"And I like you," said Joan.

And they both laughed again, feeling like children. It was a characteristic trick of Fate's to bring about this meeting.

"I don't mind telling you now," went on Tootles, all barriers down, "that I've come up here every evening for a week. It's a thousand years since I've seen the sun go to bed and watched the angels light the stars. It's making me religious. The Broadway electrics have always been between me and the sky.... Gee, but it's goin' to be great this evening." She settled herself more comfortably, leaned back against the stump of a tree and began to smile like a child at the Hippodrome in expectation of one of the "colossal effects."

Joan's curiosity was more and more piqued, but it was rather to know what than who this amazingly natural little person was. For all her youth there were lines round her mouth that were eloquent of a story begun early. Somehow, with Martin away and giving no sign, Joan was glad, and in a way comforted, to have stumbled on some one, young like herself, who had obviously faced uncertainty and stood at the crossroads. "I'd like to ask you hundreds of questions," she said impulsively. "Do you mind?"

"No, dearie. Fire away. I shan't have to tell you any fables to keep you interested. I broke through the paper hoop into the big ring when I was ten. Look! See those ducks flyin' home? The first time I saw them I thought it was a V-shaped bit of smoke running away from one of the factories round Newark."

She had told Martin that. His laugh seemed still to be in the air.

"Are you married?" asked Joan suddenly.

"Not exactly, dearie," replied Tootles, without choosing her words. But a look at the young, eager, sweet face bent towards her made her decide to use camouflage. "What I mean is, no, I'm not. Men don't marry me when it isn't absolutely necessary. I'm a small part chorus lady, if you get my point."

Joan was not quite sure that she did. Her sophistication had not gone farther up than Sixty-seventh Street or farther down than Sherry's, and it was bounded by Park Avenue on the one side and Fifth Avenue on the other. "But would you like to have been married?" All her thoughts just then were about marriage and Marty.

Tootles shook her head and gave a downward gesture with an open hand that hardly needed to be amplified. "No, not up to a few weeks ago. I've lived by the stage, you see, and that means that the men I've come across have not been men but theatricals. Very different. You may take my word. When I met my first man I didn't believe it. I thought he was the same kind of fake. But when I knew that he was a man alright,—well, I wanted to be married as much as a battered fishing smack wants to get into harbor." She was thinking of Marty too, although not of marriage any more.

"And are you going to be?"

"No, dearie. He's got a wife, it turns out. It was a bit o' cheek ever to dream of hitting a streak of such luck as that. All the same, I've won something that I shall treasure all the days of my life.... Look. Here come some of the mourners." She pointed to three crows that flapped across a sky all hung with red and gold.

Joan was puzzled. "Mourners?"

"Why, yes. Isn't this the death bed of a day?"

"I never thought of it in that way," said Joan.

"No," said Tootles, running her eyes again over Joan's well-groomed young body. "That's easy to see. You will, though, if ever you want every day to last a year. You're married, anyway."

"Not exactly," said Joan, unconsciously repeating the other girl's expression.

Tootles looked at Martin's ring. "What about that, then?"

Joan looked at it too, with a curious gravity. It stood for so much more than she had ever supposed that it would. "But I don't know whether it's going to bind us, or not."

"And you so awfully young!"

"I was," said Joan.

The girl who had never had any luck darted a keen, examining glance at the girl who had all the appearance of having been born lucky. Married, as pretty as a picture, everything out of the smartest shops, the owner, probably, of this hill and those woods, and the old house that she had peeped at all among that lovely garden—she couldn't have come up against life's sharp elbow, surely? She hoped not, most awfully she hoped not.

Joan caught the look and smiled back. There was kindness here, and comradeship. "I've nothing to tell," she said, "yet. I'm just beginning to think, that's the truth, only just. I've been very young and thoughtless, but I'm better now and I'm waiting to make up for it. I'm not unhappy, only a little anxious. Everything will come right though, because my man's a man, too."

Tootles made a long arm and put her hand on Joan's. "In that case, make up for it bigly, dearie," she said earnestly. "Don't be afraid to give. There are precious few real men about and lots of women to make a snatch at them. It isn't being young that matters. Most troubles are brought about, at your time of life, by not knowing when to stop being young. Good luck, Lady-bird. I hope you never have anything to tell. Oh, just look, just look!"

Joan followed the pointing finger, but held the kind hand. And they sat in silence watching "the fair frail palaces, the fading Alps and archipelagoes, and great cloud-continents of sunset seas." And as she sat, enthralled, the whole earth hushed and still, shadows lurking towards the east, the evening air holding its breath, the night ready behind the horizon for its allotted work, God's hand on everything, it was of Marty that Joan thought, Marty whom she must have hurt so deeply and who had gone away without a word or a sign, believing that she was still a kid. Yes, she WOULD make up for it, bigly, bigly, and he should be happy, this boy-man who was a knight.

And it was of Martin that Tootles, poor, little, unlucky Tootles, thought also. All her life she would have something to which to look back, something precious and beautiful, and his name, stamped upon her heart, would go down with her to the grave.

And they stayed there, in silence, holding hands, until the last touch of color had gone out of the sky and the evening air sighed and moved on and the night climbed slowly over the dim horizon. They might have been sisters.

And then Joan rose in a sort of panic. "I must go," she said nervously, forgetting that she had grown up. "Good night, Fairy."

Tootles stood up too. "Good night, Lady-bird. Make everything come right," and held out her hand.

Joan took it again and went forward and kissed the odd little girl who was her friend.

And a moment later Tootles saw her disappearing into the wood, like a spirit. When she looked up at the watching star and waved her hand, it seemed all misty.

XII

"And now, Mr. Harley," said Grandmother Ludlow, lashing the septuagenarian footman with one sharp look because he had spilt two or three drops of Veuve Cliquot on the tablecloth, "tell me about the present state of the money market."

Under his hostess's consistent courtesy and marked attentions George Harley had been squirming during the first half of dinner. He had led her into the fine old dining room with all the style that he could muster and been placed, to his utter dismay, on her right. He would infinitely rather have been commanded to dine with the Empress of China, which he had been told was the last word in mental and physical torture. Remembering vividly the cold and satirical scorn to which he had been treated during his former brief and nightmare visit the old lady's change of attitude to extreme politeness and even deference made him feel that he was having his leg pulled. In a brand new dinner jacket with a black tie poked under the long points of a turned-down collar, which, in his innocence, he had accepted as the mode of gentlemen and not, as he rightly supposed of waiters, he had done his best to give coherent answers to a rapid fire of difficult questions.

The most uneasy man on earth, he had committed himself to statements that he knew to be unsound, had seen his untouched plate whisked away while he was floundering among words, and started a high temperature beneath what he was perfectly certain was lurking mockery behind apparently interested attention.

If any banker at that moment had overheard him describing the state of the money market he would have won for himself a commission in the earth's large army of unconfined lunatics.

The old sportsman, sitting with Joan on his right and his daughter-in-law on his left, was more nearly merry and bright than any one had seen him since the two great changes in his household. His delight in having Joan near him again was pathetic. He had shaved for the second time that day, a most unusual occurrence. His white hair glistened with brilliantine, and there was a gardenia in his buttonhole. Some of the old fire had returned to his eyes, and his tongue had regained its once invariable knack of paying charming compliments. In his excitement and delight he departed from his rigid diet, and, his wife's attention being focussed upon George Harley, punished the champagne with something of his old vigor, and revived as a natural result many of the stories which Joan and her mother had been told ad nauseam over any number of years with so much freshness as to make them seem almost new.

Mrs. Harley, wearing a steady smile, was performing the painful feat of listening with one ear to the old gentleman and with the other to the old lady. All her sympathy was with her unfortunate and uneasy husband who looked exactly like a great nervous St. Bernard being teased by a Pekinese.

Joan missed none of the underlying humor of the whole thing. It was amusing and satisfactory to be treated as the guest of honor in a house in which she had always been regarded as the naughty and rebellious child. She was happy in being able to put her usually morose grandfather into such high spirits and moved to a mixture of mirth and pity at the sight of George Harley's plucky efforts. Also she had brought away with her from the girl she called the fairy a strengthened desire to play the game and a good feeling that Marty was nearer to her than he had been for a long and trying week. It's true that from time to time she caught in her grandmother's eyes that queer look of triumphant glee that had disturbed her when they met and the same expression of malicious spite at the corner of Gleave's sunken mouth which had made her wonder what he knew, but these things she waved aside. Instinct, and her complete knowledge of Mrs. Cumberland Ludlow's temperament, made her realize that if the old lady could find a way to get even with her for having run off she would leave no stone unturned, and that she would not hesitate to use the cunning ex-fighting man to help her. But, after all, what could they do? It would be foolish to worry.

Far from foolish, if she had had an inkling of the trap that had been laid for her and into which she was presently going to fall without suspicion.

The facts were that Gleave had seen Martin drive up to his house with Tootles, had watched them riding and walking together throughout the week, had reported what he had seen to Mrs. Ludlow and left it to her fertile imagination to make use of what was to him an ugly business. And the old lady, grasping her chance, had written that letter to Mrs. Harley and having achieved her point of getting Joan into her hands, had discovered that she did not know where Martin was and had made up her mind to show her. Revenge is sweet, saith the phrasemonger, and to the old lady whose discipline had been flouted and whose amour propre had been rudely shaken it was very sweet indeed. Her diabolical scheme, conceived in the mischievous spirit of second childhood, was to lead Joan on to a desire to show off her country house to her relations at the moment when the man she had married and the girl with whom he was amusing himself on the sly were together. "How dramatic," she chuckled, in concocting the plan. "How delightfully dramatic." And she might have added, "How hideously cruel."

But it was not until some little time after they had all adjourned to the drawing-room, and Joan had played the whole range of her old pieces for the edification of her grandfather, that she set her trap.

"If I had my time over again," she said, looking the epitome of benevolence, "I would never spend spring in the city."

"Wouldn't you, dear?" prompted Mrs. Harley, eager to make the conversation general and so give poor George a rest.

"No, my love. I would make my winter season begin in November and end in February—four good months for the Opera, the theatres, entertaining and so forth. Then on the first of March, the kind-hearted month that nurses April's violets, I would leave town for my country place and, as the poets have it watch the changing skies and the hazel blooms peep through the swelling buds and hear the trees begin to whisper and the throstles break into song. One loses these things by remaining among bricks and mortar till the end of April. Joan, my dear, give this your consideration next year. If your good husband is anything like his father, whom we knew very slightly and admired, he is a lover of the country and should be considered."

"Yes, Grandmamma," said Joan, wondering if Marty had come back and found her note on his dressing-table.

"Always supposing, of course, that next year finds you both as much in love as you are to-day,—the most devoted pair of turtle doves, as I am told." She laughed a little roguishly to disguise the sting.

"They will be," said Mrs. Harley quickly. "There is no doubt about that."

"None," said Joan, looking full at the old lady with a confident smile and a high chin. Would her grandmother never forget that escape from the window?

"Why suggest the possibility of a break?" asked Mr. Ludlow, with a touch of anger. "Really, my dear."

"A little joke, Cumberland, merely a little joke. Joan understands me, I know."

"I think so," said Joan, smiling back. Not on her, whatever happened, would she see the white feather. Some one had told the tale of her kid's rush into the heart of things and her many evenings with Palgrave and the others, when "Who cares?" was her motto.

The old lady went on, with infinite artfulness. "During the coming summer, my love, you should look out for a pleasant little house in some charming part of the country, furnish it, put men to work on the garden, and have it all ready for the following spring."

"I know just the place," put in George. "Near a fine golf course and country club with a view across the Hudson that takes your breath away."

"That might necessitate the constant attendance of a doctor," said Mrs. Ludlow drily, "which would add considerably to the expenses. I would advise the Shinnecock Hills, for instance, which are swept by sea breezes and so reminiscent of Scotland. Martin would be within a stone's throw of his favorite course, there, wouldn't he, Joan?"

"Yes, Grandmamma," said Joan, still with a high head and a placid smile, although it came to her in a flash that her statement as to where Martin was had not been believed. What if Grandmother knew where Martin had gone? How absurd. How could she?

And then Mr. Ludlow broke in again, impatiently. The effect of the champagne was wearing off. He hated feminine conversation in drawing-rooms, anyhow. "Why go searching about for a house for the child when she's got one already."

"Why, so I have," cried Joan. "Here. I'd forgotten all about it!"

Nothing could have suited the old lady so well. Her husband could not have said anything more right if he had been prompted. "Of course you have," she said, with a cackle of laughter. "I had forgotten it too. Mr. Harley, can you believe our overlooking the fact that there is a most excellent house in the family a gunshot from where we are all sitting? It's natural enough for me, who have never met Joan's young husband. But for you, my love, who spent such a romantic night there! Where are your wits?"

Joan's laugh rang out. "Goodness knows, but I really had forgotten all about it. And although I've only been in it once I've known it by sight all my life. Martin's father had it built, Papa George, and it's awfully nice and sporting, with kennels, and tennis courts, and everything."

"Yes, and beautifully furnished, I remember. I dined there several times, years ago before Mr. Gray had—" Mrs. Harley drew up short.

Mrs. Ludlow finished the sentence. "A little quarrel with me," she said. "I objected to his hounds scrambling over this property and wrote pithily to that effect. We never spoke again. My dear, while we are all together, why not personally conduct us over this country house of yours and give us an unaccustomed thrill of excitement."

"Yes, do, darling," said Mrs. Harley. "George would love to see it."

"I will," said Joan. "I'd adore to. I don't know a bit what it's like, except the hall and the library. It will come as a perfect surprise to me."

"A very perfect surprise," said Mrs. Ludlow.

Joan sprang to her feet. "Let's go now. No time like the present."

"Well," said Mrs. Harley cautiously, though equally keen.

"No, no, not to-night. Bear with your aged grandparents. Besides, the housekeeper and the other servants will probably be in bed. To-morrow now, early—"

"All right," said Joan. "To-morrow then, directly after breakfast. Fancy forgetting that one possessed a country house. It's almost alarming." And she put her hands on her grandfather's shoulders, and bent down and kissed him. She was excited and thrilled. It was her house because it was Martin's, and soon she would be Martin's too. And they would spend a real honeymoon in the place in which they had sat together in the dark and laid their whispered plans for the great adventure. How good that would be!

And when she went back to the piano and rattled off a fox trot, Grandmother Ludlow got up and hobbled out of the room, on her tapping stick, to hide her glee.

XIII

It was ten o'clock when Joan stood once more in the old, familiar bedroom in which she had slept all through her childhood and adolescence.

Nothing had been altered since the night from which she dated the beginning of her life. Her books were in the same places. Letters from her school friends were in the same neat pile on her desk. The things that she had been obliged to leave on her dressing-table had not been touched. A framed photograph of her mother, with her hands placed in the incredible way that is so dear to the photographer's heart, still hung crooked over a colonial chest of drawers. Her blue and white bath wrap was in its place over the back of a chair, with her slippers beneath it.

She opened the door of the hospitable closet. There were all the clothes and shoes and hats that she had left. She drew out a drawer in the chest. Nothing had been disturbed.... It was uncanny. She seemed to have been away for years. And yet, as she looked about and got the familiar scent of the funny little lavender sachets made by Mrs. Nye, she found it hard to believe that Marty and Gilbert Palgrave, the house in New York, all the kaleidoscope of Crystal rooms and restaurants, all the murmur of voices and music and traffic were not the elusive memories of last night's dream. But for the longing for Marty that amounted to an absorbing, ever-present homesickness, it was difficult to accept the fact that she was not still the same early-to-bed, early-to-rise country girl, kicking against the pricks, rebelling against the humdrum daily routine, spoiling to try her wings.

"Dear old room," she whispered, suddenly stretching out her arms to it. "My dear old room. I didn't think I'd miss you a little bit. But I have. I didn't think I should be glad to get back to you. But I am. What are you doing to me to make me feel a tiny pain in my heart? You're crowding all the things I did here and all the things I thought about like a thousand white pigeons round my head. All my impatient sighs, and big ambitions, and silly young hopes and fears are coming to meet me and make me want to laugh and cry. But it isn't the same me that you see; it isn't. You haven't changed, dear old room, but I have. I'm different. I'm older. I'm not a kid any more. I'm grown up. Oh, my dear, dear old room, be kind to me, be gentle with me. I haven't played the game since I went away or been honest. I've been thoughtless, selfish and untamed. I've done all the wrong things. I've attracted all the wrong people. I've sent Marty away, Marty—my knight—and I want him back. I want to make up to him bigly, bigly for what I ought to have done. Be kind to me, be kind to me."

And she closed her arms as if in an embrace and put her head down as though on the warm breast of an old friend and the good tears ran down her cheeks.

All the windows were open. The air was warm and scented. There was no sound. The silent voices of the stars sang their nightly anthem. The earth was white with magic moonshine. Joan looked out. The old creeper down which she had climbed to go to Martin that night which seemed so far away was all in leaf. With what exhilaration she had dropped her bag out. Had ever a girl been so utterly careless of consequences then as she? How wonderfully and splendidly Martinish Martin had been when she plunged in upon him, and how jolly and homelike the hall of his house—her house—had seemed to be. To-morrow she would explore it all and show it off to her family. To-morrow.... Yes, but to-night? Should she allow herself to be carried away by a sudden longing to follow her flying footsteps through the woods, pretend that Martin was waiting for her and take a look at the outside of the house alone? Why not? No one need know, and she had a sort of aching to see the place again that was so essentially a part of Martin. Martin—Martin—he obsessed her, body and brain. If only she could find Martin.

With hasty fingers she struggled with the intricate hooks of her evening frock. Out of it finally, and slipping off her silk stockings and thin shoes she went quickly to the big clothes closet, chose a short country skirt, a pair of golf stockings, thick shoes and a tam-o'-shanter, made for the drawer in which were her sport shirts and sweaters and before the old round-faced clock on the mantelpiece could recover from his astonishment became once more the Joan-all-alone for whom he had ticked away the hours. Then to the window, and hand over hand down the creeper again and away across the sleeping garden to the woods.

The fairies were out. Their laughter was blown to her like thistledown. But she was a woman now and only Martin called her—Martin who had married her for love but was not her husband yet. Oh, where was Martin?

And as she went quickly along the winding path through the trees the moon dropped pools of light in her way, the scrub oaks threw out their arms to hold her back and hosts of little shadows seemed to run out to catch at her frock. But on went Joan, just to get a sight of the house that was Martin's and hers and to cast her spirit forward to the time when he and she would live there as they had not lived in the city.

She marvelled and rejoiced at the change that had come over her,—gradually, underminingly,—a change, the seeds of which had been thrown by Alice, watered by Palgrave and forced by the disappearance of Martin, and brought to bloom in the silent hours of wakeful nights when the thought of all the diffidence and deference of Martin won her gratitude and respect. In the strong, frank and rather harsh light that had been flung on her way of life it was Martin, Martin, who stood out clean and tender and lenient—Martin, who had developed from the Paul of the woods, the boy chum, her fellow adventurer, her sexless Knight, into the man who had won her love and whom she needed and ached for and longed to find. She had been brought up with a round turn, found herself face to face with the truth of things and, deaf to the incessant jangle of the Merry-go-round, had discovered that Martin was not merely the gallant and obliging boy, playing a game, trifling on the edge of reality, but the man with the other blade of the penknife who, like his prototype in the fairy tale, had the ordained right to her as she had to him.

And as she went on through the silvered trees, with a sort of dignity, her chin high, her eyes sparkling like stars, her mouth soft and sweet, it was to see the roof under which she would begin her married life again, rightly, honestly and as a woman, crossing the bridge between thoughtlessness and responsibility with a true sense of its meaning,—not in cold blood.

She came out to the road, dry and white, bordered by coarse grasses and wild flowers all asleep, with their petals closed over their eyes, opened the gate that led into the long avenue, splashed through the patches of moonlight on the driveway and came finally to the door under which she had stood that other time with dancing eyes and racing blood and "Who cares?" ringing in her head.

There was no light to be seen in any of the front windows. The house seemed to be fast asleep. How warm and friendly and unpretentious it looked, and there was all about it the same sense of strength that there was about Martin. In which window had they stood in the dark, looking out on to a world that they were going to brave together? Was it in the right wing? Yes. She remembered that tree whose branches turned over like a waterfall and something that looked like a little old woman in a shawl bending to pick up sticks but which was an old stump covered with creepers.

She went round, her heart fluttering like a bird, all her femininity stirred at the thought of what this house must mean and shelter—and drew up short with a quick intake of breath. A wide streak of yellow light fell through open French windows across the veranda and on to the grass, all dew-covered. Some one was there ... a woman's voice, not merry, and with a break in it.... When the cat's away, the mice, in the shape of one of the servants...

Joan went on again. What a joke to peep in! She wouldn't frighten the girl or walk in and ask questions. It was, as yet, too much Marty's house for that—and, after all, what harm was she doing by sitting up on such a lovely night? The only thing was it was Martin's very own room filled with his intimate things and with his father's message written largely on a card over the fireplace—"We count it death to falter, not to die."

But she went on, unsuspecting, her hand unconsciously clasped in the stern relentless hand of Fate, who never forgets to punish.... A shadow crossed the yellow patch. There was the sound of a pipe being knocked out on one of the firedogs. A man was there, then. Should she take one look, or go back? She would go back. It was none of her business, unfortunately. But she was drawn on and on, until she could see into the long, low, masculine room.

A man was sitting on the arm of a sofa, a man with square shoulders and a deep chest, a man with his strong young face turned to the light, smiling —

"Marty," cried Joan. "Marty!" and went up and across the veranda and into the room. "Why, Marty," and held out her hand, all glad and tremulous.

And Martin got on his feet and stood in amazement, wide-eyed, and suddenly white.

"You here!" cried Joan. "I've been waiting and wondering, but I didn't call because I wanted you to come back for yourself and not for me. It's been a long week, Marty, and in every hour of it I've grown. Can't you see the change?"

And Martin looked at her, and his heart leaped, and the blood blazed in his veins and he was about to go forward and catch her in his arms with a great cry...

"Oh, hello, Lady-bird; who'd have expected to see you!"

Joan wheeled to the left.

Lying full stretched on the settee, her settee, was a girl with her hands under her bobbed hair, a blue dress caught up under one knee, her bare arms agleam, her elfin face all white and a smile round her too red lips.

("White face and red lips and hair that came out of a bottle.")

Martin said something, inarticulately, and moved a chair forward. The girl spoke again, cheerily, in the spirit of good-fellowship, astonished a little, but too comfortable to move.

But a cold hand was laid on Joan's heart, and all that rang in her brain were the words that Alice had used,—"white face and red lips and hair that came out of a bottle.... Don't YOU be the one to turn his armor into common broadcloth."

And for a moment she stood, looking from Marty to the girl and back to Marty, like one struck dumb, like one who draws up at the very lip of a chasm.... And in that cruel and terrible minute her heart seemed to break and die. Marty, Marty in broadcloth, and she had put it in his hands. She had turned him away from her room and lost him. There's not one thing that any of us can do or say that doesn't react on some one else to hurt or bless.

With a little gasp, the sense of all this going home to her, Tootles scrambled awkwardly off the settee, dropping a book and a handkerchief. This, then, this beautiful girl who belonged to a quarter of life of which she had sometimes met the men but never the women, was Martin's wife—the wife of the man whom she loved to adoration.

"Why, then, you're—you're Mrs. Gray," she stammered, her impertinence gone, her hail-fellow-well-met manner blown like a bubble.

Catching sight of the message, "We count it death to falter not to die," Joan summoned her pride, put up her chin and gave a curious little bow. "Forgive me," she said, "I'm trespassing," and not daring to look at Marty, turned and went out. She heard him call her name, saw his sturdy shadow fall across the yellow patch, choked back a sob, started running, and stumbled away and away, with the blood from her heart bespattering the grasses and the wild flowers, and the fairies whimpering at her heels,—and, at last, climbing back into the room that knew and loved and understood, threw herself down on its bosom in a great agony of grief.

"Be kind to me, old room, be kind to me. It's Joan-all-alone,—all alone."

PART THREE

THE GREAT EMOTION

I

Mrs. Alan Hosack, bearing a more than ever remarkable resemblance to those ship's figureheads that are still to be seen in the corners of old lumber yards, led the way out to the sun porch. Her lavish charms, her beaming manner, her clear blue eye, milky complexion, reddish hair, and the large bobbles and beads with which she insisted upon decorating herself made Howard Cannon's nickname of Cornucopia exquisitely right. She was followed by Mrs. Cooper Jekyll and a man servant, whose arms were full of dogs and books and newspapers.

"The dogs on the ground, Barrett," she said, "the books and papers on the table there, my chair on the right-hand side of it and bring that chair forward for Mrs. Jekyll. We will have the lemonade at once. Tell Lestocq that I shall not want the car before lunch, ask Miss Disberry to telephone to Mrs. John Ward Harrison and say that I will have tea with her this afternoon with pleasure, and when those two good little Sisters of Mercy finally arrive,—I could see them, all sandy, struggling along the road from my room, Augusta; dear me, what a life,—they are to be given luncheon as usual and the envelope that is on the hall table. That will do, I think."

The man servant was entirely convinced that it would.

"And now, make yourself comfortable, dear Augusta, and tell me everything. So very kind of you to drive over like this on such a sunny morning. Yes, that's right. Take off that lugubrious Harem veil,—the mark of a Southampton woman,—and let me see your beautiful face. Before I try to give you a chance to speak I must tell you, and I'm sure you won't mind with your keen sense of humor, how that nice boy, Harry Oldershaw, describes those things. No, after all, perhaps I don't think I'd better. For one reason, it was a little bit undergraduate, and for another, I forget." She chuckled and sat down, wabbling for a moment like an opulent blancmange.

Minus the strange dark blue thing which had hidden her ears and nose and mouth and which suggested nothing but leprosy, Mrs. Jekyll became human, recognizable and extremely good to look at. She wore her tight-fitting suit of white flannel like a girl and even in that clear detective light she did not look a day over thirty. She painted with all the delicacy of an artist. She was there, as a close friend of Alice Palgrave, to discover why Gilbert had not gone with her to the Maine coast.

"I haven't heard from you since we left town," she said, beating about the bush, "and being in the neighborhood I thought it would be delightful to catch a glimpse of you and hear your news. I have none, except that I have just lost the butler who has been with me for so long, and Edmond is having his portrait painted again for some club or institution. It's the ninth time, I believe. He likes it. It's a sort of rest cure."

"And how did you lose that very admirable butler? Illness or indiscretion?"

"Neither. Commerce, I suppose one might call it. It appears that one of these get-rich-quick munition men offered him double his wages to leave me, and Derbyshire couldn't resist it. He came to me with tears in his eyes and told me that he had to make the sacrifice owing to the increased cost of living. He has a family, you know. He said that the comic atmosphere of his new place might bring on neuritis, but he must educate his three boys. Really, there is a great deal of unsung heroism in the world, isn't there? In the meantime, I am trying to get accustomed to a Swiss, who's probably a German spy and who will set up a wireless installation on the roof." Then she dropped her baited hook. "You have a large house party, I suppose."

"Yes," said Mrs. Hosack, swinging her foot to keep the flies away. The wind was off the land.

"Primrose is so depressed if the house isn't full. And so the d'Oylys are here,—Nina more Junoesque than ever and really quite like an Amazon in bathing clothes; Enid Ouchterlony, a little bitter, I'm afraid, at not being engaged to any one yet,—men are horribly scared of an intelligent girl and, after all, they don't marry for intelligence, do they?—Harry Oldershaw, Frank Milwood and Courtney Millet, all nice boys, and I almost forgot to add, Joan Gray, that charming girl. My good man is following at her heels like a bob-tailed sheep dog. Poor old dear! He's arrived at that pathetic period of a man's life when almost any really blond girl still in her teens switches him into a second state of adolescence and makes him a most ridiculous object—what the novelists call the 'Forty-nine feeling,' I believe."

Bennett brought the lemonade and hurried away before his memory could be put to a further strain. "Tell me about Joan Gray," said Mrs. Jekyll, letting out her line. "There's probably no truth in it, but I hear that she and Martin have agreed to differ. How quickly these romantic love matches burn themselves out. I always say that a marriage made in Heaven breaks up far sooner than one made on earth. It has so much farther to fall. Whose fault is it, hers or his?"

Mrs. Hosack bent forward and endeavored to lower her voice. She was a kind-hearted woman who delighted to see every one happy and normal. "I'm very worried about those two, my dear," she answered. "There are all sorts of stories afloat,—one to the effect that Martin has gone off with a chorus girl, another that Joan only married him to get away from her grandparents and a third that they quarreled violently on the way home from church and have not been on speaking terms since. I daresay there are many others, but whatever did happen, and something evidently did, Joan is happy enough, and every man in the house is sentimental about her. Look out there, for instance."

Mrs. Jekyll followed her glance and saw a girl in bathing clothes sitting on the beach under a red and blue striped umbrella encircled by the outstretched forms of half a dozen men. Beyond, on the fringe of a sea alive with bursting breakers, several girls were bathing alone.

"H'm," said Mrs. Jekyll. "I should think that the second story is the true one. A tip-tilted nose, chestnut hair and brown eyes are better to flirt with than marry. Well, I must run away if I'm to be back to lunch. I wish I could stay, but Edmond and his artist may kill my new butler unless I intervene. They are both hotly pro-Ally. By the way, I hear that Alice Palgrave has gone to the Maine coast with her mother, who is ill again; I wonder where Gilbert is going?"

"Well, I had a very charming letter from him two days ago, asking me if he could come and stay with us. He loves this house and the beach, and I always cheer him up, he said, and he is very lonely without Alice. Of course I said yes, and he will be here this afternoon."

Whereupon, having landed her fish, Mrs. Jekyll rose to go. Gilbert Palgrave and Joan Gray,—there was truth in that story, as she had thought. She had heard of his having been seen everywhere with Joan night after night, and her sister-in-law, who lived opposite to the little house in East Sixty-seventh Street, had seen him leaving in the early hours of the morning more than once. A lucky strike, indeed. Intuition was a wonderful gift. She was highly pleased with herself.

"Good-by, my dear," she said. "I will drive over again one day this week and see how you are all getting on in this beautiful corner of the world. My love to Prim, please, and do remember me to the little siren."

And away she went, leaving Mrs. Hosack to wonder what was the meaning of her rather curious smile. Only a hidebound prejudice on the part of the Ministries of all the nations has precluded women from the Diplomatic Service.

II

"Ah, here you are," said Hosack, scrambling a little stiffly out of a hammock. "Well, have you had a good ride?"

Joan came up the steps with Harry Oldershaw, the nice boy. She was in white linen riding kit, with breeches and brown top boots. A man's straw hat sat squarely on her little head and there was a brown and white spotted tie under her white silk collar. Color danced on her cheeks, health sparkled in her eyes and there was a laugh of sheer high spirits floating behind her like the blown petals of a daisy.

"Perfectly wonderful," she said. "I love the country about here, with the little oaks and sturdy ferns. It's so springy. And aren't the chestnut trees in the village a sight for the blind? I don't wonder you built a house in Easthampton, Mr. Hosack. Are we too late for tea?"

Hosack ran his eyes over her and blinked a little as though he had looked at the sun. "Too late by an hour," he said, with a sulky glance at young Oldershaw. "I thought you were never coming back." His resentment of middle age and jealousy of the towering youth of the sun-tanned lad who had been Joan's companion were a little pitiful.

Harry caught his look and laughed with the sublime audacity of one who believes that he ranks among the Immortals. To him forty-nine seemed to be a colossal sum of years, almost beyond belief. It was pathetic of this old fellow to imagine that he had any right to the company of a girl so springlike as Joan. "If we hadn't worn the horses to a frazzle," he said, "we shouldn't have been back till dark. Have a drink, Joan?"

"Yes, water. Buckets of it. Hurry up, Harry."

The boy, triumphant at being in favor, swung away, and Joan flung her crop on to a cane sofa. "Where's everybody?" she asked.

"What's it matter," said Hosack. "Sit here and talk to me for a change. I've hardly had a word with you all day." He caught her hand and drew her into the swinging hammock. "What a pretty thing you are," he added, with a catch in his breath. "I know," said Joan. "Otherwise, probably, I shouldn't be here, should I?" She forgot all about him, and an irresistible desire to tease, at the sight of the sea which, a stone's throw from the house, pounded on the yellow sweep of sand and swooped up in large half circles of glistening water. "I've a jolly good mind to have another dip before changing. What do you say?"

"No, don't," said Hosack, a martyr to the Forty-nine-feeling. "Concentrate on me for ten minutes, if only because, damn it, I'm your host."

Joan pushed his hand away. "I've given up concentrating," she said. "I gave it a turn a little while ago, but it led nowhere, so why worry? I'm on the good old Merry-go-round again, and if it doesn't whack up to the limit of its speed I'll know the reason why. There's a dance at the Club to-night, isn't there?"

"Yes, but we don't go."

She was incredulous. "Don't go,—to a dance? Why?"

"It's rather a mixed business," he said. "The hotel pours its crowd out. It isn't amusing. We can dance here if you want to."

But her attention was caught by young Oldershaw who came out carrying a glass and a jug of iced water. She sprang up and went to meet him, the dance forgotten, Hosack forgotten. Her mood was that of a bird, irresponsible, restless. "Good for you," she said, and drank like a thirsty plant. "Nothing like water, is there?" She smiled up at him.

He was as pleased with himself as though he owned the reservoir. "Have another?"

"I should think so." And she drank again, put the glass down on the first place that came to hand, relieved him of the jug, put it next to the glass, caught hold of his muscular arm, ran him down the steps, and along the board path to the beach. "I'll race you to the sea," she cried, and was off like a mountain goat. He was too young to let her beat him and waited for her with the foam frothing round his ankles and a broad grin on his attractive face.

He was about to cheek her when she held up a finger and with a little exclamation of delight pointed to the sky behind the house. The sun was setting among a mass of royal clouds. A golden wand had touched the dunes and the tips of the scrub and all over the green of the golf course, still dotted with scattered figures, waves of reflected lusters played. To the left of the great red ball one clear star sparkled like an eye. Just for a moment her lips trembled and her young breasts rose and fell, and then she threw her head up and wheeled round and went off at a run. Not for her to think back, or remember similar sights behind the woods near Marty's place. Life was too short for pain. "Who Cares?" was her motto once more, and this time joy-riding must live up to its name.

Harry Oldershaw followed, much puzzled at Joan's many quick changes of mood. Several times during their irresponsible chatter on the beach between dips her laughter had fallen suddenly, like a dead bird, and she had sat for several minutes as far away from himself and the other men as though they were cut off by a thick wall. Yesterday, in the evening after dinner, during which her high spirits had infected the whole table, he had walked up and down the board path with her under the vivid white light of a full moon, and she had whipped out one or two such savage things about life that he had been startled. During their ride that afternoon, too, her bubbling chatter of light stuff about people and things had several times shifted into comments as to the conventions that were so careless as to make him ask himself whether they could really have come from lips so fresh and young. And why had that queer look of almost childlike grief come into her eyes a moment ago at the sight of ah everyday sunset? He was mightily intrigued. She was a queer kid, he told himself, as changeable and difficult to follow as some of the music by men with such weird names as Rachmaninoff and Tschaikowsky that his sister was so precious fond of playing. But she was unattached and frightfully pretty and always ready for any fun that was going, and she liked him more than the others, and he liked being liked, and although not hopelessly in love was ready and willing and even anxious to be walked on if she would acknowledge his existence in no other way. It was none of his business, he told himself, to speculate as to what she was trying to hide away in the back of her mind, from herself as well as from everybody else. This was his last vacation as a Yale man, and he was all out to make the most of it.

As soon as he was at her side she ran her hand through his arm and fell into step. The shadow had passed, and her eyes were dancing again. "It appears that the Hosacks turn up their exclusive noses at the club dances," she said. "What are we going to do about it?"

"There's one to-night, isn't there? Do you want to go?"

"Of course I do. I haven't danced since away back before the great wind. Let's sneak off after dinner for an hour without a word to a soul and get our fill of it. There's to be a special Jazz band to-night, I hear, and I simply can't keep away. Are you game, Harry?"

"All the way," said young Oldershaw, "and it will be the first time in the history of the Hosacks that any members of their house parties have put in an appearance at the club at night. No wonder Easthampton has nicknamed the place St. James's Palace, eh?"

Joan shrugged her shoulders. "Oh, my dear boy," she said, "life's too short for all that stuff, and there's no hobby so painful as cutting off one's nose to spite one's face. And, after all, what's the matter with Easthampton people? I'd go to a chauffeurs' ball if the band was the right thing. Wouldn't you?"

"With you," said Harry. "Democracy forever!"

"Oh, I'm not worrying about democracy. I'm out for a good time under any conditions. That's the only thing that matters. Now let's go back and change. It's too late to bathe. I'll wear a new frock to-night, made for fox-trotting, and if Mrs. Hosack wants to know where we've been when we come back as innocent as spring lambs, leave it to me. Men can't lie as well as women can."

"It won't be Mrs. Hosack who'll ask," said Harry. "Bridge will do its best to rivet her ubiquitous mind. It's the old man who'll be peeved. He's crazy about you, you know."

Joan laughed. "He's very nice and means awfully well and all that," she said, "but of course he isn't to be taken seriously. No men of middle age ought to be. They all say the same things with the same expressions as though they got them from the same books, and their gambolling makes their joints creak. It's all like playing with a fire of damp logs. I like something that can blaze and scorch. The game counts then."

"Then you ought to like me," said Harry, doing his best to look the very devil of a fellow. Even he had to join in Joan's huge burst of merriment. He had humor as well as a sense of the ridiculous, and the first made it possible for him to laugh at himself,—a rare and disconcerting gift which would utterly prevent his ever entering the Senate.

"You might grow a moustache and wax the tips, Harry," she said, when she had recovered sufficiently well to be able to speak. "Curl your hair with tongs and take dancing lessons from a tango lizard or go in for a course of sotto voce sayings from a French portrait painter, but you'd still remain the Nice Boy. That's why I like you. You're as refreshing and innocuous as a lettuce salad, and you may glare as much as you like. I hope you'll never be spoilt. Come on. We shall be late for dinner." And she made him quicken his step through the dry sand.

Being very young he was not quite sure that he appreciated that type of approval. He had liked to imagine that he was distinctly one of the bold bad boys, a regular dog and all that. He had often talked that sort of thing in the rooms of his best chums whose mantelpieces were covered with the photographs of little ladies, and he hoarded in his memory two episodes at least of jealous looks from engaged men. But, after all, with Joan, who was married, although it was difficult to believe it, it wouldn't be wise to exert the whole force of the danger that was in him. He would let her down lightly, he told himself, and grinned as he said it. She was right. He was only a nice boy, and that was because he had had the inestimable luck to possess a mother who was one in a million.

The rather pretentious but extremely civilized house that stood alone in all its glory between the sea and the sixth hole was blazing with lights as they returned to it. The color had gone out of the sky and other twinkling eyes had appeared, and the breeze, now off the sea, had a sting to it. Toad soloists were trying their voices for their evening concert in near-by water and crickets were at work with all their well-known enthusiasm. Bennett, with a sunburned nose, was tidying up the veranda, and some one with a nice light touch was playing the rhythmic jingles of Jerome Kern on the piano in the drawing-room.

Still with her hand on Harry Oldershaw's arm, Joan made her way across the lofty hall, caught sight of Gilbert Palgrave coming eagerly to meet her, and waved her hand.

"Oh, hello, Gilbert," she cried out. "Welcome to Easthampton," and ran upstairs.

With a strange contraction of the heart, Palgrave watched her out of sight. She was his dream come to life. All that he was and hoped to be he had placed forever at her feet. Dignity, individualism, egoism,—all had fallen before this young thing. She was water in the desert, the north star to a man without a compass. He had seen her and come into being.

Good God, it was wonderful and awful!

But who was that cursed boy?

III

Six weeks had dropped off the calendar since the night at Martin's house.

Facing Grandmother Ludlow in the morning with her last handful of courage Joan had told her that she had been called back to town. She had left immediately after breakfast in spite of the protests and entreaties of every one, including her grandfather, down whose wrinkled cheeks the tears had fallen unashamed. With a high head and her best wilful manner she had presented to them all in that old house the bluff of easy-mindedness only to burst like a bubble as soon as the car had turned the corner into the main road. She had gone to the little house in New York, and with a numbed heart and a constant pain in her soul, had packed some warm-weather clothes and, leaving her maid behind, hidden herself away in the cottage, on the outskirts of Greenwich, of an old woman who had been in the service of her school. As a long-legged girl of twelve she had stayed there once with her mother for several days before going home for the holidays. She felt like a wounded animal, and her one desire was to drag herself into a quiet place to die.

It seemed to her then, under the first stupendous shock of finding that Marty was with that girl, that death was the next certain thing. Day after day and night after night, cut to the quick, she waited for it to lay its cold hand upon her and snuff her out like a tired candle, whose little light was meaningless in a brutal world. Marty, even Marty, was no longer a knight, and she had put him into broadcloth.

Not in the sun, but in the shadow of a chestnut all big with bloom, her days had passed in lonely suffering. Death was in the village, that was certain. She had seen a little procession winding along the road to the cemetery the morning after her arrival. She was ready. Nothing mattered now that Marty, even Marty, had done this thing while she had been waiting for him to come and take her across the bridge, anxious to play the game to the very full, eager to prove to him that she was no longer the kid that he thought her who had coolly shown him her door. "I am here, Death," she whispered, "and I want you. Come for me."

All her first feelings were that she ought to die, that she had failed and that her disillusion as to Marty had been directly brought about by herself. She saw it all honestly and made no attempt to hedge. By day, she sat quietly, big-eyed, amazingly childlike, waiting for her punishment, watched by the practical old woman, every moment of whose time was filled, with growing uneasiness and amazement. By night she lay awake as long as she could, listening for the soft footstep of the one who would take her away. At meals, the old woman bullied for she was of the school that hold firmly to the belief that unless the people who partake of food do not do so to utter repletion a personal insult is intended. At other times she went out into the orchard and sat with Joan and, burning with a desire to cheer her up, gave her, in the greatest detail, the story of all the deaths, diseases and quarrels that had ever been known to the village. And every day the good sun warmed and encouraged the earth, drew forth the timid heads of plants and flowers, gave beauty even to the odd corners once more and did his allotted task with a generosity difficult to praise too highly. And Death paid visits here and there but passed the cottage by. At the beginning of the second week, Nature, who has no patience with any attempt to refute her laws, especially on the part of those who are young and vigorous, took Joan in hand. "What is all this, my girl?" she said, "sitting here with your hands in your lap while everybody and everything is working and making and preparing. Stir yourself, bustle up, get busy, there's lots to be done in the springtime if the autumn is to bear fruit. You're sound and whole for all that you've been hurt. If you were not, Death would be here without your calling him. Up you get, now." And, with good-natured roughness, she laid her hand under Joan's elbow, gave a hoist and put her on her feet.

Whereupon, in the natural order of things, Joan turned from self-blame to find a victim who should be held responsible for the pain that she had suffered, and found the girl with the red lips and the white face and the hair that came out of a bottle. Ah, yes! It was she who had caught Marty when he was hurt and disappointed. It was she who had taken advantage of his loneliness and dragged him clown to her own level, this girl whom she had called Fairy and who had had the effrontery to go up to the place on the edge of the woods that was the special property of Marty and herself. And for the rest of the week, with the sap running eagerly in her veins once more, she moved restlessly about the orchard and the garden, heaping coals of fire on to the all too golden head of Tootles.

Then came the feeling of wounded pride, the last step towards convalescence. Marty had chosen between herself and this girl. Without giving her a real chance to put things right he had slipped away silently and taken Tootles with him. Not she, but the girl with the red lips and the pale face and the hair that came out of a bottle had stripped Marty of his armor, and the truth of it was that Marty, yes, even Marty, was not really a knight but a very ordinary man.

Out of the orchard and the garden she went, once she had arrived at this stage, and tramped the countryside with her ears tuned to catch the alluring strains of the mechanical music of the Round-about. She had not only been making a fool of herself but had been made to look a fool, she thought. Her pain and suffering and disillusion had been wasted. All these dull and lonely days had been wasted and thrown away. Death must have laughed to see her sitting in the shadow of the apple trees waiting for a visit that was undeserved. Marty could live and enjoy himself without her. That was evident. Very well, then, she could live and enjoy herself without Marty. The earth was large enough for them both, and if he could find love in the person of that small girl she could surely find it in one or other of the men who had whispered in her ear. Also there was Gilbert Palgrave, who had gone down upon his knees.

And that was the end of her isolation, her voluntary retirement. Back she went to the City of Dreadful Nonsense, bought clothes and shoes and hats, found an invitation to join a house party at Southampton, made no effort to see or hear from Marty, and sprang back into her seat in the Merry-go-round. "Who Cares?" she cried again. "Nobody," she answered. "What I do with my life matters to no one but myself. Set the pace, my dear, laugh and flirt and play with fire and have a good time. A short life and a merry one."

And then she joined the Hosacks, drank deep of the wine of adulation, and when, at odd times, the sound of Marty's voice echoed in her memory, she forced it out and laughed it away. "Who Cares?" was his motto too,—red lips and white face and hair that came out of a bottle!

And now here was Gilbert Palgrave with the fire of love in his eyes.

IV

When Mrs. Hosack rose from the dinner table and sailed Olympically into the drawing-room, surrounded by graceful light craft in the persons of Primrose and her girl friends, the men, as usual, followed immediately. The house was bridge mad, and the tables called every one except Joan, the nice boy, and Gilbert Palgrave.

During the preliminaries of an evening which would inevitably run into the small hours, Joan went over to the piano and, with what was a quite unconscious touch of irony, played one of Heller's inimitable "Sleepless Nights," with the soft pedal down. The large imposing room, a chaotic mixture of French and Italian furniture with Flemish tapestries and Persian rugs, which accurately typified the ubiquitous mind of the hostess, was discreetly lighted. The numerous screened windows were open and the soft warm air came in tinged with the salt of the sea.

Palgrave, refusing to cut in, stood about like a disembodied spirit, with his eyes on Joan, from whom, since his arrival, he had received only a few fleeting glances. He watched the cursed boy, as he had labelled him, slip over to her, lean across the piano and talk eagerly. He went nearer and caught, "the car in half an hour," and "not a word to a soul." After which, with jealousy gnawing at his vitals, he saw Harry Oldershaw moon about for a few minutes and then make a fishlike dart out of the room. He had been prepared to find Joan amorously surrounded by the men of the party but not on terms of sentimental intimacy with a smooth-faced lad. In town she had shown preference for sophistication. He went across to the piano and waited impatiently for Joan to finish the piece which somehow fitted into his mood. "Come out," he said, then, "I want to speak to you."

But Joan let her fingers wander into a waltz and raised her eyebrows. "Do I look so much like Alice that you can order me about?" she asked.

He turned on his heel with the look of a dog at which a stone had been flung by a friend, and disappeared.

Two minutes later there was a light touch on his arm, and Joan stood at his side on the veranda. "Well, Gilbert," she said, "it's good to see you again."

"So good that I might be a man touting for an encyclopedia," he answered angrily.

She sat upon the rough stone wall and crossed her little feet. Her new frock was white and soft and very perfectly simple. It demanded the young body of a nymph,—and was satisfied. The magic of the moon was on her. She might have been Spring resting after a dancing day.

"If you were," she said, taking a delight in unspoiling this immaculate man, "I'm afraid you'd never get an order from me. Of all things the encyclopedia must be accompanied by a winning smile and irresistible manners. I suppose you've done lots of amusing things since I saw you last."

He went nearer so that her knees almost touched him. "No," he said. "Only one, and that was far from amusing. It has marked me like a blow. I've been waiting for you. Where have you been, and why haven't you taken the trouble to write me a single letter?"

"I've been ill," she said. "Yes, I have. Quite ill. I deliberately set out to hurt myself and succeeded. It was an experiment that I sha'n't repeat. I don't regret it. It taught me something that I shall never forget. Never too young to learn, eh? Isn't it lovely here? Just smell the sea, and look at those lights bobbing up and down out there. I never feel any interest in ships in the daytime, but at night, when they lie at anchor, and I can see nothing but their lonely eyes, I would give anything to be able to fly round them like a gull and peep into their cabins. Do they affect you like that?"

Palgrave wasn't listening to her. It was enough to look at her and refresh his memory. She had been more than ever in his blood all these weeks. She was like water in a desert or sunlight to a man who comes up from a mine. He had found her again and he thanked whatever god he recognized for that, but he was forced to realize from her imperturbable coolness and unaffected ease that she was farther away from him than ever. To one of his temperament and schooling this was hard to bear with any sort of self-control. The fact that he wanted her of all the creatures on earth, that she, alone among women, had touched the fuse of his desire, and that, knowing this, she could sit there a few inches from his lips and put a hundred miles between them, maddened him, from whom nothing hitherto had been impossible.

"Have I got to begin all over again?" he asked, with a sort of petulance.

"Begin what, Gilbert?" There was great satisfaction in playing with one who thought that he had only to touch a bell to bring the moon and the sun and the stars to his bidding.

"Good God," he cried out. "You're like wet sand on which a man expects to find yesterday's footmarks. Hasn't anything of me and the things I've said to you remained in your memory?"

"Of course," she said. "I shall never forget the night you took me to the Brevoort, for instance, and supplied the key to all the people with unkempt hair and comic ties."

Some one on the beach below shot out a low whistle.

A little thrill ran through Joan. In ten minutes, perhaps less, she would be dancing once more to the lunatic medley of a Jazz band, dancing with a boy who gave her all that she needed of him and asked absolutely nothing of her; dancing among people who were less than the dust in the scheme of things, so far as she was concerned, except to give movement and animation to the room and to be steered through. That was the right attitude towards life and its millions, she told herself. As salt was to an egg so was the element of false romance to this Golf Club dance. In a minute she would get rid of Palgrave, yes, even the fastidious Gilbert Palgrave, who had never been able quite to disguise the fact that his love for her was something of a condescension; she would fly in the face of the unwritten law of the pompous house on the dunes and mingle with what Hosack had called the crowd from the hotel. It was all laughable and petty, but it was what she wanted to do. It was all in the spirit of "Who Cares?" that she had caught at again. Why worry as to what Mrs. Hosack might say or Palgrave might feel? Wasn't she as free as the air to follow her whims without a soul to make a claim upon her or to hold out a hand to stop?

Through these racing thoughts she heard Palgrave talking and crickets rasping and frogs croaking and a sudden burst of laughter and talk in the drawing-room,—and the whistle come again.

"Yes," she said, because yes was as good as any other word. "Well, Gilbert, dear, if you're not an early bird you will see me again later,"—and jumped down from the wall.

"Where are you going?"

"Does that matter?"

"Yes, it does. I want you here. I've been waiting all these weeks."

She laughed. "It's a free country," she said, "and you have the right to indulge in any hobby that amuses you. Au revoir, old thing." And she spread out her arms like wings and flew to the steps and down to the beach and away with some one who had sent out a signal.

"That boy," said Palgrave. "I'm to be turned down for a cursed boy! By God, we'll know about that."

And he followed, seeing red.

He saw them get into a low-lying two-seater built on racing lines, heard a laugh flutter into the air, watched the tail light sweep round the drive and become smaller and smaller along the road.

So that was it, was it? He had been relegated to the hangers-on, reduced to the ranks, put into the position of any one of the number of extraneous men who hung round this girl-child for a smile and a word! That was the way he was to be treated, he, Gilbert Palgrave, the connoisseur, the decorative and hitherto indifferent man who had refused to be subjected to any form of discipline, who had never, until Joan had come into his life, allowed any one to put him a single inch out of his way, who had been triumphantly one-eyed and selfish,—that was the way he was to be treated by the very girl who had fulfilled his once wistful hope of making him stand, eager and startled and love-sick among the chaos of individualism and indolence, who had shaken him into the Great Emotion! Yes, by God, he'd know about that.

Bare-headed and surging with untranslatable anger he started walking. He was in no mood to go into the drawing-room and cut into a game of bridge and show his teeth and talk the pleasant inanities of polite society. All the stucco of civilization fell about him in slabs as he made his way with long strides out of the Hosacks' place, across the sandy road and on to the springy turf of the golf links. It didn't matter where he went so long as he got elbow room for his indignation, breathing space for his rage and a wide loneliness for his blasphemy....

He had stood humble and patient before this virginal girl. He had confessed himself to her with the tremendous honesty of a man made simple by an overwhelming love. She was married. So was he. But what did that matter to either of them whose only laws were self-made? The man to whom she was not even tied meant as little to her as the girl he had foolishly married meant or would ever mean to him. He had placed himself at her beck and call. In order to give her amusement he had taken her to places in which he wouldn't have been seen dead, had danced his good hours of sleep away for the pleasure of seeing her pleased, had revolutionized his methods with women and paid her tribute by the most scrupulous behavior and, finally, instead of setting out to turn her head with pearls and diamonds and carry her by storm while she was under the hypnotic influence of priceless glittering things for bodily adornment, which render so many women easy to take, he had recognized her as intelligent and paid her the compliment of treating her as such, had stated his case and waited for the time when the blaze of love would set her alight and bring her to his arms.

There was something more than mere egotism in all this,—the natural egotism of a man of great wealth and good looks, who had walked through life on a metaphorical red carpet pelted with flowers by adoring women to whom even virtue was well lost in return for his attention. Joan, like the spirit of spring, had come upon Palgrave at that time of his life when youth had left him and he had stood at the great crossroads, one leading down through a morass of self-indulgence to a hideous senility, the other leading up over the stones of sacrifice and service to a dignified usefulness. Her fresh young beauty and enthusiasm, her golden virginity and unself-consciousness, her unaffected joy in being alive, her superb health and vitality had shattered his conceit and self-obsession, broken down his aloofness and lack of scruple and filled the empty frame that he had hung in his best thoughts with her face and form.

There was something of the great lover about Palgrave in his new and changed condition. He had laid everything unconditionally at the feet of this young thing. He had shown a certain touch of bigness, of nobility, he of all men, when, after his outburst in the little drawing-room that night, he had stood back to wait until Joan had grown up. He had waited for six weeks, going through tortures of Joan-sickness that were agonizing. He had asked her to do what she could for him in the way of a little kindness, but had not received one single line. He was prepared to continue to wait because he knew his love to be so great that it must eventually catch hold of her like the licking flame of a prairie fire. It staggered him to arrive at the Hosacks' place and find her fooling with a smooth-faced lad. It outraged him to be left cold, as though he were a mere member of the house party and watch her to whom he had thrown open his soul go joy-riding with a cursed boy. It was, in a sort of way, heresy. It proved an almost unbelievable inability to realize the great thing that this was. Such love as his was not an everyday affair, to be treated lightly and carelessly. It was, on the contrary, rare and wonderful and as such to be, at any rate, respected. That's how it seemed to him, and by God he would see about it.

He drew up short, at last, on his strange walk across the undulating course. The light from the Country Club streamed across his feet, and the jangle of the Jazz band broke into his thoughts. From where he stood, surprised to find himself in civilization, he could see the crowd of dancers through the open windows of what resembled a huge bungalow, at one side of which a hundred motor cars were parked. He went nearer, drawn forward against his will. He was in no mood to watch a summer dance of the younger set. He made his way to the wide veranda and stood behind the rocking chairs of parents and friends. But not for more than fifty seconds. There was Joan, with her lovely laughing face alight with the joy of movement, held in the arms of the cursed boy. Between two chairs he went, into and across the room in which he was a trespasser, tapped young Oldershaw sharply on the arm, cut into the dance, and before the boy could recover from his surprise, was out of reach with Joan against his heart.

"Oh, well done, Gilbert," said Joan, a little breathlessly. "When Marty did that to you at the Crystal Room..."

She stopped, and a shadow fell on her face and a little tremble ran across her lips.

Smoking a cigarette on the veranda young Oldershaw waited for the dance to end. It was encored several times but being a sportsman and having achieved a monopoly of Joan during all the previous dances, he let this man enjoy his turn. He was a great friend of hers, she had said on the way to the club, and was, without doubt, a very perfect person with his wide-set eyes and well-groomed head, his smooth moustache and the cleft on his chin. He didn't like him. He had decided that at a first glance. He was too supercilious and self-assured and had a way of looking clean through men's heads. He conveyed the impression of having bought the earth,—and Joan. A pity he was too old for a year or two of Yale. That would make him a bit more of a man.

When presently the Jazzers paused in order to recuperate,—every one of them deserving first aid for the wounded,—and Joan came out for a little air with Palgrave, Harry strolled up. This was his evening, and in a perfectly nice way he conveyed that impression by his manner. He was, moreover, quite determined to give nothing more away. He conveyed that, also.

"Shall we sit on the other side?" he asked. "The breeze off the sea keeps the mosquitoes away a bit."

Refusing to acknowledge his existence Palgrave guided Joan towards a vacant chair. He went on with what he had been saying and swung the chair round.

Joan was smiling again.

Oldershaw squared his jaw. "I advise against this side, Joan," he said. "Let me take you round."

He earned a quick amused look and a half shrug of white shoulders from Joan. Palgrave continued to talk in a low confidential voice. He regarded Oldershaw's remarks as no more of an interruption than the chorus of the frogs. Oldershaw's blood began to boil, and he had a queer prickly sensation at the back of his neck. Whoo, but there'd have to be a pretty good shine in a minute, he said to himself. This man Palgrave must be taught.

He marched up to Joan and held out his arm. "We may as well get back," he said. "The band's going to begin again."

But Joan sat down, looking from one man to the other. All the woman in her revelled in this rivalry,—all that made her long-dead sisters crowd to the arenas, wave to armored knights in deadly combat, lean forward in grand stands to watch the Titanic struggles of Army and Navy, Yale and Harvard on the football field. Her eyes danced, her lips were parted a little, her young bosom rose and fell.

"And so you see," said Palgrave, putting his hand on the back of her chair, "I can stay as long as the Hosacks will have me, and one day I'll drive you over to my bachelor cottage on the dune. It will interest you."

"The only thing that has any interest at the moment is dancing," said Oldershaw loudly. "By the way, you don't happen to be a member of the club, do you, Mr. Palgrave?"

With consummate impudence Palgrave caught his eye and made a sort of policeman gesture. "Run away, my lad," he said, "run away and amuse yourself." He almost asked for death.

With a thick mutter that sounded like "My God," Oldershaw balanced himself to hit, his face the color of a beet-root,—and instantly Joan was on her feet between them with a hand on the boy's chest.

"No murder here," she said, "please!"

"Murder!" echoed Palgrave, scoffing.

"Yes, murder. Can't you see that this boy could take you and break you like a dry twig? Let's go back, all three of us. We don't want to become the center of a sight-seeing crowd." And she took an arm of each shaking man and went across the drive to where the car was parked.

And so the danger moment was evaded,—young Oldershaw warm with pride, Palgrave sullen and angry. They made a trio which had its prototypes all the way back to the beginning of the world.

It did Palgrave no good to crouch ignominiously on the step of the car which Oldershaw drove back hell for leather.

The bridge tables were still occupied. The white lane was still across the sea. Frogs and crickets still continued their noisy rivalry, but it was a different climate out there on the dunes from that of the village with its cloying warmth.

Palgrave went into the house at once with a brief "Thank you." Joan waited while Harry put the car into a garage. Bed made no appeal. Bridge bored,—it required concentration. She would play the game of sex with Gilbert if he were to be found. So the boy had to be disposed of.

"Harry," she said, when he joined her, chuckling at having come top dog out of the recent blaze, "you'd better go straight to bed now. We're going to be up early in the morning, you know."

"Just what I was thinking," he answered. "By Jove, you've given me a corking good evening. The best of my young life. You ... you certainly are, —well, I don't know how to do you justice. I'd have to be a poet." He fumbled for her hand and kissed it a little sheepishly.

They went in. "You're a nice boy, Harry," she said. There was something in his charming simplicity and muscular strength that reminded her of,—but she refused to let the name enter her mind.

"I could have broken that chap like a dry twig, too, easy. Who does he think he is?" He would have pawned his life at that moment for the taste of her lips.

She stood at the bottom of the stairs and held out her hand. "Good night, old boy," she said.

And he took it and hurt it. "Good night, Joany," he answered.

That pet name hurt her more than his eager grasp. It was Marty's own word—Marty, who—who—

She threw up her head and stamped her foot, and slammed the door of her thoughts. "Who cares?" she said to herself, challenging life and fate. "Come on. Make things move."

She saw Palgrave standing alone in the library looking at the sea. "You might be Canute," she said lightly.

His face was curiously white. "I'm off in the morning," he said. "We may as well say good-by now."

"Good-by, then," she answered.

"I can't stay in this cursed place and let you play the fool with me."

"Why should you?"

"There'll be Hosack and the others as well as your new pet."

"That's true."

He caught her suddenly by the arms. "Damn you," he said. "I wish to God I'd never seen you."

She laughed. "Cave man stuff, eh?"

He let her go. She had the most perfect way of reducing him to ridicule.

"I love you," he said. "I love you. Aren't you going to try, even to try, to love me back?"

"No."

"Not ever?"

"Never." She went up to him and stood straight and slim and bewitching, eye to eye. "If you want me to love you, make me. Work for it, move Heaven and earth. You can't leave it to me. I don't want to love you. I'm perfectly happy as I am. If you want me, win me, carry me off my feet and then you shall see what it is to be loved. It's entirely up to you, understand that. I shall fight against it tooth and nail, but I give you leave to do your best. Do you accept the challenge?"

"Yes," he said, and his face cleared, and his eyes blazed.

V

At the moment when the Nice Boy, as brown as the proverbial berry, was playing a round of golf with Joan within sound of the sea, Howard Oldershaw, his cousin, drove up to the little house in East Sixty-fifth Street to see Martin.

He, too, had caught the sun, and his round fat face was rounder and fatter than ever. He, too, had the epitome of health, good nature, and misdirected energy. He performed a brief but very perfect double shuffle on the top step while waiting for the door to open, and then barged past the constitutionally unsurprised man servant, sang out a loud woo-hoo and blew into the library like an equinoctial gale.

Pipe in mouth, and wearing a thin silk dressing gown, Martin was standing under the portrait of his father. He slipped something quickly into his pocket and turned about. It was a photograph of Joan.

"Well, you Jack-o'-Lantern," he said. "It's better late than never, I suppose."

Howard sent his straw hat spinning across the room. It landed expertly in a chair. "My dear chap, your note's been lying in my apartment for a week, snowed under my bills. I drove back this morning, washed the bricks out of my eyes and came right around. What are you grumbling about?"

"I'm not grumbling. When you didn't show up in answer to my note I telephoned, and they told me you were away. Where've you been?"

"Putting in a week at the Field Club at Greenwich," replied Howard, filling a large cigarette case from the nearest box, as was his most friendly habit. "Two sweaters, tennis morning, noon and night, no sugar, no beer, no butter, no bread, gallons of hot water—and look at me! Martin, it's a tragedy. If I go on like this, it's me for Barnum's Circus as the world's prize pig. What's the trouble?"

There was not the usual number of laughter lines round Martin's eyes, but one or two came back at the sight and sound of his exuberant friend. "No trouble," he said, lying bravely. "I got here the day you left and tried to find you. That's all. I wanted you to come down to Shinnecock and play golf. Everybody else seems to be at Plattsburg, and I was at a loose end."

"Golf's no good to me. It wouldn't reduce me any more than playing the piano with somebody dying in the next room. Been here all the week?"

"Yes," said Martin.

"What? In this fug hole, with the sun shining? Out with it, Martin. Get it off your chest, old son."

Just for an instant Martin was hugely tempted to make a clean breast of everything to this good-hearted, tempestuous person, under whose tight skin there was an uncommon amount of shrewdness. But it meant dragging Joan into open discussion, and that was all against his creed. He had inherited from his father and his father's father an absolute incapability of saying anything to anybody about his wife. And so he slammed the door of his soul and presented an enigmatical front.

"There's nothing on my chest," he said. "Business downtown has kept me here,—legal stuff and that sort of thing. But I'm free now. Got any suggestions?"

Howard accepted this. If a pal was determined not to confide and get invaluable advice, what was the use of going for him with a can opener? But one good look at the face whose every expression he knew so well convinced him that something was very much the matter. "Why, good Lord," he said to himself, "the old thing looks as if he'd been working night and day for an examination and had been plucked. I wonder which of the two girls is at the back of all this,—the wife or the other?" Rumors had reached his way about both.

"What do you want to do?" he asked.

"I don't care," said Martin. "Any damn thing so long as it's something with somebody. What's it matter?"

He didn't quite manage to hide the little quiver in his voice, and it came to Howard Oldershaw for the first time how young they both were to be floundering on the main road, himself with several entanglements and money worries, his friend married and with another complication. They were both making a pretty fine hash of things, it seemed, and just for a moment, with something of boyishness that still remained behind his sophistication, he wished that they were both back at Yale, unhampered and unencumbered, their days filled with nothing but honest sport and good lectures and the whole joy of life.

"It's like this with me, Martin," he said, with a rather rueful grin. "I'm out of favor at home just now and broke to the wide. There are one or two reasons why I should lie low for a while, too. How about going out to your place in the country? I'll hit the wily ball with you and exercise your horses, lead the simple life and, please God, lose some flesh, and guarantee to keep you merry and bright in my well-known, resilient way. What do you say, old son?"

Martin heartily appreciated Howard's sound method of swinging everything round to himself and trying to make out that it was all on his side to go out to the house in which Joan ought to be. He was not a horseman or a golfer, and the simple life had few attractions for him. Well, that was friendship.

"Thanks, old man," he said. "That's you to the life, but I vote we get a change from golf and riding. Come down to Devon with me, and let's do some sailing. You remember Gilmore? I had a letter from him this morning, asking if I'd like to take his cottage and yawl. Does that sound good?"

"Great," cried Howard. "Sailing—that's the game, and by gum, swimming's the best of all ways of dropping adipose deposit. Wire Gilmore and fix it. I'll drive you out to-morrow. By the way, I found a letter from my cousin Harry among the others. He's in that part of the world. He's frightfully gone on your wife, it appears."

Martin looked up quickly. "Where is she?" he asked.

"Why, they're both staying at the Hosacks' place at Easthampton. Didn't you know that?" He was incredulous.

"No," said Martin.

Howard metaphorically clapped his hand over his mouth. Questions were on the tip of his tongue. If Martin were not in the mood to take him into his confidence, however, there must be a good reason for it, but,—not to know where his wife was! What on earth was at the bottom of all this? "All right," he said. "I've one or two things I must do, and I'll be round in the morning, or is that too soon?"

"The sooner the better," said Martin. "I'll send the cook and Judson down by the early train. They'll have things in shape by the time we show up. I'm fed up with New York and can smell the water already. Will you dine with me to-night and see a show?"

"I can't," said Howard, and laughed.

"I see. To-morrow, then."

"Right. Great work. So long, old son. Get busy and do what you have to do to-day, then we can leave this frying pan to-morrow with nothing on our minds."

"I haven't anything to do," said Martin.

Howard picked up his hat and caught it with his head in the manner of a vaudeville artist. But he didn't go. He stood waiting, keyed to a great sympathy. There was something in Martin's voice and at the back of his eyes which made him see him plainly and suddenly as a man standing all alone and wounded. But he waited in vain. There was a curious silence,—a rather painful and embarrassing silence, during which these two lads, who had been pretending to be men, dodged each other's eyes.

And then Howard, with an uncharacteristic awkwardness, and looking very young, made a quick step forward, and with a sort of gentle roughness grasped Martin by the arm. "But you've got something to say," he said. "Good God, man, have we been pals for nothing? I hide nothing from you. I can help."

But Martin shook his head. He tried to speak and failed. There was something hard in his throat. But he put his hand very warmly on his friend's shoulder for a moment and turned away abruptly. "Joan, Joan," he cried in his heart, "what are you doing, what are we both doing? Why are we killing the days that can never come back?"

He heard Howard go out. He heard the front door close and the honk of the horn. And for a long time he stood beneath the portrait of the man who had gone so far away and who alone could have helped him.

The telephone bell rang.

Martin was spoken to by the girl that lived in the rabbit warren in West Forty-sixth Street in the rooms below those of Tootles. "Can you come round at once?" she asked. "It's about Tootles—urgent."

And Martin answered, "Yes, now, at once."

After all, then, there might be something to do.

VI

Master of all the sky, the sun fell warmly on the city, making delicious shadows, gliding giant buildings, streaming across the park, chasing the endless traffic along the Avenue, and catching at points of color. It was one of those splendid mornings of full-blown Tune, when even New York,—that paradox of cities,—had beauty. It was too early in the year for the trees to have grown blowsy and the grass worn and burnt. The humidity of midsummer was held back by the energy of a merry breeze which teased the flags and sent them spinning against the oriental blue of the spotless sky.

Martin walked to West Forty-sixth Street. There was an air of half-time about the Avenue. The ever-increasingly pompous and elaborate shops, whose window contents never seem to vary, wore a listless, uninterested expression like that of a bookmaker during the luncheon hour at the races. Their glittering smile, their enticement and solicitation, their tempting eye-play were relaxed. The cocottes of Monte Carlo at the end of the season could not have assumed a greater indifference. But there were the same old diamonds and pearls, the same old canvases, the same old photographs, the same old antiques, the same old frocks and shoes and men's shirtings, the same old Persian rugs and Japanese ware, the same cold, hard plates and china, the very same old hats and dinks and dressing-gowns and cut flowers and clubs, and all the same doormen in the uniforms that are a cross between those of admirals and generals, the men whose only exercise during the whole of the year is obtained by cutting ice and sweeping snow from just their particular patch of pavement. In all the twists and changes, revolutions and cross currents, upheavals and in-fallings that affect this world, there is one great street which, except for a new building here and there, resolutely maintains its persistent sameness. Its face is like that of a large, heavily made-up and not unbeautiful woman, veil-less and with some dignity but only two expressions, enticement and indifference. A man may be lost at the North Pole, left to die on the west coast of Africa, married in London, or forcibly detained in Siberia, but, let him return to life and New York, and he will find that whatever elsewhere Anno Domini may have defaced and civilization made different, next to nothing has happened to Fifth Avenue.

Martin had told Howard of the way he had found Joan on the hill, how she had climbed out of window that night and come to him to be rescued and how he had brought her to town to find Alice Palgrave away and married her. All that, but not one word of his having been shown the door on the night of the wedding, of her preference for Palgrave, her plunge into night life, or his own odd hut human adventure with Susie Capper as a result of the accident. But for the fact that it wasn't his way to speak about his wife whatever she did or left undone, Martin would have been thankful to have made a clean breast of everything. Confession is good for the soul, and Martin's young soul needed to be relieved of many bewilderments and pains and questionings. He wished that he could have continued the story to Howard of the kid's way Joan had treated him,—a way which had left him stultified,—of how, touched by the tragedy that had reduced the poor little waif of the chorus to utter grief and despair, he had taken her out to the country to get healing in God's roofless cathedral, and of how, treating her, because of his love and admiration of Joan, with all the respect and tenderness that he would have shown a sister, it had given him the keenest pleasure and delight to help her back to optimism and sanity. He would like to have told Howard all the simple and charming details of that good week, giving him a sympathetic picture of the elfish Tootles enjoying her brief holiday out in the open, and of her recovery under the inspiration of trees and flowers and brotherliness, to all of which she was so pathetically unaccustomed. He wouldn't have told of the many efforts made by Tootles to pay him back in the only way that seemed to her to be possible, even if he had known of them,—he had not been on the lookout for anything of that sort. Nor would he, of course, have gone into the fact that Tootles loved him quite as much as he loved Joan,—he knew nothing of that. But he would have said much of the joy that turned cold at the sight of Joan's face when she saw Tootles lying on the sofa in his den, of her rush to get away, of the short, sharp scene which followed her unexpected visit, and of his having driven Tootles back to town the following morning at her urgent request,—a curious, quiet Tootles with the marks of a sleepless night on her face. Also he would have said something of his wild despair at having been just ten minutes too late to find Joan at the house in East Sixty-fifth Street, of his futile attempts to discover where she had gone, and of the ghastly, mystifying days back in the country, waiting and wondering and writing letters that he never posted,—utterly unaware of the emotion which had prompted Joan to walk into his den that night, but quite certain of the impression that she had taken away with her.

It was with a sense of extraordinary isolation that Martin walked down Fifth Avenue. Two good things had, however, come out of his talk with Howard Oldershaw. One was the certainty of this man's friendship. The other the knowledge of the place at which Joan was staying. This last fact made him all the more anxious to get down to the cottage. Devon was only a short drive from Easthampton, and that meant the possibility of seeing and speaking to Joan. Good God, if only she could understand a little of what she meant to him, and how he craved and pined for her.

The dressmaker on the street floor of the rabbit warren had gone out of business. Failed probably, poor thing. Tootles had once said that the only people she ever saw in the shop were pressing creditors. A colored woman of bulbous proportions and stertorous breathing was giving a catlick to the dirty stairway. A smell of garlic and onions met Martin on his way to the rooms of Tootles' friend, and on the first landing he drew back to let two men pass down who looked like movie actors. They wore violet ties and tight-fitting jackets with trench belts and short trousers that should have been worn by their younger brothers. The actor on the next floor, unshaven and obviously just out of bed, was cooking breakfast in his cubby-hole. He wore the upper part of his pajamas and a pair of incredibly dirty flannel trousers. The marks of last night's grease paint were on his temples and eyebrows. He hummed a little song to the accompaniment of sizzling bacon.

When Martin knocked on the door of the apartment of the girl to whom he had never spoken except over the telephone and whose name he remembered to be Irene Stanton, a high-pitched, nasal voice cried out.

"Come right in." He went right in and was charged at by a half-bred Chow whose bark was like a gunman's laugh, and a tiny pink beast which worked itself into a state of hysterical rage. But when a high-heeled shoe was flung at them from the bedroom, followed by a volley of fruit-carrier words of the latest brand, they retired, awed and horror-stricken, to cover.

Martin found himself in a small, square living room with two windows looking over the intimate backs of other similar houses. Under the best of conditions it was not a room of very comfortable possibilities. In the hands of its present occupant, it was, to Martin's eyes, the most depressing and chaotic place he had ever seen. The cheap furniture and the cheaper wall paper went well with a long-unwhite-washed ceiling and smudged white paint. A line of empty beer bottles which stood on a mantelpiece littered with unframed photographs and dog-eared Christmas cards struck a note so blase that it might almost have been committed for a reason. On the square mission table in the center there was a lamp with a belaced pink shade at a cock-eyed angle which resembled the bonnet of a streetwalker in the early hours of the morning. An electric iron stood coldly beneath it with its wire attached to a fixture in the wall. Various garments littered the chairs and sofa, and jagged pieces of newspaper which had been worried by the dogs covered the floor.

But the young woman who shortly made her appearance was very different from the room. Her frock was neat and clean, her face most carefully made up, her shoes smart. She had a wide and winning grin, teeth that should have advertised a toothpaste, and a pair of dimples which ought to have been a valuable asset to any chorus. "Why, but you HAVE done a hustle," she said. "I haven't even had time to tidy up a bit." She cleared a chair and shook a finger at the dogs, who, sneaking out from under the sofa, were eyeing her with apprehensive affection. The Chow's mother had evidently lost her heart to a bulldog. "Excuse the look of this back attic," she added. "I've got to move, and I'm in the middle of packing."

"Of course," said Martin, eager to know why he had been sent for. "It's about Tootles, you said."

"Very much so." She sat on the edge of the table, crossed her arms, and deliberately looked Martin over with expert eyes. Knowing as much about men as a mechanic of a main-road motor-repairing shop knows about engines, her examination was acute and thorough.

Martin waited quietly, amused at her coolness, but impatient to come to cues. She was a good sort, he knew. Tootles had told him so, and he was certain that she had asked to see him out of friendship for the girl upstairs.

Her first question was almost as disconcerting and abrupt as a Zeppelin bomb. "What did you do to Tootles?"

Martin held her examining gaze. "Nothing, except give her a bit of a holiday," he said.

"I saw you go off with her that morning." She smiled and her eyes became a little more friendly. "She wrote me a letter from your place and said she'd found out what song writers meant by the word heaven."

"Did she?" said Martin. "I'm glad."

It came to her in a flash that her little pal had fallen in love with this boy and instantly she understood the mystery of Tootles' change of method and point of view—her moping, her relaxed grip on life. She meant almost nothing to the boy and knew it.

"But don't you think you might have been to see her since you brought her back?" she asked.

"I've been very worried," said Martin simply.

"Is that so?" and then, after another pause, this girl said a second astonishing thing. "I wish I didn't see in you a man who tells the truth. I wish you were just one of the ordinary sort that comes our way. I should know how to deal with you better."

"Tell me what you mean," said Martin.

"Shall I? All right, I will." She stood up with her hands on her hips. "If you'd played the usual game with little Tootles and dropped her cold, I wouldn't let you get out of this room without coming up to scratch. I'd make you cough up a good-sized check. There's such a thing as playing the game even by us strap-hangers, you know. As it is, I can see that you were on the square, that you're a bit of a poet or something and did Tootles a good turn for nothing, and honestly, I don't know the next move. You don't owe her anything, you see."

"Is money the trouble?" asked Martin.

Irene Stanton shot out an odd, short laugh. "Let me tell you something," she said. "You know what happened at the dress rehearsal of 'The Ukelele Girl'? Well, the word's gone around about her chucking the show at the last minute, and it's thumbs down for Tootles. She hadn't a nickel when she came back from your place, and since then she's pawned herself right down to the bone to pay her rent and get a few eats. She wouldn't take nothing from me because I'm out too, and this is a bad time to get into anything new. Only two things can stop her from being put out at the end of the week. One's going across the passage to the drunken fellow that writes music, and the other's telling the tale to you. She won't do either. I've never seen her the way she is now. She sits around, staring at the wall, and when I try to put some of her usual pep into her she won't listen. She's all changed since that taste of the country, and I figure she won't get on her feet again without a big yank up. She keeps on saying to herself, like a sort of song, 'Oh, Gawd, for a sight of the trees,' and I've known girls end it quick when they get that way."

Martin got up. "Where do you keep your pen and ink?" he asked. Poor old Tootles. There certainly was something to do.

Irene bent forward eagerly. "Are you going to see her through this snag?"

"Of course I am."

"Ah, that's the talk. But wait a second. We got to be tricky about this." She was excited and tremendously in earnest. "If she gets to know I've been holding out the hat to you, we're wasting time. Give me the money, see? I'll make up a peach of a story about how it came to me,—the will of a rich uncle in Wisconsin or something, you know,—and ask her to come and help me blow it in somewhere on the coast, see? She gave me three weeks' holiday once. It's my turn now, me being in luck.... But perhaps you don't trust me?"

"You trust me," said Martin, and gave her one of his honest smiles.

He caught sight of a bottle of ink on the window sill. There was a pen of sorts there also. He brought them to the table and made out a check in the name of his fellow conspirator. He was just as anxious as she was to put "a bit of pep" into the little waif who had sat beneath the portrait of his father. There was no blotting paper, so he waved it in the air before handing it over.

A rush of tears came to Irene's eyes when she saw what he had written. She held out her hand, utterly giving up an attempt to find words.

"Thank you for calling up," said Martin, doing his best to be perfectly natural and ordinary. "I wish you'd done so sooner. Poor old Tootles. Write to the Devon Yacht Club, Long Island, and let me know how you get on. We've all three been up against some rotten bad luck, haven't we? Good-by, then. I'll go up to Tootles now."

"No, no," she said, "don't. That'd bring my old uncle to life right away. She'd guess you was in on this, all right. Slip off and let me have a chance with my movie stuff." With a mixture of emotion and hilarity she suddenly waved the check above her head. "Can you imagine the fit the receiving teller at my little old bank'll throw when I slip this across as if it meant nothing to me?"

And then she caught up one of Martin's hands and did the most disconcerting thing of all. She pressed it to her lips and kissed it.

Martin got as red as a beet. "Well, then, good-by," he said, making for the door. "Good luck."

"Good-by and good luck to you. My word, but you've made optimism sprout all over my garden, and I thought the very roots of it were dead."

For a few minutes after Martin was gone, she danced about her appalling room, and laughed and cried and said the most extraordinary things to her dogs. The little pink beast became hysterical again, and the Chow leaped into a bundle of under-clothing and worried the life out of it. Finally, having hidden the check in a safe place, the girl ran upstairs to break the good news of her uncle's death to Tootles. Why, they could do the thing like ladies, the pair of them. It was immense, marvellous, almost beyond belief! That old man of Wisconsin deserved a place in Heaven.... Heaven—Devon.

It was an inspiration. "Gee, but that's the idea!" she said to herself. "Devon—and the sight of that boy. That'll put the pep back, unless I'm the original nut. And if he doesn't care about her now, he may presently. Others have."

And when she went in, there was Tootles staring at the wall, and through it and away beyond at the place Martin had called the Cathedral, and at Martin, with his face dead-white because Joan had turned and gone.

VII

It was a different Tootles who, ten days later, sat on a bank of dry ferns that overlooked a superb stretch of water and watched the sun go down. The little half-plucked bird of the Forty-sixth Street garret with the pale thin face and the large tired eyes had almost become the fairy of Joan's hill once more, the sun-tanned little brother of Peter Pan again. A whole week of the air of Devon and the smell of its pines, of the good wholesome food provided by the family with whom she and Irene were lodging, of long rambles through the woods, of bathing and sleeping, and the joy of finding herself among trees had performed that "yank" of which her fellow chorus lady had spoken.

Tootles was on her feet again. Her old zest to live had been given back to her by the wonder and the beauty of sky and water and trees. A child of nature, hitherto forced to struggle for her bread in cities, she was revived and renewed and refreshed by the sweet breath and the warm welcome of that simple corner of God's earth to which Irene had so cunningly brought her. Her starved, city-ridden spirit had blossomed and become healthy out there in the country like a root of Creeping Jenny taken from a pot on the window-sill of a slum house and put back into good brown earth.

The rough and ready family with whom they were lodging kept a duck farm, and it was to this white army of restless, greedy things that Tootles owed her first laugh. Tired and smut-bespattered after a tedious railway journey she had eagerly and with childish joy gone at once to see them fed, the old and knowing, the young and optimistic, and all the yellow babies with uncertain feet and tiny noises. After that, a setting sun which set fire to the sky and water and trees, melting and mingling them together, and Tootles turned the corner. The motherless waif slept that night on Nature's maternal breast and was comforted.

The warm-hearted Irene was proud of herself. Devon—Heaven—it was indeed an inspiration. The only fly in her amber came from the fact that Martin was away. But when she discovered that he and his friend had merely gone for a short trip on the yawl she waited with great content for their return, setting the seeds in Tootles' mind, with infinite diplomacy and feminine cunning, of a determination to use all her wiles to win even a little bit of love from Martin as soon as she saw him again.

Playing the part of one who had unexpectedly benefited from the will of an almost-forgotten relative she never, of course, said a word of why she had chosen Devon for this gorgeous holiday. Temporarily wealthy it was not necessary to look cannily at every nickel. Before leaving New York she had bought herself and Tootles some very necessary clothes and saw to it that they lived on as much of the fat of the land as could be obtained in the honest and humble house in which she had found a large two-bedded room. Her cigarettes were Egyptian now and on the train she had bought half a dozen new novels at which she looked with pride. Hitherto she had been obliged to read only those much-handled blase-looking books which went the round of the chorus. Conceive what that meant! Also she had brought with her a bottle of the scent that was only, so far as she knew, within reach of leading ladies. Like the cigarettes and the books, this was really for Tootles to use, but she borrowed a little from time to time.

As for Irene Stanton, then, she was having, and said so, the time of her young life. She richly deserved it, and if her kindness and thoughtfulness, patience and sympathy had not been entered in the big volume of the Recording Angel that everlasting young woman must have neglected her pleasant job for several weeks.

And, as for Tootles, it is true that her bobbed hair still owed its golden brilliance to a bottle, but the white stuff on her face had been replaced by sunburn, and her lips were red all by themselves.

She was watching the last of the great red globe when her friend joined her. There had been a race of sloops that afternoon, and there was unusual animation on the quay and at the little club house. A small power boat, on which were the starter and judges and others, had just put in with a good deal of splutter and fuss. On the stoop of the club a small band was playing, and a bevy of young people were dancing. Following in the wake of the last sloop a yawl with a dingey in tow was coming towards the quay.

Seeing that Tootles was in one of her ecstatic moods and was deaf to remarks, Irene saved her words to cool her porridge and watched the incoming yawl. She did so at first without much interest. It was merely a sailboat to her city eyes, and her good lines and good management meant nothing. But as she came nearer something familiar in the cut of the man at her helm caught her attention. Surely those broad shoulders and that deep chest and small head could belong only to Martin Gray? They did, they did. It was that boy at last, that boy about whom Tootles had gone dippy, that boy whose generosity had made their holiday possible, that boy the first sight of whom would put the last touch to Tootles' recovery—that boy who, if her friend set her mind and feminine charm to work, might, it seemed to the practical Irene, make her future safe. Strap-hangers had very few such chances.

With a tremendous effort she sat wordless and waited, knowing that Martin must come that way to his cottage. With all her sense of the dramatic stirred she watched the business of coming to anchor with some impatience and when finally the dingey was hauled in and the two men got aboard, loosed off and rowed to shore, excitement sent the blood tingling through her veins. She heard them laugh and look up towards the club, now almost deserted; cars were being driven inland in quick succession. She watched them, hatless and sun-tanned, come nearer and nearer. She got up as if to go, hesitated, caught Martin's eye, gave an exclamation of well-acted amazement and waved her hand. "Well," she cried out, "for Heaven's sake! I never thought you meant this little old Devon!"

Howard had long ago caught sight of the two girls and wondered if they were pretty, hoping they would remain until he could decide the point for himself. They were, both of them, and Martin knew them. Good enough. He stood by while Martin greeted the one who spoke and then saw the other wake suddenly at the sound of his friend's voice, stumble to her feet and go forward with a little cry.

"Why, Tootles," said Martin warmly. "I never thought of seeing you here. How well you look."

It was like dreaming true. Tootles could only smile and cling to his hand.

"By Jove, the other girl," thought Howard, with what, after all, was only an easy touch of intuition. The girl's face told her story. "What will this mean?" Then there were introductions, questions and answers, laughter, jokes, a quick exchange of glances between Martin and Irene, in which he received and acknowledged her warning, and a little silence.

"Come up to the cottage and have dinner with us," said Martin, breaking it rather nervously. "Can you?"

Tootles nodded. Devon—Heaven. How perfectly the words rhymed.

"You couldn't keep us away with a stick," said Irene. This was the way things should go. Also, the jovial, fat person with the roving eyes might brighten things considerably for her.

"Great work!" Said Howard.

And then, taking Tootle's arm and breaking into enthusiastic details of the sailing trip, Martin led the way up to the cottage among the firs. It was good to have been able to put little Tootles into spirits again.

Howard followed with Irene. "Gee whiz!" he said to himself, "some dimples!"

A few miles away as the crow flies Gilbert Palgrave In his bedroom in St. James's Palace cursed himself and life because Joan was still as difficult to win as sunshine was to bottle.

And up in the sky that hung above them all the angels were lighting the stars.

VIII

Martin was not given to suspicion. He accepted people at their face value and believed in human nature. It never occurred to him, then, that the apparently ingenuous and disarming Irene, with her straight glance and wide smile, had brought Tootles to Devon except by accident or for anything but health and peace. He was awfully glad to see them. They added to the excellent effect upon his spirits which had been worked by the constant companionship of the irrepressible Howard, before whose habitual breeziness depression could stand little chance.

Also he had youth and health and plenty to do in gorgeous weather, and so his case, which he had been examining rather morbidly, assumed a less painful aspect. His love and need of Joan remained just as strong, but the sense of martyrdom brought about by loneliness and self-analysis left him. Once more he assured himself that Joan was a kid and must have her head until she became a woman and faced facts. Over and over again he repeated to himself the creed that she had flung into the teeth of fate, and in this he found more excuse than she deserved for the way in which she had used him to suit her purpose and put him into the position of a big elder brother whose duty it was to support her, in loco parentis, and not interfere with her pastimes. However much she fooled and flirted, he had an unshakable faith in her cleanness and sweetness, and if he continued to let her alone, to get fed up with what she called the Merry-go-round, she would one day come home and begin all over again. She was a kid, just a kid as she had said, and why, after all, should she be bullied and bully-ragged before she had had time to work it off? That's how he argued.

Meanwhile, he was, thankfully enough, no longer alone. Here were Howard and the two girls and the yawl and the sun, and he would keep merry and bright until Joan came back. He was too proud and sensitive to go to Joan and have it all out with her and thus dispel what had developed into a double misunderstanding, and too loyal to go to Joan's mother and tell his story and beg for help. Like Joan and Howard, and who knows how many other young things in the world, he was paying the inevitable penalty for believing that he could face the problems of life unassisted, unadvised and was making a dreadful hash of it in consequence. He little knew that his kindness to Tootles had made Joan believe that he had exchanged his armor for broadcloth and put her in a "who cares?" mood far more dangerous than the one which had sent her into the night life of New York, or that, owing to Tootles, she was, at that very moment, for the fun of the thing, driving Gilbert Palgrave to a state of anger and desperation which might lead to tragedy. Poor young things, misguided and falsely proud and at a loose end! What a waste of youth and spring which a few wise words of counsel would retrieve and render blessed.

And as for Tootles, with her once white face and red lips and hair that came out of a bottle, Martin was to her what Joan was to Palgrave and for the same reason. Irene's hints and innuendos had taken root. Caring nothing for the practical side of her friend's point of view,—the assured future business,—all her energies were bent to attract Martin, all that was feminine in her was making a huge effort to win, by hook or crook, somehow soon, an answer, however temporary, to her love. Never mind what happened after these summer weeks were over. What matter if she went mad so that she had her day? She had never come across any man like this young Martin, with his clean eyes and sensitive soul and honest hands, his, to her, inconceivable capacity of "being brother," his puzzling aloofness from the lure of sex. She didn't understand what it meant to a boy of Martin's type to cherish ideals and struggle to live up to a standard that had been set for him by his father. In her daily fight for mere self-preservation, in which joy came by accident, any such thing as principle seemed crazy. Her street—Arab interpretation of the law of life was to snatch at everything that she could reach because there was so much that was beyond her grasp. Her love for Martin was the one passion of her sordid little life, and she would be thankful and contented to carry memories back to her garret which no future rough-and-tumble could ever take away or blot out.

For several days after the first of many dinners with the boys, Tootles played her cards with the utmost care. The foursome became inseparable, bathing, sailing and motoring from morning to night. If there was any truth in the power of propinquity, it must have been discovered then. Howard attached himself to Irene whom he found something more than merry and amusing,—a girl of indomitable courage and optimism, in fact. He liked her immensely. And so Tootles paired off with Martin and had innumerable opportunities of putting forward the challenge of sex. She took them all, but with the most carefully considered subtlety. She descended to nothing obvious, as was to be expected from one of her type, which was not famous for such a thing as self-restraint. She paid great attention to her appearance and kept a close watch on her tongue. She played what she imagined was the part of a little lady, toned down her usual exuberance, her too loud laugh and her characteristic habit of giving quick and smart back answers. But in all her long talks with Martin she hinted ever so lightly that she and he had not been thrown together from opposite poles without a reason. She tried to touch his mind with the thought that it was to become what she said it might the night of the accident,—a romance, a perfectly private little affair of their own, stolen from their particular routine, which could be ended at a moment's notice. She tried to wrap the episode up in a page of poetry which might have been torn from a little book by Francois Villon and give it a wistfulness and charm that she thought would appeal to him. But it was not until one more than usually exquisite night, when the spirit of July lingered in the air and the warmth of the sun still lay among the stars, that she made her first step towards her goal. Howard and Irene had wandered down to the water, and she was left with Martin sitting elfishly among the ferns on the bank below the cottage and above the silver lapping water. Martin, very much alive to the magic spell of the night, with the young sap stirring in his veins, lay at her feet, and she put her hand caressingly on his head and began to talk in a half whisper.

"Boy, oh, boy," she said, "what shall I do without you when this dream comes to an end?"

"Dream again," said Martin.

"Down there in the city, so far away from trees?"

"Why not? We can take our dreams with us wherever we go. But it isn't coming to an end yet."

"How long will it last?"

"Until the sun gets cold," said Martin, catching her mood, "and there's a chill in the air."

She slipped down a little so that he should see the light in her eyes. There was hardly an inch between their lips, and the only sound was the beating of her heart. Youth and July and the scent of honeysuckle.

"I thought I was dead when you helped me out of that wreck," she went on in a quivering voice, and her long-fingered hand on his face. "I think I must be really dead to-night. Surely this is too sweet to be life."

"Dear little Tootles," said Martin softly. She was so close that he could feel the rise and fall of her breasts. "Don't let's talk of death. We're too young."

The sap was stirring in his veins. She was like a fairy, this girl, who ought never to have wandered into a city.

"Martin," she said, "when the sun gets cold and there's a chill in the air will you ever come back to this hour in a dream?"

"Often, Tootles, my dear."

"And will you see the light in my eyes and feel my hands on your face and my lips on your lips?"

She bent forward and put them there and drew back with a shaking sob and scrambled up and fled.

She had seen the others coming, but that was not why she had torn herself away. One flash of sex was enough that night. The next time he must do the kissing.

Eve and July and the scent of honeysuckle!

Breakfast was on the table. To Irene, who came down in her dressing gown with her hair just bundled up and her face coated with powder, eight o'clock was an unearthly hour at which to begin the day. In New York she slept until eleven, read the paper until twelve, cooked and disposed of a combined breakfast-lunch at one, and if it was a matinee day, rushed round to the theater, and if it wasn't, killed time until her work called her in the evening. A boob's life, as she called it, was a trying business, but the tyranny of the bustling woman with whom she lodged was such that if breakfast was not eaten at eight o'clock it was not there to eat. Like an English undergraduate who scrambles out of bed to attend Chapel simply to avoid a fine, this product of Broadway theaterdom conformed to the rule of Mrs. Burrell's energetic house because the good air of Devon gave her a voracious appetite. Then, too, even if she missed breakfast, she had to pay for it, "so there you are, old dear."

Tootles, up with the lark as usual, was down among the ducks, giving Farmer Burrell a useful hand. She delighted in doing so. From a country grandfather she had inherited a love of animals and of the early freshness of the morning that found eager expression, now that she had the chance of giving it full rein. Then, too, all that was maternal in her nature warmed at the sight and sound of all those new, soft, yellow things that waddled closely behind the wagging tails of their mothers, and it gave her a sort of sweet comfort to go down on her knees and hold one of these frightened babies against her cheek.

Crying out, "Oo-oo, Tootles," from halfway down the cinder path, Irene, stimulated by the aroma of hot coffee and toast, and eggs and bacon, returned to the living room and fell to humming, "You're here and I'm here."

Tootles joined her immediately, a very different looking little person from the tired-eyed, yawning girl of the city rabbit warren. Health was in her eyes and a little smile at the corners of her mouth. Quick work was made of the meal to the intermittent duck talk of Mrs. Burrell who came in and out of the kitchen through a creaking door,—a normal, noisy soul, to whom life was a succession of laborious days spent between the cooking stove and the washtub with a regular Saturday night, in her best clothes, at the motion-picture theater at Sag Harbor to gape at the abnormality of Theda Bara and scream with uncontrolled mirth at the ingenious antics of Charlie Chaplin. An ancient Ford made possible this weekly dip into these intense excitements.

And then the two girls left the living room with its inevitable rocking chairs and framed texts and old heating stove with a funnel through the wall and went out into the sun.

"Well, dearie," said Irene, sitting on the edge of the stoop, within sound of the squeaking of a many-armed clothes drier, teased by a nice sailing wind. "Us for the yawl to-day."

"You for the yawl," said Tootles. "I'm staying here to help old man Burrell. It's his busy day."

Irene looked up quickly. "What's the idea?"

"Just that,—and something else. I don't want to see Martin till this evening. I moved things last night, and I want him to miss me a bit."

"Ah," said Irene. "I guessed it meant something when you made that quick exit when we moved up. Have you got him, dearie?"

Tootles shot out a queer little sigh and nodded.

"That's fine. He's not like the others, is he? But you've played him great. Oh, I've seen it all, never you fear. Subtle, old dear, very subtle. Shouldn't have had the patience myself. Go in and win. He's worth it." Tootles put her hands over her face and a great sob shook her.

In an instant, Irene had her in her arms. "Dear old Tootles," she said, "it means an awful lot to you, don't it? Don't give way, girlie. You've done mighty well so far. Now follow it up, hot and fast. That boy's got a big heart and he's generous and kind, and he won't forget. I brought you here for this, such a chance as it was, and if I can see you properly fixed up and happy, my old uncle's little bit of velvet will have come in mighty useful, eh? Got a plan for to-night?"

Tootles nodded again. "If I don't win to-night," she said, "it's all over. I shall have to own that he cares for me less than the dust. I shall have to throw up my hands and creep away and hide. Oh, my God, am I such a rotten little freak as all that, Irene? Tell me, go on, tell me."

"Freak? You! For Heaven's sake. Don't the two front rows give nobody but you the supper signal whenever the chorus is on?"

"But they're not like Martin. He's,—well, I dunno just what he is. For one thing there's that butterfly he's married to. He's never said as much as half a word about her to me, but the look that came into his eyes when he saw her the night I told you about,—I'd be run over by a train for it any time. He's a man alright and wants love as bad as I do. I know that, but sometimes, when I watch his face, when neither of us is talking, there's a queer smile on it, like a man who's looking up at somebody, and he sets his jaw and squares his shoulders just as if he had heard a voice telling him to play straight. Many times I've seen it, Irene, and after that I have to begin all over again. I respect him for it, and it makes me love him more and more. I've never had the luck to meet a man like him. The world would be a bit less rotten for the likes of you and me if there were more of him about, I tell you. But it hurts me like the devil because it makes me feel no better than a shoe with the buttons off and the heel all worn down, and I ask myself what's the blooming use. But last night I kissed him, and I saw his eyes glint for the first time and to-night,—to-night, Irene, I'm going to play my last card. Yes, that's what I'm going to do, play the last card in the pack."

"How?" asked Irene eagerly, sympathy and curiosity bubbling to the top.

Tootles shook her head. "It isn't lucky to go talking about it." she said, with a most wistful smile. "You'll know whether it's the heights or the depths for me when you see me in the morning."

"In the morning? Shan't you be..."

"Don't ask. Just wish me luck and go and have a good day with the boys. I shall be waiting for you at the cottage. And now I'm off down to the ducks. Say I've got a headache and don't let 'em come round and try to fetch me. So long, Irene; you've been some pal to me through this and I shall never forget."

Whereupon Tootles went off to lend the unloquacious Burrell a helping hand, and Irene ran up to the bedroom to dress.

From the pompous veranda of the Hosack place Gilbert Palgrave, sick with jealousy, watched Joan swimming out to the barrels with that cursed boy in tow. And he, too, had made up his mind to play his last card that night.

Man and woman and love,—the old, inevitable story.

IX

The personnel of the Hosacks' house party had changed.

Mrs. Noel d'Oyly had led her little husband away to Newport to stay with Mrs. Henry Vanderdyke, where were Beatrix and Pelham Franklin, with a bouncing baby boy, the apple of Mr. Vanderdyke's eye. Enid Ouchterlony had left for Gloucester, Massachusetts, where her aunt, Mrs. Horace Pallant, entertained in an almost royal fashion and was eager to set her match-making arts to work on behalf of her only unmarried niece. Enid had gone to the very edge of well-bred lengths to land Courtney Millet, but Scots ancestry and an incurable habit of talking sensibly and rather well had handicapped her efforts. She had confided to Primrose with a sudden burst of uncharacteristic incaution that she seemed doomed to become an old man's darling. Her last words to the sympathetic Primrose were, "Oh, Prim, Prim, pray that you may never become intellectual. It will kill all your chances." Miss Hosack was, however, perfectly safe.

Milwood, fired by a speech at the Harvard Club by Major General Leonard Wood, had scratched all his pleasant engagements for the summer, and was at Plattsburg learning for the first time, at the camp which will some day occupy an inspiring chapter in the history of the United States, the full meaning of the words "duty" and "discipline." Their places had been taken by Major and Mrs. Barnet Thatcher and dog, Regina Waterhouse and Vincent Barclay, a young English officer invalided out of the Royal Flying Corps after bringing down eight German machines. A cork leg provided him with constant amusement. He had a good deal of property in Canada and was making his way to Toronto by easy stages. A cheery fellow, cut off from all his cherished sports but free from even the suggestion of grousing. Of his own individual stunts, as he called them, he gave no details and made no mention of the fact that he carried the D.S.O. and the Croix de Guerre in his bag. He had met the Hosacks at the American Embassy in London in 1913. He was rather sweet on Primrose.

The fact that Joan was still there was easily accounted for. She liked the place, and her other invitations were not interesting. Hosack didn't want her to go either, but of course that had nothing to do with it, and so far as Mrs. Hosack was concerned, let the bedroom be occupied by some one of her set and she was happy enough. Indeed, it saved her the brain fag of inviting some one else, "always difficult with so many large houses to fill and so few people to go round, my dear."

Harry Oldershaw was such a nice boy that he did just as he liked. If it suited him he could keep his room until the end of the season. The case of Gilbert Palgrave was entirely different. A privileged, spoiled person, who made no effort to be generally agreeable and play up, he was rather by way of falling into the same somewhat difficult category as a minor member of the British Royalty. His presence was an honor although his absence would have been a relief. He chose to prolong his visit indefinitely and there was an end of it.

Every day at Easthampton had, however, been a nightmare to Palgrave. Refusing to take him seriously, Joan had played with him as a cat plays with a mouse. Kind to him one minute she had snubbed him the next. The very instant that he had congratulated himself on making headway his hopes had been scattered to the four winds by some scathing remarks and her disappearance for hours with Harry Oldershaw. She had taken a mischievous delight in leading him on with winning smiles and charming and appealing ways only to burst out laughing at his blazing protestations of love and leave him inarticulate with anger and wounded vanity. "If you want me to love you, make me," she had said. "I shall fight against it tooth and nail, but I give you leave to do your best." He had done his best. With a totally uncharacteristic humbleness, forgetting the whole record of his former easy conquests, and with this young slim thing so painfully in his blood that there were times when he had the greatest difficulty to retain his self-control, he had concentrated upon the challenge that she had flung at him and set himself to teach her how to love with all the thirsty eagerness of a man searching for water. People who had watched him in his too wealthy adolescence and afterwards buying his way through life and achieving triumphs on the strength of his, handsome face and unique position would have stared in incredulous amazement at the sight of this love-sick man in his intense pursuit of a girl who was able to twist him around her little finger and make him follow her about as if he were a green and callow youth. Palgrave, the lady-killer; Palgrave, the egoist; Palgrave, the superlative person, who, with nonchalant impertinence, had picked and chosen. Was it possible?

Everything is possible when a man is whirled off his feet by the Great Emotion. History reeks with the stories of men whose natures were changed, whose careers were blasted, whose honor and loyalty and common sense were sacrificed, whose pride and sense of the fitness of things were utterly and absolutely forgotten under the stress of the sex storm that hits us all and renders us fools or heroes, breaking or making as luck will have it and, in either case, bringing us to the common level of primevality for the love of a woman. Nature, however refined and cultivated the man, or rarified his atmosphere, sees to this. Herself feminine, she has no consideration for persons. To her a man is merely a man, a creature with the same heart and the same senses, working to the same end from the same beginning. Let him struggle and cry "Excelsior!" and fix his eyes upon the heights, let him devote himself to prayer or go grimly on his way with averted eyes, let him become cynic or misogynist, what's it matter? Sooner or later she lays hands upon him and claims him as her child. Man, woman and love. It is the oldest and the newest story in the world, and in spite of the sneers of thin-blooded intellectuals who think that it is clever to speak of love as the particular pastime of the Bolsheviki and the literary parasites who regard themselves as critics and dismiss love as "mere sex stuff," it is the everlasting Story of Everyman.

Young and new and careless, obsessed only with the one idea of having a good time,—never mind who paid for it,—Joan knew nothing of the danger of trifling with the feelings of a high-strung man who had never been denied, a man over-civilized to the point of moral decay. If she had paused in her determined pursuit of amusement and distraction to analyze her true state of mind she might have discovered an angry desire to pay Fate out for the way in which he had made things go with Martin by falling really and truly in love with Gilbert. As it was, she recognized his attraction and in the few serious moments that forced themselves upon her when she was alone she realized that he could give her everything that would make life easy and pleasant. She liked his calm sophistication, she was impressed, being young, by his utter disregard of laws and conventions, and she was flattered at the unmistakable proofs of his passionate devotion. But she would have been surprised to find beneath her careless way of treating herself and everybody round her an unsuspected root of loyalty towards Alice and Martin that put up a hedge between herself and Gilbert. There was also something in the fine basic qualities of her undeveloped character that unconsciously made her resent this spoiled man's assumption of the fact that, married or not, she must sooner or later fall in with his wishes. She was in no mood for self-analysis, however, because that meant the renewal of the pain and deep disappointment as to Martin which was her one object to hide and to forget. So she kept Gilbert in tow, and supplied her days with the excitement for which she craved by leading him on and laughing him off. It is true that once or twice she had caught in his eyes a look of madness that caused her immediately to call the nice boy to her support and make a mental note of the fact that it would be wise never to trust herself quite alone with him, but with a shrug of the shoulders she continued alternately to tease and charm, according to her mood.

She did both these things once again when she came up from the sea to finish the remainder of the morning in the sun. Seeing Gilbert pacing the veranda like a bear with a sore ear, she told Harry Oldershaw to leave her to her sun bath and signalled to Gilbert to come down to the edge of the beach. The others were still in the sea. He joined her with a sort of reluctance, with a look of gall and ire in his eyes that was becoming characteristic. There was all about him the air of a man who had been sleeping badly. His face was white and drawn, and his fingers were never still. He twisted a signet ring round and round at one moment and worried at a button on his coat the next. His nerves seemed to be outside his skin. He stood in front of Joan antagonistically and ran his eyes over her slim young form in its wet bathing suit with grudging admiration. He was too desperately in love to be able to apply to himself any of the small sense of humor that was his in normal times and hide his feelings behind it. He was very far from being the Gilbert Palgrave of the early spring,—the cool, satirical, complete man of the world.

"Well?" he asked.

Joan pretended to be surprised. "Well what, Gilbert dear? I wanted to have a nice little talk before lunch, that's all, and so I ventured to disturb you."

"Ventured to disturb me! You're brighter than usual this morning."

"Ah I? Is that possible? How sweet of you to say so. Do sit down and look a little less like an avenging angel. The sand's quite warm and dry."

He kicked a little shower of it into the air. "I don't want to sit down," he said. "You bore me. I'm fed up with this place and sick to tears of you."

"Sick to tears of me? Why, what in the world have I done?"

"Every conceivable and ingenious thing that I might have expected of you. Loyalty was entirely left out of your character, it appears. Young Oldershaw and the doddering Hosack measure up to your standard. I can't compete."

Joan allowed almost a minute to go by in silence. She felt at the very tip-top of health, having ridden for some hours and gone hot into the sea. To be mischievous was natural enough. This man took himself so seriously, too. She would have been made of different stuff or have acquired a greater knowledge of Palgrave's curious temperament to have been able to resist the temptation to tantalize.

"Aren't you, by any chance, a little on the rude side this morning, Gilbert?"

"If you call the truth rude," he said, "yes."

"I do. Very. The rudest thing I know."

He looked down at her. She was leaning against the narrow wooden back of a beach chair. Her hands were clasped round her white knees. She wore little thin black shoes and no stockings. A tight rubber bathing cap which came low down on her forehead gave her a most attractively boyish look. She might have been a young French Pierrot in a picture by Sem or Van Beers. He almost hated her at that moment, sitting there in all the triumph of youth, untouched by his ardor, unaffected by his passion.

"You needn't worry," he said. "You won't get any more of it from me. So that you may continue to amuse yourself undisturbed I withdraw from the baby hunt. I'm off this afternoon."

He had cried "Wolf!" so many times that Joan didn't believe him.

"I daresay a change of air will do you good," she said. "Where are you going?"

He shrugged his shoulders. "What's it matter? Probably to that cottage of mine to play hermit and scourge myself for having allowed you to mortify me and hold me up to the ridicule of your fulsome court of admirers."

"Yes, that cottage of yours. You've forgotten your promise to drive me over to see it, haven't you?"

Palgrave wheeled round. This was too much of a good thing. "Be careful, or my rudeness will become more truthful than even you will be able to swallow. Twice last week you arranged for me to take you over and both times you turned me down and went off with young Oldershaw."

"What IS happening to my memory?" asked Joan.

"It must be the sea air."

He turned on his heel and walked away.

In an instant she was up and after him, with her hand on his arm.

"I'm awfully sorry, Gilbert," she said. "Do forgive me."

"I'd forgive you if you were sorry, but you're not."

"Yes, I am."

He drew his arm away. "No. You're not really anything; in fact you're not real. You're only a sort of mermaid, half fish, half girl. Nothing comes of knowing you. It's a waste of time. You're not for men. You're for lanky youths with whom you can talk nonsense, and laugh at silly jokes. You belong to the type known in England as the flapper—that weird, paradoxical thing with the appearance of flagrant innocence and the mind of an errand boy. Your unholy form of enjoyment is to put men into false positions and play baby when they lay hands on you. Your hourly delight is to stir passion and then run into a nursery and slam the door. You dangle your sex in the eyes of men and as soon as you've got them crazy, claim chastity and make them ashamed. One of these days you'll drive a man into the sort of mad passion that will make him give you a sound thrashing or seduce you. I don't want to be that man. Oldershaw is too young for you to hurt and Hosack too old, and apparently Martin Gray has chucked you and found some human real person. As for me, I've had enough. Good morning."

And once more, having delivered himself coldly and clearly of this brutally frank indictment he went up the steps to the veranda and into the house.

There was not even the tail of a smile on Joan's face as she watched him go.

Lunch was not quite the usual pleasant, happy-go-lucky affair that day. The gallant little Major, recently married to the fluffy-minded Mrs. Edgar Lee Reeves and her peevish little dog, sat on the right of the overwhelmingly complacent Cornucopia. With the hope of rendering himself more youthful for this belated adventure with the babbling widow he had been treated by a hair specialist. The result was, as usual, farcically pathetic. His nice white hair which had given him a charming benignity and cleanness had been turned into a dead and musty black which made him look unearthly and unreal. His smart and carefully cherished moustache which once had laid upon his upper lip like cotton wool had been treated with the same ink-colored mixture. His clothes, once so perfectly suitable, were now those built for a man of Harry Oldershaw's youthful lines and gave him the appearance of one who had forced himself into a suit made for his son. It was of a very blue flannel with white lines,—always a trying combination. His tie and socks were en suite and his gouty feet were martyrized to this scheme of camouflage by being pressed into a pair of tight brown and white shoes. Having been deprived of his swim for fear that his youthfulness might come off in the water and with the rather cruel badinage of his old friend Hosack still rankling in his soul, the poor little old gentleman was not in the best of tempers. Also he had spent most of the morning exercising Pinkie-Winkie while his wife had been writing letters, and his nerves were distinctly jaded. The pampered animal which had taken almost as solemn a part of his marriage vows as the bride herself had insisted upon making a series of strategic attacks against Mrs. Hosack's large, yellow-eyed, resentful Persian Tom, and his endeavors to read the morning paper and rescue Pinkie from certain wreckage had made life a bitter and a restless business. He was unable to prevent himself from casting his mind back to those good bachelor days of the previous summer when he had taken his swim with the young people, enjoyed his sunbath at the feet of slim and beautiful girls, and looked forward to a stiff cocktail in his bathhouse like a natural and irresponsible old buck.

Gilbert Palgrave faced him, an almost silent man who, to Cornucopia's great and continually voiced distress, allowed her handsomely paid cook's efforts to go by contemptuously untouched. It rendered her own enthusiastic appetite all the more conspicuous.

For two reasons Hosack was far from happy. One was because Mrs. Barnet Thatcher was seated on his right pelting him with brightness and the other because Joan, on his left, looked clean through his head whenever he tried to engage her in sentimental sotto voce.

Gaiety was left to Prim and the wounded Englishman and to young Oldershaw and the towering Regina who continually threw back her head to emit howls of laughter at Barclay's drolleries while she displayed the large red cavern of her mouth and all her wonderful teeth. After every one of these exhausting paroxysms she said, with her characteristic exuberance of sociability, "Isn't he the best thing?"

"Don't you think he's the most fascinating creature?" to any one whose eye she caught,—a nice, big, beautiful, insincere girl who had been taught at her fashionable school that in order to succeed in Society and help things along she must rave about everything in extravagant language and make as much noise as her lungs would permit.

Joan's unusual lack of spirits was noticed by every one and especially, with grim satisfaction, by Gilbert Palgrave. With a return of optimism he told himself that his rudeness expressed so pungently had had its effect. He congratulated himself upon having, at last, been able to show Joan the sort of foolish figure that she cut in his sight and even went so far as to persuade himself that, after all, she must do something more than like him to be so silent and depressed.

His deductions were, however, as hopelessly wrong as usual. His drastic criticism had been like water on a duck's back. It inspired amusement and nothing else. It was his remark that Martin Gray had chucked her and found some human real person that had stuck, and this, with the efficiency of a surgeon's knife, had cut her sham complacence and opened up the old wound from which she had tried so hard to persuade herself that she had recovered. Martin-Martin-what was he doing? Where was he, and where was that girl with the white face and the red lips and the hair that came out of a bottle?

The old overwhelming desire to see Martin again had been unconsciously set blazing by this tactless and provoked man. It was so passionate and irresistible that she could hardly remain at the table until the replete Cornucopia rose, rattling with beads. And when, after what seemed to be an interminable time, this happened and the party adjourned to the shaded veranda to smoke and catch the faint breeze from the sea, she instantly beckoned to Harry and made for the drawing-room.

In this furniture be-clogged room all the windows were open, but the blazing sun of the morning had left it hot and stuffy. A hideous squatting Chinese goddess, whose tongue, by a mechanical appliance, lolled from side to side, appeared to be panting for breath, and the cut flowers in numerous pompous vases hung their limp heads. It was a gorgeously hot day.

Young Oldershaw bounded in, the picture of unrealized health. His tan was almost black, and his teeth and the whites of, his eyes positively gleamed. He might have been a Cuban.

"Didn't I hear you tell Prim last night that you'd had a letter from your cousin?"

"Old Howard? Yes." He was sorry that she had.

"Is Martin with him?" It was an inspiration, an uncanny piece of feminine intuition.

Young Oldershaw was honest. "He's staying with Gray," he said reluctantly.

"Where?"

"At Devon."

"Devon? Isn't that the place we drove to the other day—with a little club and a sort of pier and sailboats gliding about?"

"Yes. They've got one."

Ah, that was why she had had a queer feeling of Martinism while she had sat there having tea, watching the white sails against the sky. On one of those boats bending gracefully to the wind Martin must have been.

"Where are they living?"

"In a cottage that belongs to a pal of Gray's, so far as I could gather."

In a cottage, together! Then the girl whom she had called "Fairy,"—the girl who was human and real, according to Gilbert, couldn't be, surely couldn't be, with them.

"Will you drive me over?" she asked.

"When?"

"Now."

"Why, of course, Joan, if I—must," he said. It somehow seemed to him to be wrong and incredible that she had a husband,—this girl, so free and young and at the very beginning of things, like himself, and whom he had grown into the habit of regarding as his special—hardly property, but certainly companion and playmate.

"If you're not keen about it, Harry, I'll ask Mr. Hosack or a chauffeur. Pray don't let me take you an inch out of your way."

In an instant he was off his stilts and on his marrow bones. "Please don't look like that and say those things. You've only got to tell me what you want and I'll get it. You know that."

"Thank you, Harry, the sooner the better, then," she said, with a smile that lit up her face like a sunbeam. She must see Martin, she must, she must! The old longing had come back. It was like a pain. And being with Howard Oldershaw in that cottage he was alone, and being alone he had got back into his armor. SHE had a clean slate.

"Hurry, hurry," she said.

And when Harry hurried, as he did then, though with a curious misgiving, there were immediate results. Before Joan had chosen a hat, and for once it was difficult to make a choice, she heard his whistle and from the window of her bedroom saw him seated, hatless and sunburnt to the roots of his fair hair, in his low-lying two-seater.

It was, at his pace, a short run eastward over sandy roads, lined with stunted oaks and thick undergrowth of poison ivy, scrub and ferns; characteristic Long Island country with here a group of small untidy shacks and there a farm and outhouses with stone walls and scrap heaps, clothes drying on a line, chickens on the ceaseless hunt and a line of geese prowling aimlessly, easily set acackle,—a primitive end-of-everywhere sort of country just there, with sometimes a mile of half burned trees, whether done for a purpose or by accident it would be difficult to say. At any rate, no one seemed to care. It all had the look of No Man's Land,—unreclaimed and unreclaimable.

For a little while nothing was said. Out of a clear sky the sun beat down upon the car and the brown sand of the narrow road. Many times the boy shot sidelong glances at the silent girl beside him, burning to ask questions about this husband who was never mentioned and who appeared to him to be something of a myth and a mystery. He didn't love Joan, because it had been mutually agreed that he shouldn't. But he held her in the sort of devoted affection which, when it exists between a boy and a girl, is very good and rare and even beautiful and puts them close to the angels.

Presently, catching one of these deeply concerned glances, she put her little shoulder against his shoulder in a sisterly way. "Go on, then, Harry," she said. "Ask me about it. I know you want to know."

And he did. Somehow he felt that he ought to know, that he had the right. After all he had stopped himself from loving her at her urgent request, and their friendship was the best thing that he had ever known. And he began with, "When did you do it?"

"Away back in history," she said, "or so it seems. It's really only a few months."

"A few months! But you can hardly have been with him any time."

"I have never really been with him," she said. She wanted him to know everything. Now that the wound was open again and Martin in possession of her once more, she felt that she must talk about it all to some one, and who could be better than Harry, who was so like a brother?

The boy couldn't believe that she meant what she implied but would have bitten off his tongue rather than put a direct question. "Is he such a rotter?" he asked instead.

"He's not a rotter. He's just Martin—generous, sensitive, dead straight and as reliable as a liner. You and he were made in twin molds."

He flushed with pleasure—but it was like meeting a new Joan, a serious, laughterless Joan, with an odd little quiver in her voice and tears behind her eyes. He felt a new sense of responsibility by being confided in. Older, too. It was queer—this sudden switch from thoughtless gaiety to something which was like illness in a house and which made Joan almost unrecognizable.

He began again. "But then—" and stopped.

"I'm the rotter," she said. "It's because of me that he's in Devon and I'm at Easthampton, that he's sailing with your cousin, and I'm playing the fool with Gilbert. I was a kid, Harry, and thought I might go on being a kid for a bit, and everything has gone wrong and all the blame is mine."

"You're only a kid now," said Harry, trying to find excuses for her. He resented her taking all the blame.

She shook her head. "No, I'm not. I'm only pretending to be. I came to Easthampton to pretend to be. All the time you've known me I've been pretending,—pretending to pretend. I ceased to be a kid before the spring was over,—when I came face to face with something I had driven Martin to do and it broke me. I've been bluffing since then,—bluffing myself that I didn't care and that it wasn't my fault. I might have kept it up a bit longer,—even to the end of the summer, but Gilbert said something this morning that took the lynch pin out of the sham and brought it all about my ears."

And there was another short silence,—if it could be called silence with the whirring of the engine and the boy driving with the throttle out.

"You care for him, then?" he asked finally, looking at her.

She nodded and the tears came.

It was a great shock to him, somehow; he couldn't quite say why. This girl had, as she had said, played the fool with Gilbert,—led the man on and teased him into desperation. He loathed the supercilious fellow and didn't give a hang how much he suffered. Anyway, he was married and ought to have known better. But what hit was the fact that all the while she had loved this Martin of hers,—she, by whom he dated things, who had given him a new point of view about girls and who was his own very best pal. That was not up to her form and somehow hurt.

And she saw that it did and was deeply sorry and ashamed. Was she to have a bad effect on every man she met? "I won't make excuses, Harry," she said. "They're so hopeless. But I want you to know that I sprang into marriage before I'd given a thought to what it all meant, and I took it as a lark, a chapter in my adventure, something that I could easily stop and look at after I'd seen and done everything and was a little breathless. I thought that Martin had gone into it in the same spirit and that for the joke of the thing we were just going to play at keeping house, as we might have played at being Indians away in the woods. It was the easiest way out of a hole I was in and made it possible for me not to creep back to my grandmother and take a whipping like a dog. Do you understand?"

The boy nodded. He had seen her do things and heard her say things on the spur of the moment that were almost as unbelievable.

His sympathy and quick perception were like water to her. And it was indescribably good to be believed without incredulous side-looks and suspicions, half-smiles such as Hosack would have given,—and some of the others who had lost their fineness in the world.

"And when Martin,—who was to me then just what you are, Harry dear, —came up to my room in his own particular natural way, I thought it was hard luck to be taken so literally and not be left alone to find my wings for a little. I had just escaped from a long term of subjection, and I wanted to have the joy of being free—quite absolutely free. Still not thinking, I sent him away and like a brick he went, and I didn't suppose it really mattered to him, any more than it did to me, and honestly if it had mattered it wouldn't have made any difference because I had promised myself to hit it up and work off the marks of my shackles and I was full of the 'Who Cares?' feeling. And then Gilbert Palgrave came along and helped to turn my head. Oh, what a perfect little fool I was, what a precocious, shallow, selfish little fool. And while I was having what I imagined was a good time and seeing life, Martin was wandering about alone, suffering from two things that aren't good for boys,—injustice and ingratitude. And then of course I woke up and saw things straight and knew his value, and when I went to get him and begin all over again he wasn't mine. I'd lost him."

The boy's eyebrows contracted sharply. "What a beastly shame," he said, "I mean for both of you." He included Martin because he liked him now, reading between the lines. He must be an awfully decent chap who had had a pretty bad time.

"Yes," said Joan, "it is, for both of us." And she was grateful to him for such complete understanding,—grateful for Martin, too. They might have been brothers, these boys. "But for you, Easthampton would have been impossible," she added. "I don't mean the house or the place or the sea, which is glorious. I mean from what I have forced myself to do. I came down labelled 'Who Cares?' caring all the time, and just to share my hurt with some one I've made Gilbert care too. He's in an ugly mood. I feel that he'll make me pay some day—in full. But I'm not afraid to be alone now and drop my bluff because I believe Martin is waiting for me and is back in armor again with your cousin. And I believe the old look will come into his eyes when he sees me, and he'll hear me ask him to forgive and we'll go back and play at keeping house in earnest. Harry, I believe that. Little as I deserve it I'm going to have another chance given to me,—every mile we go I feel that! After all, I'm awfully young and I've kept my slate clean and I ought to be given another chance, oughtn't I?"

Harry nodded and presently brought the car to a stop under the shadow of the little clubhouse. Half a dozen other cars were parked there, and a colored chauffeur was sitting on the steps of the back entrance, fast asleep with his chin on his chest. The small but vigorous orchestra was playing a fox-trot on the far veranda, and the sound of shuffling feet resembled that of a man cleaning something with sandpaper. There was an army of flies on the screen door of the kitchen and on several galvanized iron bins stuffed with ginger-ale bottles and orange peel.

"We'll leave the car here," said Harry, "and go and have a look for the cottage. It'll be easy to find. There aren't many of 'em, if I remember right."

Joan took his arm. She had begun to tremble. "Let's go this way first," she said, going the right way by instinct.

"If they're in," said Harry, "and I should guess they are.—there's no wind,—I'll draw old Howard off for an hour or so."

"Yes, please do, Harry."

And they went up the sandy incline, over the thick undergrowth, and the sun blazed down on the shining water, and half a dozen canvas-covered catboats near the little pier. Several people were sitting on it in bathing clothes, and some one was teaching a little girl to swim. The echo of her gurgling laughter and little cries came to them clearly. The sound of music and shuffling feet grew fainter and fainter. Gardiner's Island lay up against the horizon like a long inflated sand bag. There were crickets everywhere. Three or four large butterflies gamboled in the shimmering air.

Away out, heading homewards, Martin's yawl, with Irene lying full stretch on the roof of the cabin, and Howard whistling for a wind, crept through the water, inch by inch.

With the tiller under one arm and a pipe in his mouth, long empty, sat Martin, thinking about Joan. Hearing voices, Tootles looked up from a book that she was trying to read. She had been lying in the hammock on the stoop of Martin's cottage for an hour, waiting for Martin. It had taken her a long time to do her hair and immense pains to satisfy herself that she looked nice,—for Martin. Her plan was cut and dried in her mind, and she had been killing time with all the impatience and throbbing of nerves of one who had brought herself up to a crisis which meant either success and joy, or failure and a drab world. She couldn't bear to go through another day without bringing about a decision. She felt that she had to jog Fate's elbow, whatever was to be the insult. She had discovered from a casual remark of

Howard's that Martin, those hot nights, had taken to sleeping on the boat. Her plan, deliberately conceived as a follow-up to what had happened out under the stars the night before, was to swim out to it and wait for him in the cabin. She knew, no one so well, that it was in the nature of a forlorn hope, but she was desperate. She loved him intransitively, to the utter extinction of the little light of modesty which her hand-to-mouth existence had left burning. She wanted love or death, and she was going to put up this last fight for love with all the unscrupulousness of a lovesick woman.

She saw two people coming towards the cottage, a tall, fair, sun-tanned youth, hatless and frank-eyed like Martin, and—

She got up. A cold hand seemed suddenly to have been placed on her heart. Joan,—it was Joan, the girl who, once before, at Martin's house, had sent the earth spinning from under her feet and put Martin suddenly behind barbed wire. What hideous trick was this of Fate's? Why was this moment the one chosen for the appearance of this girl,—his wife? This moment,—her moment?

Fight? With tooth and nail, with all the cunning and ingenuity of a member of the female species to protect what she regarded as her own. She and her plan against the world,—that was what it was. Thank God, Martin was not in sight. She had a free hand.

She had not been seen. A thick honeysuckle growing up the pillar had hidden her. She slipped into the house quickly, her heart beating in her throat. "I'll try this," said Harry. "Wait here." He left Joan within a few feet of the stoop, went up the two steps, and not finding a bell, knocked on the screen door. In less than an instant he saw the girl with bobbed hair come forward. "I'm sorry to trouble you," he said, with a little bow, "I thought Mr. Gray might live here," and turned to go. Obviously it was the wrong house.

Very clearly and distinctly Tootles spoke. "Mr. Gray does live here. I'm Mrs. Gray. Will you leave a message?"

Harry wheeled round. He felt that the bullet which had gone through his back had lodged in Joan's heart. He opened his mouth to speak but no word came. And Tootles spoke again, even more clearly and distinctly. She intended that her voice should travel.

"My husband won't be back for several days," she said, "but I shall be very glad to tell him that you called if you will leave your name."

"It—it doesn't matter," said Harry, stammering. After an irresolute, unhappy pause, he turned to go—

He went straight to Joan. She was standing with her eyes shut and both hands on her heart, as white as a white rose. She looked like a young slim tree that had been struck by lightning.

"Joan," he said, "Joan," and touched her arm. There was no answer.

"Joan," he said, "Joany."

And with a little sob she tottered forward.

He caught her, blazing with anger that she had been so hurt, inarticulate with indignation and a huge sympathy, and with the one strong desire to get her away from that place, picked her up in his arms,—a dead delicious weight,—and carried her down the incline of sand and undergrowth to his car, put her in ever so gently, got in himself, backed the machine out, turned it and drove away.

And Tootles, breathing hard and shaking, stood on the edge of the stoop, and with tears streaming down her face, watched the car become a speck and disappear.

XI

The sun had gone down, and the last of its lingering glory had died before the yawl managed to cajole her way back to her mooring.

Dinner was ready by the time the hungry threesome, laughing and talking, arrived at the cottage. Howard, spoiling for a cocktail, made for the small square dining-room, and Irene, waving her hand to Tootles, cried out, "Cheero, dearie, you missed a speedy trip, I don't think," and took her into the house to tidy up in the one bathroom. Martin drew up short on the edge of the stoop, listened and looked about, holding his breath. It was most odd, but—there was something in the still air that had the sense of Joan in it.

After a moment, during which his very soul asked for a sight of her, he stumped into the living room and rang the bell impatiently.

The imperturbable Judson appeared at once, his eyebrows slightly raised.

"Has any one been here while I've been away?" asked Martin.

"No, sir. No one except Miss Capper, who's been reading on the stoop."

"You're quite sure?"

"You never can be quite sure about anything in this life, sir, but I saw no one."

"Oh," said Martin. "All right, then." But when he was alone, he stood again, listening and looking. There was nothing of Joan in the room. A mixture of honeysuckle and tobacco and the aroma of cooking that had slipped through the swing door into the the kitchen. That was all. And Martin sighed deeply and said to himself "Not yet. I must go on waiting," and went upstairs to his bedroom. He could hear Irene's voice above the rush of water in the bathroom and Howard's, outside, raised in song. In the trees outside his window a bird was piping to its mate, and in the damp places here and there the frogs had already begun to try their voices for their community chorus. It was a peaceful earth, thereabouts falsely peaceful. An acute ear could easily have detected an angry roar of guns that came ever nearer and nearer, and caught the whisper of a Voice calling and calling.

When Martin returned to the wood-lined sitting room with its large brick chimney, its undergraduate chairs and plain oak furniture, its round thick blue and white mats and disorderly bookcase, Tootles was there, a Tootles with a high chin, a half defiant smile, and honeysuckle at her belt.

"Tootles."

"Yes?"

"Have you been alone all the afternoon?"

"Yes." (Fight? Tooth and nail.) "Except for the flies.... Why, boy?"

"Oh, nothing. I thought—I mean, I wondered—but it doesn't matter. By gum, you have made the room look smart, haven't you? Good old Tootles. Even a man's room can be made to look like something when a girl takes an interest in it."

If she had been a dog she would have wagged her tail and crinkled up her nose and jumped up to put her nozzle against his hand. As it was she flushed with pleasure and gave a little laugh. She was a thousandfold repaid for all her pains. But, during the first half of a meal made riotous by the invincible Howard and the animated Irene, Tootles sat very quiet and thoughtful and even a little awed. How could Martin have sensed the fact that she had been there?... Could she,—could she possibly, even with the ever-ready help of nature,—hope to win against such a handicap? She would see. She would see. It was her last card. But during all the rest of the meal she saw the picture of a muscular sun-tanned youth carrying that pretty unconscious thing down the incline to a car, and, all against her will, she was sorry. That girl, pampered as she was, outside the big ring of hard daily effort and sordid struggle as she always had had the luck to be, loved, too. Gee, it was a queer world.

The stoop called them when they left the boxlike dining room. It was still hot and airless. But the mosquitoes were out with voracious appetite and discretion held them to the living room.

Irene flung herself on the bumpy sofa with a cigarette between her lips and a box near to her elbow. "This's the life," she said. "I shall never be able to go back to lil' old Broadway and grease paint and a dog kennel in Chorusland."

"Sufficient for the day," said Howard, loosening his belt. "If a miracle man blew in here right now with a million dollars in each hand and said: 'Howard Guthrie Oldershaw,'—he'd be sure to know about the Guthrie, —'this is all yours if you'll come to the city,' I'd..."

Irene leaned forward with her mouth open and her round eyes as big as headlights. "Well?"

"Take it and come right back."

"You disappoint me, Funny-face. Go to the piano and hit the notes. That's all you're fit for."

It was a baby grand, much out of tune, but Howard, bulging over the stool, made it sound like an orchestra,—a cabaret orchestra, and ran from Grieg to Jerome Kern and back to Gounod, syncopating everything with the gusto and the sense of time that is almost peculiar to a colored professional. Then he suddenly burst into song and sang about a baby in the soft round high baritone of all men who run to fat and with the same quite charming sympathy. A useful, excellent fellow, amazingly unself-conscious and gifted.

Martin was infinitely content to listen and lie back in a deep straw chair with a pipe between his teeth, the memories of good evenings at Yale curling up in his smoke. And Tootles, thinking and thinking, sat, Puck-like, at his feet, with her warm shoulders against his knees. Not in her memory could she delve for pleasant things, not yet. Eh, but some day she might be among the lucky ones, if—if her plan went through—

Howard lit another cigarette at the end of the song, but before he could get his hands on the notes again Irene bounded to her feet and went over to the piano. "Say, can you play 'Love's Epitome'?" she pronounced it "Eppy-tomy."

"Can a duck swim?" asked Howard, resisting a temptation to emit a howl of mirth. She was too good a sort to chaff about her frequent maltreatment of the language.

"Go ahead, then, and I'll give you all a treat." He played the sentimental prelude of this characteristic product of the vaudeville stage, every note of which was plagiarized from a thousand plagiarisms and which imagined that eternity rhymed with serenity and mother with weather. With gestures that could belong to no other school than that of the twice-dailies and the shrill nasal voice that inevitably goes with them, Irene, with the utmost solemnity, went solidly through the whole appalling thing, making the frequent yous "yee-ooo" in the true "vawdville" manner.

To Tootles it was very moving, and she was proud of her friend. Martin almost died of it, and Howard was weak from suppressed laughter. It was the first time that Irene had shown the boys what she could do, and she was delighted at their enthusiastic applause. She would have rendered another of the same sort gladly enough,—she knew dozens of them, if Tootles had not given her a quick look and risen to her feet.

"Us for the downey," she said, and put the palm of her hand on Martin's lips. He kissed it.

"Not yet," said Howard. "It's early."

"Late enough for those who get up at dawn, old dear. Come on, Irene."

And Irene, remembering what her friend had said that morning, played the game loyally, although most reluctant to leave that pleasant atmosphere, and said "Good night." And she was in such good voice and Howard played her accompaniment like a streak. Well, well.

Tootles took her hand away gently, gave Martin a little disturbing smile, put her arm round the robust shoulders of her chum, opened the screen door and was gone.

Howard immediately left the piano. He had only played to keep things merry and bright. "Me for a drink," he said. "And I think I've earned it."

Martin's teeth gleamed as he gave one of his silent laughs.

"How well you know me, old son," he said.

"Of course. But—why?"

"I like Tootles awfully. She's one in a million. But somehow it's—oh, I dunno,—mighty difficult to talk to her."

"Poor little devil," said Howard involuntarily.

"But she's having a real good time—isn't she?"

"Is she?" He helped himself to a mild highball in reluctant deference to his weight.

"I've never seen her look so well," said Martin.

Wondering whether to tell the truth about her state of mind, which his quick sophisticated eyes had very quickly mastered, Howard drank, and decided that he wouldn't. It would only make things uncomfortable for Martin and be of no service to Tootles. If she loved him, poor little soul, and he was not made of the stuff to take advantage of it, well, there it was. He, himself, was different, but then he had no Joan as a silent third. No, he would let things alone. Poor old Tootles.

"Great weather," he said, wrenching the conversation into a harmless generality. "Are you sleeping on the yawl to-night?"

"Yes," replied Martin. "It's wonderful on the water. So still. I can hear the stars whisper."

"Most of the stars I know get precious noisy at night," said Howard, characteristically unable to let such a chance go by. Then he grew suddenly grave and sat down. "Martin, I'm getting frightfully fed up with messing about in town. I'm going to turn a mental and physical somersault and get a bit of self-respect."

"Oh? How's that, old man."

"It's this damn war, I think. I've been reading a book in bed by a man called Philip Gibbs. Martin, I'm going to Plattsburg this August to see if they can make something of me."

Martin got up. "I'm with you," he said. "If ever we get into this business I'm going to be among the first bunch to go. So we may as well know something. Well, how about turning in now? There'll be a wind to-morrow. Hear the trees?" He filled his pocket with cigarettes and slung a white sweater over his shoulder.

"All right," said Howard. "I shall read down here a bit. I won't forget to turn out and lock up." He had forgotten one night and Judson had reported him.

"Good night, old son."

"Good night, old man."

XII

He was not given much to reading, but when Martin left the cottage and stood out in the liquid silver of the moon under the vast dome which dazzled with stars, and he caught the flash of fireflies among the undergrowth that were like the lanterns of the fairies a line came into his mind that he liked and repeated several times, rather whimsically pleased with himself for having found it at exactly the right moment. It was "the witching hour of night."

He remained on top of the incline for a little while, moved to that spirit of the realization of God which touches the souls of sensitive men when they are awed by the wonder and the beauty of the earth. He stood quite still, disembodied for the moment, uplifted, stirred, with all the scents and all the whisperings about him, humble, childlike, able, in that brief flight of ecstasy, to understand the language of another world.

And then the stillness was suddenly cut by a scream of vacuous laughter, probably that of an exuberant Irish maid-servant, to whom silences are made to break, carrying on, most likely, a rough flirtation with a chauffeur.

It brought Martin back to earth like the stick of a rocket. But he didn't go down immediately to the water. He sat there and nursed his knees and began to think. Whether it was Howard's unexpected talk of Plattsburg and of being made something of or not he didn't know. What he did know was that he was suddenly filled with a sort of fright.... "Good God," he said to himself, "time's rushing away, and I'm nearly twenty-six. I'm as old as some men who have done things and made things and are planted on their feet. What have I done? What am I fit to do? Nearly twenty-six and I'm still playing games like a schoolboy!... What's my father saying? 'We count it death to falter not to die' ... I've been faltering—and before I know anything about it I shall be thirty—half-time.... This can't go on. This waiting for Joan is faltering. If she's not coming to me I must go to her. If it's not coming right it must end and I must get mended and begin again. I can't stand in father's shoes with all he worked to make in my hands like ripe plums. It isn't fair, or straight. I must push up a rung and carry things on for him. Could I look him in the face having slacked? My God, I wish I'd watched the time rush by! I'm nearly twenty-six ... Joan—to-morrow. That's the thing to do." He got up and strode quickly down to the water. "If she's going to be my wife, that's a good step on. And she can help me like no one but my father. And then I'll make something of myself. If not ... if not,—no faltering, Gray,—then I'll do it alone for both their sakes."

He chucked his sweater into the dingey, shoved it off the beach and sprang in and rowed strongly towards the yawl. Somehow he felt broader of back and harder of muscle for this summing up of things, this audit of his account. He was nearly twenty-six and nothing was done. That was the report he had to make to his conscience, that was what he had to say to the man who smiled down upon him from his place in the New York house.... Good Lord, it was about time that he pulled himself together.

The yawl was lying alone, aloof from the other small craft anchored near the pier. Her mast seemed taller and her lines more graceful silhouetted against the sky, silvered by the moon. It was indeed the witching hour of night.

He got aboard and tied up the dingey, cast a look round to see that everything was shipshape, took in a deep breath and went into the cabin. He was not tired and never felt less like sleep. His brain was clear as though a fog had risen from it, and energy beat in him like a running engine. He would light the lamp, get into his pajamas and think about to-morrow and Joan. He was mighty glad to have come to a decision.

Stooping, he lit the lamp, turned and gave a gasp of surprise.

There, curled up like a water sprite on the unmade bunk lay Tootles in bathing clothes, holding a rubber cap in her hand, her head, with its golden bobbed hair, dented into a cushion.

For a moment she pretended to be asleep, but anxiety to see how Martin was looking was too much for her. Also her clothes were wet and not very comfortable. She opened her eyes and sat up.

"My dear Tootles!" said Martin, "what's the idea? You said you were going home to bed." She would rather that he had been angry than amused. "It was the night," she said, "and something in the air. I just had to bathe and swam out here. I didn't think you'd be coming yet. I suppose you think I'm bug-house."

"No, I don't. If I hadn't taken my bathing suit to the cottage to be mended I'd have a dip myself. Cigarette?" He held one out.

But she shook her head. How frightfully natural and brotherly this boy was, she thought. Was her last desperate card to be as useless as all the rest of the pack? How could it be! They might as well be on a desert island out there on the water and she the only woman on it.

"Feel a bit chilly? You'd better put on this sweater."

She took it from him but laid it aside. "No. The air's too warm," she said. "Oh, ho, I'm so sleepy," and she stretched herself out again with her hands under her head.

"I'm not," said Martin. "I'm tremendously awake. Let's talk if you're not in a hurry to get back."

"I'm very happy here," she answered. "But must we have that lamp? It glares and makes the cabin hot."

"The moon's better than all the lamps," said Martin, and put it out. He sat on his bunk and the gleam of his cigarette came and went. It was like a big firefly in the half dark cabin. "To-morrow," he said to himself, with a tingle running through his blood, "to-morrow—and Joan."

Tootles waited for him to speak. She might as well have been miles away for all that she affected him. He seemed to have forgotten that she was alive.

He had. And there was a long silence.

"To-morrow,—and Joan. That's it. I'll go over to Easthampton and take her away from that house and talk to her. This time I'll break everything down and tell her what she means to me. I've never told her that."

"He doesn't care," thought Tootles. "I'm no more than an old shoe to him."

"If I'd told her it might have made a difference. Even if she had laughed at me she would have had something to catch hold of if she wanted it. By Jove, I wish I'd had the pluck to tell her."

"He even looks at me and doesn't see me," she went on thinking, her hopes withering like cut flowers, her eagerness petering out and a great humiliation creeping over her. "What's the matter with me? Some people think I'm pretty. Irene does ... and last night, when I kissed him there was an answer.... Has that girl come between us again?"

And so they went on, these two, divided by a thousand miles, each absorbed in individual thought, and there was a long queer silence.

But she was there to fight, and having learned one side of men during her sordid pilgrimage and having an ally in Nature, she got up and sat down on the bunk at his side, snuggling close.

"You are cold, Tootles," he said, and put his arm round her.

And hope revived, like a dying fire licked by a sudden breeze, and she put her bobbed head on his broad shoulder.

But he was away again, miles and miles away, thinking back, unfolding all the moments of his first companionship with Joan and looking at them wistfully to try and find some tenderness; thinking forward, with the picture of Joan's face before him and wondering what would come into her eyes when he laid his heart bare for her gaze.

Waiting and waiting, on the steady rise and fall of his chest,—poor little starved Tootles, poor little devil,—tears began to gather, tears as hot as blood, and at last they broke and burst in an awful torrent, and she flung herself face down upon the other bunk, crying incoherently to God to let her die.

And once more the boy's spirit, wandering high in pure air, fell like the stick of a rocket, and he sprang up and bent over the pitiful little form,—not understanding because Joan held his heart and kept it clean.

"Tootles," he cried out. "Dear old Tootles. What is it? What's happened?"

But there was only brotherliness in his kind touch, only the same solicitude that he had shown her all along. Nothing else. Not a thing. And she knew it, at last, definitely. This boy was too different, too much the other girl's—curse her for having all the luck.

For an instant, for one final desperate instant, she was urged to try again, to fling aside control and restraint and with her trembling body pressed close and her eager arms clasped about his neck, pour out her love and make a passionate stammering plea for something,—just something to put into her memory, her empty loveless memory,—but suddenly, like the gleam of a lamp in a tunnel, her pride lit up, the little streak of pride which had taken her unprofaned through all her sordid life, and she sat up, choked back her sobs, and dried her face with the skirt of her bathing dress.

"Don't mind me," she said. "It's the night or something. It got on my nerves, I suppose, like—like the throb of an organ. I dunno. I'm all right now, anyway." And she stood in front of him bravely, with her chin up, but her heart breaking, and her attempt to make a laugh must surely have been entered in the book of human courage.

But before Martin could say anything, she slipped into the cockpit, balanced herself on the ledge of the cabin house, said "Good night, old dear," and waved her hand, dived into the silver water and swam strongly towards the beach.

XIII

It began to dawn upon Hosack that Joan had slipped away with Harry Oldershaw from the fact that Palgrave first became restless and irritable, then had a short sharp spat with Barclay about the length of the line on the Western front that was held by the British and finally got up and went into the house and almost immediately prowled out alone for a sulky walk along the beach.

Chortling as he watched him, although annoyed that he, himself, was not going to have an opportunity of saying soft things to Joan for some hours, Hosack made himself comfortable, lit another cigar and pondered sleepily about what he called "the infatuation of Gilbert the precious."

"I can sympathize with the feller's being gone on the girl," he said to himself, undisturbed by Regina's frequent bursts of loud laughter at young Barclay's quiet but persistent banter, "but dammit, why make a conspicuous ass of himself? Why make the whole blessed house party, including his hostess, pay for his being turned down in favor of young Harry? Bad form,

I call it. Any one would imagine that he was engaged to be married to Joan and therefore had some right to a monopoly by the way he goes on, snarling at everybody and showing the whites of his eyes like a jealous collie. Everybody's talking, of course, and making jokes about him, especially as it's perfectly obvious that the harder he hunts her the more she dodges him.... Curious chap, Gilbert. He goes through life like the ewe lamb of an over-indulgent mother and when he takes a fancy to a thing he can't conceive why everybody doesn't rush to give it him, whatever the cost or sacrifice.... If young Harry hadn't been here to keep her amused and on the move I wonder if Joan would have been a bit kinder to our friend G. P.? She's been in a weird mood, as perverse as April. I don't mind her treating me as if I was a doddering old gentleman so long as she keeps Gilbert off.... A charming, pretty, heart-turning thing. I'd give something to know the real reason why that husband of hers lets her run loose this way. And where's her mother, and why don't those old people step in?—such a child as she is. Well, it's a pretty striking commentary on the way our young people are brought up, there's no doubt about it. If she was my daughter, now—but I suppose she'd tell me to go and hang myself if I tried to butt in. Divorce and a general mess-up-the usual end, I take it."

He shook his head, and his ash dropped all over his clothes and he began to nod. He would have given a great deal to put his feet on a chair and a handkerchief over his face and sink into a blissful nap. The young people had gone off somewhere, and there were only his wife, the Major, and the bride on the veranda. And, after all, why shouldn't he? Cornucopia could always be relied upon to play up—her conversational well was inexhaustible, and as for Mrs. Thatcher—nothing natural ever stopped the incessant wagging of her tongue.

But it was not to be. He heard a new voice, the squeak of a cane chair suddenly pushed back, looked up to see the Major in an attitude of false delight and out came Mrs. Cooper Jekyll followed,—as he inwardly exclaimed,—"by the gentle Alice Palgrave, by all that's complicating! Well, I'm jiggered."

"Well," cried Cornucopia, extending her ample hand. "This IS a surprise."

"Yes, I intended it to be," said Mrs. Jekyll, more than ever Southampton in her plague veil and single eyeglass, "just to break the aloofness of your beach life."

"And dear Alice, too,—neater than ever. How very nice to see you, my dear, and how's your poor mother?"

Her little hand disappearing between Mrs. Hosack's two podgy members like the contents of a club sandwich, Alice allowed herself to be kissed on both cheeks, murmured an appropriate response, greeted the Thatchers, waved to Hosack who came forward as quickly as he could with pins and needles in one leg and threw a searching glance about for Gilbert.

Every one caught it and gathered instinctively that Mrs. Jekyll had been making mischief. She had certainly succeeded in her desire to break the aloofness. The presence of Alice at that moment, with Gilbert behaving like a madman, was calculated to set every imagination jumping.

"Um, this won't make G. P. any better tempered," thought Hosack, not without a certain sense of glee.

Mrs. Jekyll disclosed her nose and mouth, which, it seemed, were both there and in perfect condition. "I was in town yesterday interviewing butlers,—that Swiss I told you about refused to be glared at by Edmond and left us on the verge of a dinner party, summing us all up in a burst of pure German,—and there was Alice having a lonely lunch at the Ritz, just back from her mother's convalescent chair. I persuaded her to come to me for a few days and what more natural than that she should want to see what this wonderful air has done for Gilbert—who has evidently become one of the permanent decorative objects of your beautiful house."

"Cat," thought Mrs. Thatcher.

"And also for the pleasure of seeing so many old friends," said Alice. "What a gorgeous stretch of sea!" She bent forward and whispered congratulations to the Major's bride. Her quiet courage in the face of what she knew perfectly well was a universal knowledge of the true state of Gilbert's infatuation was good to watch. With his one brief cold letter in her pocket and Mrs. Jekyll's innuendoes,—"all in the friendliest spirit,"—raking her heart, her self-control deserved all the admiration that it won from the members of the house party. To think that Joan, her friend and schoolfellow in whose loyalty she had had implicit faith should be the one to take Gilbert away from her.

With shrewd eyes, long accustomed to look below the surface of the thin veneer of civilization that lay upon his not very numerous set, Hosack observed and listened for the next half an hour, expecting at any moment to see Joan burst upon the group or Gilbert make his appearance, sour, immaculate and with raised eyebrows. He studied Mrs. Jekyll, with her brilliantly made-up face, her apparent lack of guile, and her ever-watchful eye. He paid tribute to his copious wife for her determined babble of generalities, well-knowing that she was bursting with suppressed excitement under the knowledge that Alice had come to try and patch up a lost cause. He chuckled at the feline manners of the little lady whom they had all known so long as Mrs. Edgar Lee Reeves, her purring voice, her frequent over-emphasis of exuberant adjectives, her accidental choice of the sort of verb that had the effect of smashed crockery, her receptiveness to the underlying drama of the situation and the cunning with which she managed to hide her anxiety to be "on" in the scene which must inevitably come. He examined his old friend, Thatcher, under whose perfect drawing-room manners, felicitous quips and ready laughter there was an almost feminine curiosity as to scandal and the inadvertent display of the family wash. And, having a certain amount of humor, he even turned an introspective eye inwards and owned up to more than a little excitement as to what was going to happen when Gilbert realized that Mrs. Jekyll had brought his wife over to rescue him. Conceive Gilbert being rescued! "All of us as near the primeval as most of us are to lunacy," he told himself. "Education, wealth, leisure and all the shibboleths of caste and culture,—how easily they crack and gape before a touch of nature. Brooks Brothers and Lucile do their derndest to disguise us, but we're still Adam and Eve in a Turkish bath.... Somehow I feel,—I can't quite say why,—that this comedy of youth in which the elements of tragedy have been dragged in by Gilbert, is coming to a head, and unless things run off at a sudden tangent I don't see how the curtain can fall on a happy ending for Joan and the husband who never shows himself and the gentle Alice. Spring has its storms and youth its penalties. I'm beginning to believe that safety is only to be found in the dull harbor of middle-age, curse it, and only then with a good stout anchor."

It was at the exact moment that Joan and Harry went together up the incline towards Martin's cottage at Devon, eyed by Tootles through the screen door, that Gilbert came back to the veranda and drew up short at the sight of his wife.

XIV

It was when Gilbert, after a most affectionate greeting and ten minutes of easy small talk, led her away from the disappointed group, that Alice made her first mistake.

"You don't look at all well, Gilbert," she said anxiously.

The very fact that he knew himself to be not at all well made him hate to be told so. An irritable line ran across his forehead. "Oh, yes, I'm well," he said, "never better. Come along to the summer house and let's put a dune between us and those vultures."

He led her down a flight of stone steps and over a stretch of undulating dry sand to the place where Hosack invariably read the morning paper and to which his servants led their village beaux when the moon was up, there to give far too faithful imitations of the hyena. And there he sat her down and stood in front of her, enigmatically, wondering how much she knew. "If it comes to that," he said, "you look far from well yourself, Alice."

And she turned her pretty, prim face up to him with a sudden trembling of the lips. "What do you expect," she asked, quite simply, "when I've only had one short letter from you all the time I've been away."

"I never write letters," he said. "You know that. How's your mother?"

"But I wrote every day, and if you read them you'd know."

He shifted one shoulder. These gentle creatures could be horribly disconcerting and direct. As a matter of fact he had failed to open more than two of the collection. They were too full of the vibration of a love that had never stirred him. "Yes, I'm glad she's better. I'm afraid you've been rather bored. Illness is always boring."

"I can only have one mother," said Alice.

Palgrave felt the need of a cigarette. Alice, admirable as she was, had a fatal habit, he thought, of uttering bromides.

And she instantly regretted the remark. She knew that way of his of snapping his cigarette case. Was that heavily be-flowered church a dream and that great house in New York only part of a mirage? He seemed to be the husband of some other girl, barely able to tolerate this interruption. She had come determined to get the truth, however terrible it might be. But it was very difficult, and he was obviously not going to help her, and now that she saw him again, curiously worn and nervous and petulant, she dreaded to ask for facts under which her love was to be laid in waste.

"No wonder you like this place," she said, beating about the bush.

"I don't. I loathe it. The everlasting drumming of the sea puts me on edge. It's as bad as living within sound of the elevated railway. And at night the frogs on the land side of the house add to the racket and make a row like a factory in full blast. I'd rather be condemned to a hospital for incurables than live on a dune." He said all this with the sort of hysteria that she had never noticed in him before. He was indeed far from well. Hardly, in fact, recognizable. The suave, imperturbable Gilbert, with the quiet air of patronage and the cool irony of the polished man of the world,—what had become of him? Was it possible that Joan had resisted him? She couldn't believe such a thing.

"Then why have you stayed so long?" she asked, with this new point of view stirring hope.

"There was nowhere else to go to," he answered, refusing to meet her eyes.

This was too absurd to let pass. "But nothing has happened to the house at Newport, and the yacht's been lying in the East River since the first of June and you said in your only letter that the two Japanese servants have been at the cottage near Devon for weeks!"

"I'm sick of Newport with all its tuft-hunting women, and the yacht doesn't call me. As for the cottage, I'm going there to-morrow, possibly to-night."

Alice got up quickly and stood in front of him. There was a spot of color on both her cheeks, and her hands were clasped together. "Gilbert, let's both go there. Let's get away from all these people for a time. I won't ask you any questions or try and pry into what's happened to you. I'll be very quiet and help you to find yourself again."

She had made another mistake. His sensitiveness gave him as many quills as a porcupine. "Find myself," he said, quoting her unfortunate words with sarcasm. "What on earth do you mean by that, my good child?"

She forced back her rising tears. Had she utterly lost her rights as a wife? He was speaking to her in the tone that a man uses to an interfering sister. "What's to become of me?" she asked.

"Newport, of course. Why not? Fill the house up. I give you a free hand."

"And will you join me there, Gilbert?"

"No. I'm not in the mood."

He turned on his heel and went to the other side of the summer house, and flicked his half-smoked cigarette into the scrub below. A frog took a leap. When he spoke again it was with his back to her. "Don't you think you'd better rejoin Mrs. Jekyll? She may be impatient to get off."

But Alice took her courage in both hands. If this was to be the end she must know it. Uncertainty was not to be endured any longer. All her sleepless nights and fluctuations of hope and despair had marked her, perhaps for life. Hers was not the easily blown away infatuation of a debutante, the mere summer love of a young girl. It was the steady and devoted love of a wife, ready to make sacrifices, to forgive inconstancies, to make allowances for temporary aberrations and, when necessary, to nurse back to sanity, without one word or look of reproach, the husband who had slipped into delinquency. Not only her future and his were at stake, but there were the children for whom she prayed. They must be considered.

And so, holding back her emotion, she followed him across the pompous summer house in which, with a shudder, she recognized a horrible resemblance to a mausoleum, and laid her little hand upon his arm.

"Gilbert," she said, "tell me the truth. Be frank with me. Let me help you, dear."

Poor little wife. For the third time she had said the wrong thing. "Help"—the word angered him. Did she imagine that he was a callow youth crossed in love?

He drew his arm away sharply. There was something too domestic in all this to be borne with patience. Humiliating, also, he had to confess.

"When did I ever give you the right to delve into my private affairs?" he asked, with amazing cruelty. "We're married,—isn't that enough? I've given you everything I have except my independence. You can't ask for more than that,—from me."

He added "from me" because the expression of pain on her pretty face made him out to be a brute, and he was not that. He tried to hedge by the use of those two small words and put it to her, without explanation, that he was different from most men,—more careless and callous to the old-fashioned vows of marriage, if she liked, but different. That might be due to character or upbringing or the times to which he belonged. He wasn't going to argue about it. The fact remained. "I'll take you back," he added.

But she blocked the way. "I only want your love," she said. "If you've taken that away from me, nothing else counts."

He gave a sort of groan. Her persistence was appalling, her courage an indescribable reproach. For a moment he remained silent, with a drawn face and twitching fingers, strangely white and wasted, like a man who had been through an illness,—a caricature of the once easy-going Gilbert Palgrave, the captain of his fate and the master of his soul.

"All right then," he said, "if you must know, you shall, but do me the credit to remember that I did my best to leave things vague and blurred." He took her by the elbow and put her into a chair. With a touch of his old thoughtfulness and rather studied politeness he chose one that was untouched by the sun that came low over the dune. Then he sat down and bent forward and looked her full in the eyes.

"This is going to hurt you," he said, "but you've asked for the truth, and as everything seems to be coming to a head, you'd better have it, naked and undisguised. In any case, you're one of the women who always gets hurt and always thrives on it. You're too earnest and sincere to be able to apply eye-wash to the damn thing we call life, aren't you?"

"Yes, Gilbert," she answered, with the look of one who had been placed in front of a firing squad, without a bandage over her eyes.

There was a brief pause, filled by what he had called the everlasting drumming of the sea.

"One night, in Paris, when I was towering on the false confidence of twenty-one,"—curious how, even at that moment, he spoke with a certain self-consciousness,—"I came out of the Moulin Rouge alone and walked back to the Maurice. It was the first time I'd ever been on the other side, and I was doing it all in the usual way of the precocious undergraduate. But the 'gay Paree' stuff that was specially manufactured to catch the superfluous francs of the pornographic tourist and isn't really in the least French, bored me, almost at once. And that night, going slowly to the hotel, sickened by painted women, chypre and raw champagne I turned a mental somersault and built up a picture of what I hoped I should find in life. It contained a woman, of course—a girl, very young, the very spirit of spring, whose laugh would turn my heart and who, like an elusive wood nymph, would lead me panting and hungry through a maze of trees. I called it the Great

Emotion and from that night on I tried to find the original of that boyish picture, looking everywhere with no success. At twenty-nine, coming out of what seemed to be the glamor of the impossible, I married you to oblige my mother,—you asked for this,—and imagined that I had settled into a conventional rut. Do you want me to go on with it?"

"Please, Gilbert," said Alice.

He shrugged his shoulders as much as to say, "Well, if you enjoy the Christian martyr business it's entirely your lookout."

But he dropped his characteristic habit of phrase making and became more jerky and real. "I respected you, Alice," he went on. "I didn't love you but I hoped I might, and I played the game. I liked to see you in my house. You fitted in and made it more of a home than that barrack had ever been. I began to collect prints and first editions, adjust myself to respectability and even to look forward with pride to a young Gilbert."

Alice gave a little cry and put her hand up to her breast. But he was too much obsessed by his own pain to notice hers.

"And then,—it's always the way,—I saw the girl. Yes, by God, I saw the girl, and the Great Emotion blew me out of domestic content and the pleasant sense of responsibility and turned me into the panting hungry youth that I had always wanted to be." He stopped and got up and walked up and down that mausoleum, with his eyes burning and the color back in his face.

"And the girl is Joan?" asked Alice in a voice that had an oddly sharp note for once.

"Yes," he said. "Joan.... She's done it," he added, no longer choosing his words. "She's got me. She's in my blood. I'm insane about her. I follow her like a dog, leaping up at a kind word, slinking away with my tail between my legs when she orders me to heel. My God, it's hell! I'm as near madness as a poor devil of a dope fiend out of reach of his joy. I wish I'd never seen her. She's made me loathe myself. She's put me through every stage of humiliation. I'd rather be dead than endure this craving that's worse than a disease. You were right when you said that I'm ill. I am ill. I'm horribly ill. I'm ... I'm..."

He stammered and his voice broke, and he covered his face with his hands.

And instantly, with the maternal spirit that goes with all true womanly love ablaze in her heart, Alice went to him and put her arms about his neck and drew his head down on her shoulder.

And he left it there, with tears.

A little later they sat down again side by side, holding hands.

As Hosack had told himself, and Gilbert had just said, things seemed to be coming to a head. At that moment Tootles was strung up to play her last card, Joan was being driven back by Harry from the cottage of "Mrs. Gray" and Martin, becalmed on the water, with an empty pipe between his teeth, was thinking about Joan.

Palgrave was comforted. The making of his confession was like having an abscess lanced. In his weakness, in his complete abandonment of affectation, he had never been so much of a man.

There was not to Alice, who had vision and sympathy, anything either strange or perverse in the fact that Gilbert had told his story and was not ashamed. Love had been and would remain the one big thing in her own life, the only thing that mattered, and so she could understand, even as she suffered, what this Great Emotion meant to Gilbert. She adopted his words in thinking it all over. They appealed to her as being exactly right.

She too was comforted, because she saw a chance that Gilbert, with the aid of the utmost tact and the most tender affection, might be drawn back to her and mended. She almost used Hosack's caustic expression "rescued." The word came into her mind but was instantly discarded because it was obvious that Joan, however impishly she had played with Gilbert, was unaffected. Angry as it made her to know that any girl could see in Gilbert merely a man with whom to fool she was supremely thankful that the complication was not as tragic as it might have been. So long as Joan held out, the ruin of her marriage was incomplete. Hope, therefore, gleamed like a distant light. Gilbert had gone back to youth. It seemed to her that she had better treat him as though he were very young and hurt.

"Dearest," she said, "I'm going to take you away."

"Are you, Alice?"

"Yes. We will go on the yacht, and you shall read and sleep and get your strength back."

He gave a queer laugh. "You talk like a mother," he said, with a catch in his voice.

She went forward and kissed him passionately.

"I love you like a mother as well as a wife, my man," she whispered. "Never forget that."

"You're,—you're a good woman, Alice; I'm not worthy of you, my dear."

It pained her exquisitely to see him so humble.... Wait until she met Joan. She should be made to pay the price for this! "Who cares?" had been her cry. How many others had she made to care?

"I'll go back to Mrs. Jekyll now," she went on, almost afraid that things were running too well to be true, "and stay at Southampton to-night. To-morrow I'll return to New York and have everything packed and ready by the time you join me there. And I'll send a telegram to Captain Stewart to expect us on Friday. Then we'll go to sea and be alone and get refreshment from the wide spaces and the clean air."

"Just as you say," he said, patting her hand. He was terribly like a boy who had slipped and fallen.

Then she got up, nearer to a breakdown than ever before. It was such a queer reversal of their old positions. And in order that he shouldn't rise she put her hands on his shoulders and stood close to him so that his head was against her breast.

"God bless you, dearest boy," she said softly. "Trust in me. Give all your troubles to me. I'm your wife, and I need them. They belong to me. They're mine. I took them all over when you gave me my ring." She lifted his face that was worn as from a consuming fire and kissed his unresponsive lips. "Stay here," she added, "and I'll go back. To-morrow then, in New York."

He echoed her. "To-morrow then, in New York," and held her hand against his forehead.

Just once she looked back, saw him bent double and stopped. A prophetic feeling that she was never to hear his voice again seized her in a cold grip,—but she shook it off and put a smile on her face with which to stand before the scandal-mongers.

And there stood Joan, looking as though she had seen a ghost.

XV

Alice marched up to her, blazing with anger and indignation. She was not, at that moment, the gentle Alice, as everybody called her, Alice-sit-by-the-fire, equable and pacific, believing the best of people. She was the mother-woman eager to revenge the hurt that had been done to one who had all her love.

"Ah," she said, "you're just in time for me to tell you what I think of you."

"Whatever you may think of me," replied Joan, "is nothing to what I think of myself."

But Alice was not to be diverted by that characteristic way of evading hard words, as she thought it. She had seen Joan dodge the issues like that before, many times, at school. They were still screened from the veranda by a scrub-supported dune. She could let herself go.

"You're a thief," she blurted out, trembling and out of all control for once. "Not a full-blown thief because you don't steal to keep. But a kleptomaniac who can't resist laying hands on other women's men. You ought not to be allowed about loose. You're a danger, a trap. You have no respect for yourself and none for friendship. Loyalty? You don't know the meaning of the word. You're not to be trusted out of sight. I despise you and never want to see you again."

Could this be Alice,—this little fury, white and tense, with clenched hands and glinting eyes, animal-like in her fierce protectiveness?

Joan looked at her in amazement. Hadn't she already been hit hard enough? But before she could speak Alice was in breath again. "You can't answer me back,—even you, clever as you are. You've nothing to say. That night at my house, when we had it out before, you said that you were not interested in Gilbert. If that wasn't a cold-blooded lie what was it? Your interest has been so great that you've never let him alone since. You may not have called him deliberately, but when he came you flaunted your sex in his face and teased him just to see him suffer. You were flattered, of course, and your vanity swelled to see him dogging your heels. There's a pretty expressive word for you and your type, and you know it as well as I do. Let me pass, please."

Joan moved off the narrow board-walk without a word.

And Alice passed, but piqued by this unexpected silence, turned and went for her once most intimate friend again. If she was callous and still in her "Who Cares?" mood words should be said that could never be forgotten.

"I am Mrs. Gray. My husband won't be back for several days," These were the only words that rang in Joan's ears now. Alice might as well have been talking to a stone.

"Things are coming to a head," Alice went on, unconsciously using Gilbert's expression and Hosack's.

"And all the seeds that you've carelessly sown have grown into great rank weeds. Ask Mrs. Jekyll what you've driven Martin into doing if you're curious to know. She can tell you. Many people have seen. But if you still don't care, don't trouble, because it's too late. Go a few yards down there and look at that man bent double in the summer house. If you do that and can still cry out 'Who Cares?' go on to the hour when everything will combine to make you care. It can't be far away."

"I'm Mrs. Gray. My husband won't be back for several days." Like the song of death the refrain of that line rose above the sound of the sea and of Alice's voice. Joan could listen to nothing else.

And Alice caught the wounded look in the eyes of the girl in whom she had once had faith and was recompensed. And having said all that she had had in her mind and more than she had meant to say, she turned on her heel, forced herself back into control and went smiling towards the group on the veranda. And there Joan remained standing looking as though she had seen a ghost,—the ghost of happiness.

"Mrs. Gray,—and her husband Martin.... But what have I got to say,—I, who refused to be his wife? It only seemed half true when I found them together before, although that was bad enough. But this time, now that my love for Martin has broken through all those days of pretending to pretend and that girl is openly in that cottage, nothing could be truer. It isn't Martin who has taken off his armor. It's I who have cut the straps and made it fall from his shoulders Oh, my God, if only I hadn't wanted to finish being a kid."

She moved away, at last, from the place where Alice had left her and without looking to the right or left walked slowly down to the edge of the sea. Vaguely, as though it was something that had happened in a former life, she remembered the angry but neat figure of Alice and a few of the fierce words that had got through to her. "Rank weeds ... driven Martin ... too late.... Who Cares?" Only these had stuck. But why should Alice have said them? It was all unnecessary. She knew them. She had said them all on the way back from Devon, all and many more, seated beside that nice boy, Harry, in his car.... She had died a few feet from the stoop of the cottage, in the scent of honeysuckle and Come back to something that wasn't life to be tortured with regrets. All the way back she had said things to herself that Alice, angry and bitter as she had seemed to be, never could have invented. But they too were unnecessary. Saying things now was of no more use than throwing stones into the sea at any time. Rank weeds ... driven Martin ... too late ... who cares—only who cares should have come first because everything else was the result.

And for a little while, with the feeling that she was on an island, deserted and forgotten, she stood on the edge of the sea, looking at a horizon that was utterly blank. What was she to do? Where was she to go? ... Not yet a woman, and all the future lay about her in chaos.... Once more she went back in spirit to that room of Martin's which had been made the very sanctum of Romance by young blood and moonlight and listened to the plans they had made together for the discovery of a world out of which so many similar explorers had crept with wounds and bitterness.

"I'm going to make my mark," she heard Martin cry. "I'm going to make something that will last. My father's name was Martin Gray, and I'll make it mean something out here for his sake."

"And I," she heard herself say, "will go joy-riding on that huge Round-about. I've seen what it is to be old and useless, and so I shall make the most of every day and hour while I'm young. I can live only once, and I shall make life spin whichever way I want it to go. If I can get anybody to pay my whack, good. If not, I'll pay it myself,—whatever it costs. My motto's going to be a good time as long as I can get it and who cares for the price!"

Young fool, you young fool!

The boy followed her to the window, and the moonlight fell upon them both.

"Yes, you'll get a bill all right. How did you know that?"

And once more she heard her answer. "I haven't lived with all those old people so long for nothing. But you won't catch me grumbling if I get half as much as I'm going out for. Listen to my creed, Martin, and take notes if you want to keep up with me.... I shall open the door of every known Blue Room, hurrying out if there are ugly things inside. I shall taste a little of every known bottle, feel everything there is to feel except the thing that hurts, laugh with everybody whose laugh is catching, do everything there is to do, go into every booth in the big Bazaar, and when I'm tired and there's nothing left, slip out of the endless procession with a thousand things stored in my memory. Isn't that the way to live?"

"Young fool, you young fool," she cried, with the feeling of being forgotten and deserted, with not one speck on the blank horizon. "You've failed—failed in everything. You haven't even carried out your program. Others have paid,—Martin and Gilbert and Alice, but the big bill has come in to you ... Who cares? You do, you do, you young fool, and you must creep out of the procession with only one thing stored in your memory,—the loss of Martin, Martin."

It was a bad hour for this girl-child who had tried her wings too young.

And when Gilbert straightened up and gave thanks to God for the woman who had never stirred him, but whose courage and tenderness had added to his respect, he too turned towards the sea with its blank horizon,—the sea upon which he was to be taken by his good wife for rest and sleep, and there was Joan ... young, and slight and alluring, with her back to him and her hands behind her back, and the mere sight of her churned his blood again, and set his dull fire into flames. Once more the old craving returned, the old madness revived, as it always would when the sight and sound of her caught him, and all the common sense and uncommon goodness of the little woman who had given him comfort rose like smoke and was blown away.... To win this girl he would sacrifice Alice and barter his soul. She was in his blood. She was the living picture of his youthful vision. She only could satisfy the Great Emotion.... There was the plan that he had forgotten, —the lunatic plan from which, even in his most desperate moment, he had drawn back, afraid,—to cajole her to the cottage away from which he would send his servants; make, with doors and windows locked, one last passionate appeal, and then, if mocked and held away, to take her with him into death and hold her spirit in his arms.

To own himself beaten by this slip of a girl, to pack his traps and leave her the field and sneak off like a beardless boy,—was that the sort of way he did things who had had merely to raise his voice to hear the approach of obsequious feet? ... Alice and the yacht and nothing but sea to a blank horizon? He laughed to think of it. It was, in fact, unthinkable.

He would put it to Joan in a different way this time. He would hide his fire and be more like that cursed boy. That would be a new way. She liked new things.

He left the summer house, only the roof of which was touched by the last golden rays of the sun, and with curious cunning adopted a sort of caricature of his old light manner. There was a queer jauntiness in his walk as he made his way over the sand, carrying his hat, and a flippant note in his voice when he arrived at her side.

"Waiting for your ship to come home?" he asked.

"It's come," she said.

"You have all the luck, don't you?"

She choked back a sob.

He saw the new look on her face. Something,—perhaps boredom,—perhaps the constant companionship of that cursed boy,—had brought her down from her high horse. This was his chance! ...

"You thought I had gone, I suppose?"

"Yes," she said.

"To-morrow suits me best. I'm off to-morrow,—I've not decided where. A long journey, it may be. If you're fed up with these people what do you say to my driving you somewhere for dinner? A last little dinner to remind us of the spring in New York?"

"Would you like me to very much?"

He steadied his voice. "We might be amused, I think."

"That doesn't answer my question," she said.

"I'd love you to," he answered. "It would be fair, too. I've not seen much of you here."

Yes, it would be fair. Let her try, even at that late stage of the game, to make things a little even. This man had paid enough.

"Very well," she said. "Let's go." It would be good to get away from prying eyes and the dull ache of pain for a few hours.

He could hardly believe his ears. Joan,—to give him something! It was almost incredible.

She turned and led the way up. The sun had almost gone. "I'll get my hat at once," she said, "I'll be ready in ten minutes."

His heart was thumping. "I'll telephone to a place I know, and be waiting in the car."

"Let me go in alone," she said. "We don't want to be held up to explain and argue. You're sure you want me to come?" She drew up and looked at him.

He bowed to hide his face. "Of all things on earth," he said.

She ran on ahead, slipped into the house and up to her room.

Exultant and full of hope, Gilbert waited for a moment before following her in. Going straight to the telephone room he shut the door, asked for the number of his cottage and drummed the instrument with his fingers.

At last!

"Is that you, Itrangi? ... Lay some sort of dinner for two,—cold things with wine. It doesn't matter what, but at once. I shall be over in about an hour. Then get out, with the cook. I want the place to myself to-night. Put the door key on the earth at the left-hand corner of the bottom step. Telephone for a car and go to the hotel at Sag Harbor. Be back in the morning about nine. Do these things without fail. I rely upon you."

He hardly waited for the sibilant assurance before putting back the receiver. He went round to the garage himself. This was the first time he had driven Joan in his car. It might be the last.

Harry was at the bottom of the stairs as Joan came down.

"You're not going out?" he asked. She was still in day clothes, wearing a hat.

"Yes, I am, Harry."

"Where? Why?"

She laid her hand on his arm. "Don't grudge Gilbert one evening,—his last. I've been perfectly rotten to him all along."

"Palgrave? Are you going out with Palgrave?"

"Yes, to dine somewhere. I want to, Harry, oh, for lots of reasons. You know one. Don't stop me." Her voice broke a little.

"But not with Palgrave."

"Why?"

"I saw him dodge out of the telephone room a minute ago. He looked—queer. Don't go, Joan."

"I must," she said and went to the door. He was after her and caught hold of her arm.

"Joan, don't go. I don't want you to."

"I must," she said again. "Surely you can understand? I have to get away from myself."

"But won't I do?"

"It's Gilbert's turn," she said. "Let go, Harry dear." It was good to know that she hadn't hurt this boy.

"I don't like it. Please stay," but he let her go, and watched her down the steps and into the car, with unaccountable misgiving. He had seen Gilbert's face.

And he saw it again under the strong light of the entrance—triumphant.

For minutes after the car had gone, with a wave from Joan, he stood still, with an icy hand on his heart.

"I don't like it," he repeated. "I wish to God I'd had the right to stop her."

She thought that he didn't love her, and he had done his best to obey. But he did love her, more than Martin, it seemed, more than Gilbert, he thought, and by this time she was well on her way to—what?

PART FOUR

THE PAYMENT

I

It was one of those golden evenings that sometimes follows a hot clear day—one of those rare evenings which linger in the memory when summer has slipped away and which come back into the mind like a smile, an endearment or a broad sweet melody, renewing optimism and replenishing faith. The sun had gone, but its warm glow lingered in a sky that was utterly unspotted. The quiet unruffled trees in all the rich green of early maturity stood out against it almost as though they were painted on canvas. The light was so true that distances were brought up to the eye. Far-away sounds came closely to the ear. The murmur from the earth gathered like that of a multitude of voices responding to prayers.

Palgrave drove slowly. The God-given peace and beauty that lay over everything quieted the stress and storm of his mind. Somehow, too, with Joan at his side on the road to the cottage in which he was to play out the second or the last act of the drama of his Great Emotion, life and death caught something of the truth and dignity of that memorable evening—the sounds of life and the distance of death. If he was not to live with Joan he would die with her. There was, to him, in the state of mind into which this absorbing passion had worked him, no alternative. Love, that he had made his lodestar in early youth and sought in vain, had come at last. Marriage, convention, obligations, responsibility, balance and even sanity mattered nothing. They were swept like chaff before this sex-storm. Ten years of dreams were epitomized in Joan. She was the ideal that he had placed on the secret altar of his soul. She struck, all vibrant with youth, the one poetic note that was hidden in his character behind vanity and sloth, cynicism and the ingrained belief that whatever he desired he must have. And as he drove away from Easthampton and the Hosack house he left behind him Alice and all that she was and meant. She receded from his mind like the white cliffs of a shore to which he never intended to return. He was happier than he had ever been. In his curious exaltation, life, with its tips and downs, its pettiness, its monotony, lay far below him, as the moving panorama of land does to a flying man. His head was clear, his plan definite. He felt years younger—almost boyish. Laughter came easy—the sort of reasonless laughter that comes to tired men as they start out on a holiday. He saw the strangeness of it all with some wonder and much triumph. The Gilbert Palgrave who had been molded by money and inertia and autocracy was discarded, and the man with Joan at his side was the young Gilbert whom he had caught sight of that night in Paris, when, on his way home under the stars, Joan, with her brown hair and laughing eyes, tip-tilted nose and the spirit of spring in her breath, had come out of his inner consciousness and established herself like a shape in a dream.

His heart turned when he looked at Joan's face. Was its unusual gravity due to the fact that she had come to the end of fooling—that she, too, had sensed the finality or the beginning? He thought so. He believed so. She looked younger than ever, but sweeter, less flippant, less triumphantly irresponsible. She sat, like a child, with her hands in her lap, her mouth soft, an odd wistfulness in her eyes with their long curling lashes. A black straight-brimmed straw hat sat well down on her small head and put a shadow on her face. The slim roundness of her arms showed through the white silk shirt, and her low collar proved all the beauty of her throat and neck. She looked more than ever unplucked, untouched, like a rosebud.

On the tip of his tongue there were words of adoration, not fastidious and carefully chosen, but simple, elemental words such as a farmhand might blunder out in the deep shadow of a lane, after dark. But he held them back. He would wait until after they had dined together and all round them there were silence and solitude. He drove still more slowly in order to give the two Japanese servants time to carry out his instructions and remove themselves. That cottage, which he had bought on the spur of the moment, fitted out with elaborate care and used only twice, for two weeks since, was to justify itself, after all. Who knows? He might have bought it two years before under an inspiration. Even then, months and months before he met Joan or knew of her existence, this very evening might have been mapped out He was a fatalist, and it fell into his creed to think so.

He didn't wonder why Joan was silent or ask himself jealously of what she was thinking. He chose to believe that she had arrived at the end of impishness, had grown weary of Harry Oldershaw and his cubbish ways and had turned to himself naturally and with relief, choosing her moment with the uncanny intuition that is the gift of women. She was only just in time. To-morrow would have found him following the faithful Alice on her forlorn hope—the incurable man.

It was only when they turned into the narrow sandy road that was within a quarter of a mile of the club at Devon that Joan came out of the numbness that had settled upon her and recognized things that were stamped with the marks of an afternoon that was never to be forgotten. Martin—Martin—and it was all her fault.

"But why are you coming this way?" she asked, drawing back into her seat.

"Because my cottage is just here," said Gilbert.

"At Devon?"

"Yes. Why not? I had a fancy for playing hermit from time to time. I saw the sun set behind the water,—a Byron sunset,—and in the hope of seeing just such another I bought this shack. I did those things once for want of something better. Look at it," he said, and turned the car through a rustic gate, alive with honeysuckle.

It was a bungalow, put up on a space cleared among a wood of young trees that was carpeted with ferns. It might have been built for a poet or a novelist or just an ordinary muscular man who loved the water and the silences and the sense of being on the edge of the world. It was a bungalow of logs, roughly constructed and saved from utter banality by being almost completely clothed in wisteria. It was admirably suited to two men who found amusement in being primitive or to a romantic honeymoon couple who wanted to fancy themselves on a desert island. Better still, it might have been built for just that night, for Palgrave and the girl who had taken shape in his one good dream.

Joan got out of the opulent car and watched Gilbert run it round to the side of the house. There was no garage and not even a shed to give it cover. Gilbert left it in the open, where it remained sulky and supercilious, like a grand piano in an empty kitchen.

Joan had noticed this place twice that day—on the way out to find Martin, and again on the way back from having heard the voice of the girl with the white face and the red lips and the hair that came out of a bottle. Martin—Martin—and it was all her fault.

She wondered for a moment why no one came to open the door. Some one was there because smoke was coming out of a chimney. But she refused to be impatient. She had decided to give Gilbert one evening—to be nice to him for one evening. He was terribly humble. Fate had dealt her a smashing blow on the heart, and she had returned to consciousness wistfully eager to make up at least to this man as well as she could for the pain that she had caused. There was only this one evening in which to do so because to-morrow she was going back to the old house, the old people, the old servants and the old days, a failure, having fallen off the Round-about, of which she had spoken so much. She was going back a sort of cripple to the place from which she had escaped to put the key into life; once more to read to her grandfather, to obey the orders of her grandmother, to sleep in the warm kind arms of her old bedroom, to go among the flowers and trees among which she had grown up, herself old and tired and ashamed and broken-hearted, with her gold ring burning into her finger and the constant vision of Martin's shining armor lying bent and rusty before her eyes. What an end to her great adventure!

Gilbert came up. He walked without his usual affectation of never permitting anything to hurry him. All about him there was still a sort of exaltation. His eyes were amazingly bright. His face had lost its cynicism. Ten years seemed to have fallen from his shoulders like a pack. He was a youth again, like Martin and Harry and Howard. Joan noticed all this and was vaguely surprised—and glad, because obviously she was giving him pleasure. He deserved it after her impish treatment of him. What a fool she had been.

He said, bending down, "We keep the key here," and picked it up, unlocked the door and stood back for her to pass.

"Oh, isn't this nice!" said Joan.

"Do you like it? It amused me to make it comfortable."

"Comfortable! But it's like a picture."

Gilbert laughed boyishly. Her enthusiasm delighted him. To make the long low living room with its big brick chimney and open fireplace absolutely right had dispelled his boredom—little as he had intended to use it. The whole thing was carried out on the lines of the main room in an English shooting box. The walls were matchboarded and stained an oak color, and the floor was polished and covered with skins. Old pewter plates and mugs, and queer ugly delightful bits of pottery were everywhere—on shelves, on the wide mantelpiece, and hanging from the beams. Colored sporting prints covered the walls, among stuffed fish and heads of deer with royal antlers and beady eyes with a fixed stare. The furniture was Jacobean—the chairs with ladder backs and cane seats; a wide dresser, lined with colored plates; a long narrow table with rails and bulging legs. Two old oak church pews were set on each side of the fireplace filled with cushions covered with a merry chintz. There were flowers everywhere in big bowls—red rambler roses, primula, sweet williams, Shasta daisies, and scarlet poppies. All the windows were open, and there was nothing damp or musty in the smell of the room. On the contrary, the companionable aroma of tobacco smoke hung in the air mixed with the sweet faint scent of flowers. The place seemed "lived-in"—as well it might. The two Japs had played gentlemen there for some weeks. The table was laid for two, and appetizing dishes of cold food, salad and fruit were spread out on the dresser and sideboard, with iced champagne and claret cup.

"The outside of the cottage didn't suggest all this comfort," said Joan.

"Comfort's the easiest thing in the world when you can pay for it. There's one bedroom half the size of this and two small ones. A bathroom and kitchen beyond. There's water, of course, and electric light, and there's a telephone. I loathe the telephone, the destroyer of aloofness, the missionary that breaks into privacy." He switched on the lights in several old lanterns as he spoke. The day had almost disappeared.

He went over to her and stood smiling.

"Well, isn't this better than a road-house reeking of food and flies and made hideous by a Jazz band?"

"Much better," she said.

The delightful silence was broken by the crickets.

"Martin—Martin," she thought, "and it was all my fault."

A sort of tremble ran over Gilbert as he looked at her. Agony and joy clashed in his heart. He had suffered, gone sleepless, worn himself out by hard, grim exercise in order, who knew how many times, to master his almost unendurable passion. He had killed long nights, the very thought of which made him shudder, by reading books of which he never took in a word. He had stood up in the dark, unmanned, and cursed himself and her and life. He had denounced her to himself and once to her as a flapper, a fool-girl, an empty-minded frivolous thing encased in a body as beautiful as spring. He had thrown himself on his knees and wept like a young boy who had been hurt to the very quick by a great injustice. He had faced himself up, and with the sort of fear that comes to men in moments of physical danger, recognized madness in his eyes. But not until that instant, as she stood before him unguarded in his lonely cottage, so slight and sweet and unexpectedly gentle, her eyes as limpid as the water of a brook, her lips soft and kind and unkissed, her whole young body radiating virginity, did he really know how amazingly and frighteningly he loved her. But once again he held back a rush of adoring words and a desire to touch and hold and claim. The time had not come yet. Let her warm to him. Let him live down the ugliness of the mood that she had recently put him into, do away with the impression he must have given her of jealousy and petulance and scorn. Let her get used to him as a man who had it in him to be as natural and impersonal, and even as cubbish, as some of the boys she knew. Later, when night had laid its magic on the earth, he would make his last bid for her kisses—or take her with him across the horizon.

"How do you like that?" he asked, and pointed to a charmingly grotesque piece of old Staffordshire pottery which made St. George a stunted churchwarden with the legs of a child, his horse the kind of animal that would be used in a green grocer's cart and the dragon a cross between a leopard and a half-bred bulldog.

"Very amusing," she said, going over to it.

And the instant her back was turned, he opened a drawer in a sideboard and satisfied himself that the thing which might have to put them into Eternity together lay there, loaded.

II

"And now," he said gayly, "let's dine and, if you don't mind, I will buttle. I hate servants in a place like this." He went to the head of the table and drew back a chair.

Joan sat down, thanking him with a smile. It was hard to believe that, with the words of that girl still ringing in her ears and the debris of her hopes lying in a heap about her feet, she was going through the process of being nice to this man who had his claims. It was unreal, fantastic. It wasn't really happening. She must be lying face down on some quiet corner of Mother Earth and watering its bosom with tears of blood. Martin—Martin! It was all her fault.

Tomorrow she would be back again in the old house, with the old people and the old dogs and the old trees and follow her old routine—old, old. That was the price she must pay for being a kid when she should have been a woman.

Palgrave stood at the sideboard and carved a cold chicken decorated with slips of parsley. "Have you ever gone into a room in which you've never been before and recognized everything in it or done some thing for the first time that you suddenly realize isn't new to you?"

"Yes, often," replied Joan. "Why?"

"You've never sat in that chair until this minute and this chicken was probably killed this morning. But I've seen you sitting in just that attitude at that table and cut the wing of this very bird and watched that identical smile round your lips when I put the plate in front of you." He put it in front of her and the scent of her hair made him catch his breath. "Oh, my God!" he said to himself. "This girl—this beautiful, cool, bewitching thing—the dew of youth upon her, as chaste as unsunned snow—Oh, my God...."

But Joan had caught the scent of honeysuckle, and back into her brain came that cottage splashed with sun, the lithe figure of Harry Oldershaw with his face tanned the color of mahogany and the clear voice of "Mrs. Gray."

Gilbert filled her glass with champagne cup, carved for himself and sat at the foot of the table. "The man from whom I bought this place," he said, saying anything to make conversation and keep himself rig idly light and, as he hoped, like Oldershaw, "owns a huge ready-made clothes store on Broadway—appalling things with comic belts and weird pockets."

"Oh!" said Joan. Always, for ever, the scent of honeysuckle would bring that picture back. Martin—Martin.

"He makes any amount of money by dressing that portion of young America which sells motors and vacuum cleaners and gramaphone records and hangs about stage doors smoking cheap cigarettes."

"Yes?" Joan listened but heard nothing except that high clear voice coming through the screen door.

"He built this cottage as an antidote and spent his week-ends here entirely alone with the trees and crickets, trying to write poetry. He was very pleased with it and believed that this atmosphere was going to make him immortal."

"I see,"—but all she saw was a porch covered with honeysuckle, a hammock with an open book face downwards in it and the long shadow of Harry Oldershaw flung across the white steps.

Gilbert went on—pathetically unable to catch the unaffected young stuff of the nice boy and his kind. He had never been young.

"He had had no time during his hard struggle to read the masters, and when, without malice, I quoted a chunk of Grey's 'Elegy' to him, the poor devil's jaw fell, he withdrew his blank refusal to sell the place to me, pocketed my cheque, packed his grip, and slouched off then and there, looking as if a charge of dynamite had blown his chest away. His garments,

I notice, are as comic as ever, and I suppose he is now living in a turretted house with stucco walls and stone lions at New Rochelle, wedded to Commerce and a buxom girl who talks too much and rag-times through her days."

Joan joined in his laugh. She was there to make up for her unkindness. She would do her best under the circumstances. She hoped he would tell lots of long stories to cover her wordlessness.

Gilbert emptied his glass and filled it again. He was half conscious of dramatizing the episode as it unrolled itself and thrilled to think that this might be the last time that he would eat and drink in the only life that he knew. Death, upon which he had looked hitherto with horror, didn't scare him if he went into it hand in hand with Joan. With Alice trying, in her persistently gentle way, to cure him, life was unthinkable. Life with Joan—there was that to achieve. Let the law unravel the knots while he and she wandered in France and Italy, she triumphantly young, and he a youth again, his dream come true.... Would she have come with him to-night if she hadn't grown weary of playing flapper? She knew what she meant to him. He had told her often enough. Too often, perhaps. He had taken the surprise of it away, discounted the romance..

He got up and gave her some salad and stood by her for a moment. He was like a moth hovering about a lamp.

She smiled up at him again—homesick for the old bedroom and the old trees, eager to sit in her grand father's room and read the paper to him. He was old and out of life and so was she. Oh, Martin, Martin. Why couldn't he have waited a little while longer?

The shock of touching her fingers as she took the salad plate sent the blood to Gilbert's brain. But he reined himself in. He was afraid to come to the point yet. Life was too good like this. The abyss yawned at their feet. He would turn his back to it and see only the outstretched landscape of hope.

They ate very little, and Joan ignored her glass. Gilbert frequently filled his own, but he might just as well have been drinking water. He was already drunk with love.

Finally, after a long silence, Joan pushed her chair back and got up.

Instantly he was in front of her, with his back to the door. "Joan," he said, and held out his hands in supplication.

"Don't you think we ought to drive home now?" she asked.

"Home?"

"Yes. It must be getting late."

"Not yet," he said, steadying his voice. "Time is ours. Don't hurry."

He went down suddenly on to his knees and kissed her feet.

At any other time, in any other mood, the action would have stirred her sense of the ridiculous. She would have laughed and whipped him with sarcasm. He had done exuberant things before and left her unmoved except to mirth. But this time she raised him up without a word, and he answered her touch with curious unresistance, like a man hypnotized and stood speechless, but with eyes that were filled with eloquence.

"Be good to-night, Gilbert," she said. "I've ... I've been awfully hurt to-day and I feel tired and worn—not up to fencing with you."

The word "fencing" didn't strike home at first, nor did he gather at once from her simple appeal that she had not come in the mood that he had persuaded himself was hers.

"This is the first time that you've given me even an hour since you drew me to the Hosacks," he said. "Be generous. Don't do things by halves."

She could say nothing to that. She was there only because of a desire to make up ever so little for having teased him. He had been consistently generous to her. She had hoped, from his manner, that he was simply going to be nice and kind and not indulge in romantics. She was wrong, evidently. It was no new thing, though. She was well accustomed to his being dramatic and almost foreign. He had said many amazing things but always remained the civilized man, and never attempted to make a scene. She liked him for that, and she had tried him pretty high, she knew. She did wish that he would be good that night, but there was nothing to say in reply to his appeal. And so she went over to one of the pews and sat down among the cushions.

"I'll give you another hour, then," she said.

But the word had begun to rankle. "Fencing!—Fencing! ..."

He repeated it several times.

She watched him wander oddly about the room, thinking aloud rather than speaking to her. How different he had become. For the first time it dawned upon her that the whole look of the man had undergone a change. He held himself with less affectation. His petulance had gone. He was like a Gilbert Palgrave who had been ill and had come out of it with none of his old arrogance.

He took up a cigarette and began wandering again, muttering her unfortunate word. She was sorry to have hurt his feelings. It was the very last thing that she had wanted to do. "Aren't there any matches?" she asked. "Ring for some."

She was impatient of indecision.

He drew up and looked at her. "Ring? Why? No one will come."

"Are we the only people in the house, then?"

"Yes," he said. "That's part of my plan."

"Plan?" She was on her feet. "What do you mean? Have you thought all this out and made a scheme of it?"

"Yes; all out," he said. "The moment has come, Joan."

No longer did the scent of honeysuckle take Joan back to the sun-bathed cottage and the voice behind the door. No longer did she feel that all this wasn't really happening, that it was fantastic. Stark reality forced itself upon her and brought her into the present as though some one had turned up all the lights in a dark room. She was alone with the man whom she had driven to the limit of his patience. No one knew that she was there. It was a trick into which she had fallen out of a new wish to be kind. A sense of self-preservation scattered the dire effects of everything that had happened during the afternoon. She must get out, quickly. She made for the door.

But Gilbert was there first. He locked it, drew out the key, put it in his pocket and before she could turn towards the door leading to the other rooms, he was there. He repeated the process with peculiar deftness and when he saw her dart a look at the windows, he shook his head.

"You can't jump through those screens," he said.

"It isn't fair," she cried.

"Have you been fair?"

"I shall shout for help."

"The nearest cottage is too far away for any one to hear you."

"What are you going to do?"

He went back to her. He was far too quiet and dignified and unlike himself. She could have managed the old vain Gilbert. A scoffing laugh, and he would have withered. But this new Gilbert, who looked at her with such a curious, exalted expression—what was she to do with him?

"Joan," he said, "listen. This is the end or the beginning. I haven't locked the doors and sent the servants away to get you into a vulgar trap. I might have done it a few weeks ago, but not as I am now. This is my night, my beautiful Joan. You have given it to me. After all this fencing, as you call it, you are here with me alone, as far away from the old foolishness as if you were out at sea. What I have to say is so much a private thing, and what I may have to do so much a matter to be treated with the profoundest solemnity that we must run no risk of disturbance. Do you begin to understand, little Joan?"

"No," she said.

"I will explain it to you, then. You are very young and have been very thoughtless. You haven't stopped to think that you have been playing with a soul as well as a heart. I have brought you here to-night to face things up simply and quietly and finally, and leave it to you to make a choice."

"A choice?"

"Yes, between life with me or death in my arms."

III

All that was healthy and normal in Joan broke into revolt. There was something erotic, uncanny about all this. Life or death? What was he talking about? Her pride, too, which had never been put to such a test, was up in arms against the unfairness and cunning of the way in which she had been taken advantage of. She had meant to be kind and pay something of her debt to this man, and it was a vulgar trap, whatever he said in excuse. Let him dare to touch her. Let him dare. She would show him how strong she was and put up such a fight as would amaze him. Just now she had placed herself among those old people and old trees, because she had suffered. But she was young, tingling with youth, and her slate was clean, notwithstanding the fool game that she had played, and she would keep it clean, if she had to fight her way out.

She took up her stand behind the table, alert and watchful.

"I don't get you when you go in for melodrama," she said. "I much prefer your usual way of talking. Translate for me." She spoke scornfully because hitherto she had been able to turn him off by scorn.

But it didn't work this time. It was not anger that came into his eyes, only an unexpected and disconcerting reproach. He made no attempt to go near her. He looked extraordinarily patient and gentle. She had never seen him like this before. "Don't stand there," he said. "Come and sit down and let's go into this sensibly, like people who have emerged from stupidity. In any case you are not going back to Easthampton to-night."

She began to be frightened. "Not going back to Easthampton?"

"No, my dear."

She left her place behind the table and went up to him. Had all the world gone wrong? Had her foolishness been so colossal that she was to be broken twice on the same day? "Gilbert," she said. "What is it? What do you mean? Why do you say these odd things in this queer way? You're—you're frightening me, Gilbert."

Young? She was a child as she stood there with her lovely face upturned. It was torture to keep his hands off her and not take her lips. But he did nothing. He stood steady and waited for his brain to clear. "Odd things in a queer way? Is that how I strike you?"

"Yes. I've never seen you in this mood before. If you've brought me here to make me say I'm sorry, I will, because I am sorry. I'd do anything to have all these days over again—every one since I climbed out of my old bedroom window. If you said hard things to me all night I should deserve them all and I'll pay you what I can of my debt, but don't ask me to pay too much. I trusted you by coming here alone. Don't go back on me, Gilbert."

He touched her cheek and drew his hand away.

"But I haven't brought you here to make you humble yourself," he said. "There's nothing small in this. What you've done to me has left its marks, of course, deep marks. I don't think you ever really understood the sort of love mine is. But the hour has gone by for apologies and arguments and regrets. I'm standing on the very edge of things. I'm just keeping my balance on the lip of eternity. It's for you to draw me back or go tumbling over with me. That's why you're here. I told you that. Are you really so young that you don't understand?"

"I'm a kid, I'm a kid," she cried out, going back to her old excuse. "That's the trouble."

"Then I'll put it into plain words," he said, with the same appalling composure. "I've had these things in my mind to say to you for hours. I can repeat them like a parrot. If the sort of unimaginative people who measure everybody by themselves were to hear what I'm going to say, I suppose they would think I'm insane. But you won't. You have imagination. You've seen me in every stage of what I call the Great Emotion. But you've not treated me well, Joan, or taken me seriously, and this is the one serious thing of my life."

He was still under control, although his voice had begun to shake and his hands to tremble. She could do nothing but wait for him to go on. The crickets and the frogs filled in the short silence.

"And now it's come to this. I can be played with no longer. I can't wait for you any more. Either you love me, or you don't. If you do, you must be as serious as I am, tear up your roots such as they are and come away with me. Your husband, who counts for as little as my wife, will set the law in action. So will Alice. We will wander among any places that take your fancy until we can be married and then if you want to come back, we will. But if you don't and won't love me, I can't live and see you love any other man. I look upon you as mine. I created you for myself ten years ago. Not being able to live without you, I am not made of the stuff to leave you behind me. I shall take you and if there's another life on the other side, live it with you. If not, then we'll snuff out together. Like all great lovers, I'm selfish, you see. That's what I meant when I talked just now about choice."

He moved away, quietly, and piled several cushions into a corner of one of the pews. The look of exaltation was on his face again.

"Sit here, my dream girl," he added, with the most wonderful tenderness, "and think it over. Don't hurry. The night belongs to us." He found a match and lit a cigarette and stood at one of the windows looking out at the stars.

But Joan was unable to move. Her blood was as cold as ice. As though a searchlight had suddenly been thrown on to Gilbert, she saw him as he was. "Unimaginative people will think I'm insane." ... SHE didn't think he was insane, imaginative as he said she was. She KNEW it. If she had been able to think of one thing but Martin and that girl and her own chaos, she must have guessed it at Easthampton from the look in his eyes when he helped her into his car.... He had lost his balance, gone over the dividing hue between soundness and unsoundness. And it was her fault for having fooled with his feelings. Everything was her fault, everything. And now she stood on what Gilbert had called the lip of Eternity. "Who Cares?" had come back at her like a boomerang. And as to a choice between giving herself to Gilbert or to death, what was the good of thinking that over? She didn't love this man and never could. She loved Martin, Martin. She had always loved Martin from the moment that she had turned and found him on the hill. She had lost him, that was true, He had been unable to wait. He had gone to the girl with the white face and the red lips and the hair that came out of a bottle. She had sent him to her, fool that she had been. Already she had decided to creep back to the old prison house and thus to leave life. Without Martin nothing mattered. Why put up a fight for something that didn't count? Why continue mechanically to live when living meant waiting for death? Why not grasp this opportunity of leaving it actually, at once, and urge Gilbert on to stop the beating of her wounded and contrite heart? ... Death, the great consoler. Sleep, endless sleep and peace.

But as she stood there, tempted, with the weight of Martin's discarded armor on her shoulders and the sense of failure hanging like a millstone round her neck, she saw the creeper bursting into buds on the wall beneath the window of her old room, caught the merry glint of young green on the trees below her hill, heard the piping of birds to their nesting mates, the eager breeze singing among the waving grasses and the low sweet crooning of baby voices—felt a tiny greedy hand upon her breast, was bewildered with a sudden overwhelming rush of mother-longing ... young, young? Oh, God, she was young, and in the springtime with its stirring sap, its call to life and action, its urge to create, to build, its ringing cry to be up and doing, serving, sowing, tending—the pains of winter forgotten, hope in the warming sun.

She must live. Even without Martin she must live. She was too young for death and sleep and peace. Life called and claimed and demanded. It had need of the young for a good spring, a ripe summer, a golden autumn. She must live and work and justify.

But how?

There was Gilbert watching the stars with a smile, calmly and quietly and horribly waiting for her to make a choice, having slipped over on the other side of the dividing line. A scream of fear and terror rose to her throat. This quiet, exalted man, so gentle and determined, with the look in his eyes of one who intended to own one way or the other—Live? How was she to live? He had given her a choice between something that was impossible and something that all Nature held her back from. She was locked into a lonely house as far away from help as though they were out at sea.

"We hold it death to falter not to die." The words seemed suddenly to stand out in blazing letters over the mantelpiece, as they did in Martin's room—Martin, Martin.... With a mighty effort she wound the reins round her hands and pulled herself up. In this erotic and terrible position she must not falter or show fear or exaggerate this man's sudden derangement by cries or struggles. He must be humored, kept gentle and quiet, and she must pray for help. God loved young things, and if she had forgotten Him until the very moment of great danger, He might forgive. She must, with courage and practicality, gain time so that some one might be sent. The servants might return. Harry Oldershaw might have followed them. He hadn't liked the look of Gilbert. He had said so. But if that was too good, there was Martin, Martin...

She saw herself sitting in a dressing gown on the arm of a chair in Martin's room in the little New York house. She heard Martin come along the passage with his characteristic light tread and saw him draw up short. He looked anxious. "You wanted me?" she heard him say.

"I did and do, Marty. But how did you guess?"

"I didn't guess. I knew."

"Isn't that wonderful? Do you suppose I shall always be able to get you when I want you very much?"

"Yes, always."

"Why?"

"I dunno. It's like that. It's something that can't be explained...."

Gilbert turned and smiled at her. She smiled back. Martin was not far away, Martin. "How quiet the night is," she said, and went over to a window. Hope gleamed like a star. And then, with all her strength and urgency she gave a silent cry. "Martin, Martin. I want you, so much, oh, so much. Come to me, quickly, quickly. Martin, Martin."

IV

The crickets and the frogs vied with each other to fill the silence with sound. The moon was up and had laid a silver carpet under the trees. Fireflies flashed their little lights among the undergrowth like fairies signalling.

Joan had sent her S. O. S. into the air and with supreme confidence that it would reach Martin wherever he might be, left the window, went to the pew in which Gilbert had arranged the cushions and sat down... Martin had grown tired of waiting for her. She had lost him. But twice before he had answered her call, and he would come. She knew it. Martin was like that. He was reliable. And even if he held her in contempt now, he had loved her once. Oh, what it must have cost him to leave her room that night—it seemed so long ago—she had clung to being a kid and had conceived it to be her right to stay on the girlhood side of the bridge. To be able to live those days over again—how different she would be.

Without permitting Gilbert to guess what she was doing, she must humor him and gain time. She gave thanks to God that he was in this gentle, exalted mood, and was treating her with a sort of reverence. Behind the danger and the terror of it all she recognized the wonder of his love.

"Gilbert," she said softly.

"Well, my little spring girl?"

"Come and sit here, where I can see you."

"You have only to tell me what I'm to do," he said and obeyed at once.

How different from the old affected Gilbert—this quiet man with the burning eyes who sat with his elbows on his knees and his back bent towards her and the light of one of the lanterns on his handsome face. She had played with a soul as well as with a heart, and also, it appeared, with a brain. How fatal had been her effect upon men—Martin out of armor and Gilbert on the wrong side of the thin dividing line. Men's love—it was too big and good a thing to have played with, if she had only stopped to think, or some one had been wise and kind enough to tell her. Who cares? These two men cared and so did she, bitterly, terribly, everlastingly.

Would Martin hear—oh, would he hear? Martin, Martin!

There was a long, strange silence.

"Well, my little Joan?"

"Well, Gilbert?"

He picked up her hand and put his lips to it. "Still thinking?" he asked, with a curious catch in his voice.

"Yes, Gilbert, give me time."

He gave back her hand. "The night is ours," he said, but there was pain in his eyes.

And there they sat, these two, within an arm's reach, on the edge of the abyss. And for a little while there was silence—broken only by the crickets and the frogs and the turning of many leaves by the puffs of a sudden breeze.

Was she never going to hear the breaking of twigs and the light tread outside the window? Martin, Martin.

And then Gilbert began to speak. "I can see a long way to-night, Joan," he said, in a low voice. "I can see all the way back to the days when I was a small boy—years away. It's a long stretch."

"Yes, Gilbert," said Joan. (Martin, Martin, did you hear?)

"It's not good for a boy to have no father, my sweet. No discipline, no strong hand, no man to imitate, no inspiration, no one to try and keep step with. I see that now. I suffered from all that."

"Did you, Gilbert?" Oh, when would the twigs break and the light step come? Martin, Martin.

"A spoilt boy, a mother's darling, unthrashed, unled. What a cub at school with too much money! What a conceited ass at college, buying deference and friends. I see myself with amazement taking to life with an air of having done it all, phrase-making and paying deference to nothing but my excellent profile. God, to have those years over again! We'd both do things differently given another chance, eh, Joan?"

"Yes, Gilbert." He wasn't coming. He wasn't coming. Martin, Martin.

She strained her ears to catch the sound of breaking twigs. The crickets and the frogs had the silence to themselves. She got up and went to the window, with Gilbert at her elbow. She felt that he was instantly on his feet. Martin's face was not pressed against the screen. He had heard. She knew that he had heard, because she was always able to make him hear. But he didn't care. When he had come before it was for nothing. She had lost him. She was un-Martined. She was utterly without help. She must give up. What was the good of making a fight for it now that Martin cared so little as to turn a deaf ear to her call? He had even forgotten that he had loved her once. Death was welcome then. Yes, welcome. But there was one way to make some sort of retribution—just one. She would remain true to Martin.

Gilbert touched her on the arm. "Come, Joan," he said. "The night's running away. Is it so hard to decide?"

But against her will Nature, to whom life is so precious, put words into her mouth. "I want you to try and understand something more about me," she said eagerly.

"The time has gone for arguing," he replied, stiffening a little.

"I'm not going to argue," she went on quickly, surprised at herself, deserted as she was. "I only want you to think a little more deeply about all this."

He drew his hand across his forehead. "Think? I've thought until my brain's hot, like an overheated engine."

She leaned forward. Spring was fighting her battle. "I'm not worth a love like yours," she said. "I'm too young, too unserious. I'm not half the woman that Alice is."

"You came to me in spirit that night in Paris. I placed yuu in my heart. I've waited all these years."

"Yes, but there's Alice—no, don't turn away. Let me say what's in my mind. This is a matter of life or death, you said."

He nodded. "Yes, life or death, together."

"Alice doesn't disappoint," she went on, the words put upon her lips. "I may, I shall. I already have, remember. This is your night, Gilbert, not mine, and whichever step we decide to take matters more to you than to me. Let it be the right one. Let it be the best for you."

But he made a wild sweeping gesture. His patience was running out. "Nothing is best for me if you're not in it. I tell you you've got me, whatever you are. You have your choice. Make it, make it. The night won't last for ever."

Once more she listened for the breaking twig and the light step. There was nothing but the sound of the crickets and the frogs. Martin had forgotten. He had heard, she was sure of that, but he didn't care. Nature had its hand upon her arm, but she pushed it away. Her choice was easy, because she wouldn't forget. She would be true to Martin.

"I've made my choice," she said.

"Joan, Joan—what is it?"

"I don't love you."

He went up to her, with his old note of supplication. "But I can teach you, Joan, I can teach you, my dear."

"No. Never. I love Martin. I always have and always shall."

"Oh, my God," he said.

"That's the truth.... Please be quick. I'm very tired!" She drew herself up like a young lily.

For a moment he stood irresolute, swaying. Everything seemed to be running past him. He was spinning like a top. He had hoped against hope, during her silence and her argument. But now to be told not only that she would never love him but that she loved another man....

He staggered across the room to the sideboard, opened the drawer, and the thing glistened in his hand.

Joan was as cold as ice. "I will be true," she whispered to herself. "I will be true. Martin, oh, Martin."

With a superhuman effort Gilbert caught hold of himself. The cold thing in his hand helped him to this. His mouth became firm again and his face gentle and tender. And he stood up with renewed dignity and the old strange look of exaltation. "I claim you then," he said. "I claim you, Joan. Here, on this earth, we have both made mistakes. I with Alice. You with Martin Gray. In the next life, whatever it may be, we will begin again together. I will teach you from the beginning. Death and the Great Emotion. It will be very beautiful. Shut your eyes, my sweet, and we will take the little step together." The thing glistened in his grasp.

And Joan shut her eyes with her hands to her breast. "I love you, Martin," she whispered. "I love you. I will wait until you come."

And Gilbert cried out, in a loud ringing voice, "Eternity, oh, God!" and raised his hand.

There was a crash, a ripping of window screen. Coatless, hatless, his shirt gaping at the neck, his deep chest heaving, Martin swept into the room like a storm, flung himself in front of Joan, staggered as the bullet hit him, cried out her name, crumpled into a heap at her feet.

And an instant later lay beneath the sweet burden of the girl whose call he had answered once again and to whom life broke like a glass ball at the sight of him and let her through into space.

V

"You may go in," said the doctor.

And Joan, whiter than a lily, rose from the corner in which she had been crouching through all the hours of the night and went to the doorway of the room to which Martin had been carried by the Nice Boy and Gilbert, the man who had been shocked back to sanity.

On a narrow bed, near a window through which a flood of sunlight poured, lay Martin from whom Death had turned away,—honest, normal, muscular, reliable Martin, the bullet no longer in his shoulder. His eyes, eager and wistful, lit up as he saw her standing there and the brown hand that was outside the covers opened with a sort of quiver.

With a rush Joan went forward, slipped down on her knees at the side of the bed, broke into a passion of weeping and pressed her lips to that outstretched hand.

Making no bones about it, being very young and very badly hurt, Martin cried too, and their tears washed the bridge away and the barriers and misunderstandings and criss-crosses that had sprung up between them during all those adolescent months.

"Martin, Martin, it was all my fault."

"No, it wasn't, Joany. It was mine. I wasn't merely your pal, ever. I loved and adored you from the very second that I found you out on the hill. You thought it was a game, but it wasn't. It was the real thing, and I was afraid to say so."

She crept a little nearer and put her head on his chest. "I was all wrong, Marty, from the start. I was a fool and a cheat, and you and Gilbert and Alice have paid my bill. I've sent Gilbert back to Alice, and they'll forget, but it will take me all my life to earn my way back to you." She flung her arm across his body, and her tears fell on his face.

"Oh, God," he cried out, "don't you understand that I love you, Joany? Send all your bills to me. They're mine, because I'm yours, my baby, just all yours. You were so young and you had to work it off. I knew all that and waited. Didn't you know me well enough to be dead sure that I would wait?"

The burden on her shoulders fell with a crash, and with a great cry of pent-up gratitude and joy her lips went down to his lips.

But the doctor was not so old that he had forgotten love and youth, and he left those two young clinging things alone again and went back into the sun.

CPSIA information can be obtained
at www.ICGtesting.com
Printed in the USA
LVHW012320210423
745024LV00007B/116

9 781805 474425